NO GOLD WITHOUT THE DRAGON

Wisdom Teachings
of a Quantum Healer

HEATHER LINN

SACRED DRAGON
PUBLISHING™

Los Angeles, California

© 2024 Heather Linn

All rights reserved. No part of this publication may be reproduced, stored in a retrieval system, or transmitted, in any form or by any means, electronic, mechanical, recorded, photocopied, or otherwise, without the prior written permission of the publisher, except by a reviewer who may quote brief passages in a review.

Sacred Dragon Publishing™
An imprint of Sacred Dragon Publishing Services LLC
Los Angeles, California
SacredDragonPublishing.com

ISBN: 978-1-7366793-8-8 (Paperback)
ISBN: 978-1-7366793-9-5 (ebook)
ISBN: 979-8-9876749-0-1 (Hardback)

First published 2022. Second Edition 2024.

Cover and Interior Design: Atelier Mayalen Design and Ryan Forsythe
Author photos: Sharday Swanepoel

The information presented in this work is the author's opinion and does not constitute any health or medical advice. The content of this work is for informational purposes only and is not intended to diagnose, treat, cure, or prevent any condition or disease or is meant as a substitute for consultation with a licensed practitioner.

Publisher's Cataloging-in-Publication (Provided by Cassidy Cataloguing Services, Inc.).
  Names: Linn, Heather, 1964- author.
  Title: No gold without the dragon : wisdom teachings of a quantum healer / Heather Linn.
  Description: Second edition. | Los Angeles, California : Sacred Dragon Publishing, [2024] | Includes bibliographical references.
  Identifiers: ISBN: 978-1-7366793-8-8 (paperback) | 979-8-9876749-0-1 (hardcover) | 978-1-7366793-9-5 (ebook)
  Subjects: LCSH: Energy medicine. | Self-actualization (Psychology) | Women healers. | Quantum theory. | Consciousness. | Change (Psychology) | BISAC: BODY, MIND & SPIRIT / General. | BODY, MIND & SPIRIT / Healing / General. | BODY, MIND & SPIRIT / Inspiration & Personal Growth.
  Classification: LCC: RZ421 .L56 2024 | DDC: 615.852--dc23

Printed in the United States of America

DEDICATION

For my beloved husband and sons,
who keep my feet on the ground and my heart bathed in love.

For my soul sisters,
keep shining your bright lights.

For all the awakening souls.

CONTENTS

INTRODUCTION	1
Chapter 1: AWAKENING	9
Chapter 2: DRAGON FIRE	47
Chapter 3: ALCHEMY	79
Chapter 4: ANSWERING THE CALL	111
Chapter 5: SOUL ROOTS	149
Chapter 6: INITIATION	183
Chapter 7: LIGHT	221
Chapter 8: SHADOW	269
Chapter 9: WINGS	307
EPILOGUE	345
BOOK CLUB QUESTIONS	351
GRATITUDES	353
ABOUT THE AUTHOR	357
INVITATION TO CONNECT	358

AUTHOR'S NOTE

Throughout this book, I refer to family, friends, and spiritual mentors who played an important role on my journey. Fictitious names have been used to protect their identities unless permission was given to use a true name.

This book contains detailed case studies and short anecdotes describing my healing work based on actual sessions with clients. Without exception, the real names and personal details of these individuals have been changed to protect their identities.

I have also taken great care to ensure that everyone has given consent to have their healing stories and fictionalized personal information included in this book.

INTRODUCTION

If you have ever wondered what your soul purpose is or felt you had a calling, you will understand the constant tug and pull to dance to this higher tune, to carve a pathway through the thicket of daily life and soul-shape your destiny. It's a lifelong dance, and the path might never be entirely clear. But when we hear the call, answer it we must. It may not be answered in a day, a year, or even one lifetime, but allowing your heart to open to the question and falling into the vast mystery will lead you toward your treasure.

This is my story about answering the call to become a healer and work as a quantum healer in South Africa and globally. Spanning several decades, the narrative chronicles my lifelong quest to honor this purpose and walk a path of heart in service of others through all of life's challenges, from a dramatic wake-up call, a painful separation from the father of my children and a brush with cancer, to my initiations as a healer.

There are many paths to becoming a healer; mine was a rather circuitous one. As the wounded healer archetype, I had to go deep within, many times over, to survey the damage and find the buried treasures in order to assist others on their healing journeys. It was also a mystical path. From as far back as I can remember, mystical experiences were part of my reality. From a young age, I found myself dipping into non-ordinary reality and *walking between worlds*. It took time to make sense of the mystery, to the extent that is ever possible, and figure out what was required to walk my soul path.

No Gold Without the Dragon reveals a path that was not neatly laid out but was forged through a series of mystical experiences, initiations, and years of learning my craft, honing my skills in the slow-burning fires of transformation. The title points to the hard lessons along the way. I had to face the dragon in many guises to honor my calling and become a healer worthy of the role.

How I answered the call and wove my path is a transformation story for everyone longing to sing their soul song, and perhaps especially for women who are returning to themselves, finding their unique gifts, and offering them to the world. As we unplug from patriarchy, the collective awakening of the divine feminine is bursting forth with diverse richness and beauty. This is a time for our awakening stories to be thrown to the winds and widely dispersed.

I am sharing my story as an archetypal journey, loosely structured on the Heroine's Journey. In this, I have been inspired by the work of many remarkable trailblazers, notably Clarissa Pinkola Estés, Maureen Murdock, and Dr. Sharon Blackie. I'm particularly indebted to Maureen Murdock's formulation of the Heroine's Journey in her book *The Heroine's Journey: Woman's Quest for Wholeness* for my understanding of how it differs from the classic Hero's Journey described in Joseph Campbell's seminal work, *The Hero with a Thousand Faces*.[1] In my rendition of this archetypal journey, I have also drawn upon Dr. Sharon Blackie's revisioning of the Heroine's Journey in her book *If Women Rose Rooted*, which positions the heroine as a pilgrim and an eco-heroine.[2] Throughout this book, I've used Maureen Murdock's terminology to describe the Heroine's Journey with some variation for my interpretation of the journey's flow.

While the Heroine's Journey places women at the center, it is as much an instructive process of awakening for anyone, regardless of gender, as we reset our collective compass for a post-patriarchal era. As the

---

1 Maureen Murdock, *The Heroine's Journey: Woman's Quest for Wholeness* (USA: Shambala Publications, 1990); Joseph Campbell, *The Hero with a Thousand Faces* (USA: Pantheon Books, 1949).

2 Sharon Blackie, *If Women Rose Rooted: A Life-Changing Journey to Authenticity and Belonging* (United Kingdom: September Publishing, 2016).

mother of sons, I have seen first-hand how boys and young men are engaging with their life journeys in much more divergent ways than the traditional Hero's Journey conceives. Still, the current reality is that the divine feminine energies are predominantly arising *through* women. Most of my clients and course participants are women. While I don't wish to exclude men, this story inevitably speaks more directly to women engaging with their own Heroine's Journey to transform and find their authentic voice.

While there are many similarities, the heroine's experience of the archetypal journey deviates from the hero's well-known path in several important respects. The sweeping arc of the Heroine's Journey is less grand adventure and more deep awakening than the classic Hero's Journey. The heroine's awakening to spiritual aridity is a variation of the hero's call to adventure, though her orientation at this stage of her journey is inward, not outward. When the heroine receives the call to awaken, she must leave this known world and transcend her comfort zone. She must turn away from distractions and free herself from assorted traps that drain her energy. When she steps across the threshold into unknown territory, like the hero, she too must face challenges and temptations, not least the temptation to run back to her sheltering comfort zone, no matter how life-sapping it might be.

If she continues into the unknown, the Heroine's Journey takes on its own form. Instead of slaying the dragon when it appears on the path, the heroine is more curious about its nature and what might be hidden in the dark cave. She pays homage to the dragon with great humility and finds out what she can learn from the beast within. Secretly, she would like to befriend the dragon or perhaps make it her guru.

While writing this book, I was curious to discover that this notion of befriending the dragon—or any archetypal beast—also appears in the African wisdom tradition. In a branch of African shamanism, lion shamans—many of whom are women—have a special affinity with lions. In her book, *Mystery of the White Lions*, Linda Tucker describes the relationship of female lion shamans with lions in the bushveld:

> *Lion-taming earth goddesses are associated with attunement rather than conflict with the lion. Unlike the lion-hero tradition associated with the initiation into manhood, each female deity reveals how the physical domination of lions and the befriending of the beast is one and the same expression. This is well illustrated in the tarot card entitled "Strength," which depicts a female (rather than a male) figure in command of a lion—not through slaying the beast but through working in unison with its power.*[3]

This fascinating account of the African lion-heroine places her in a fundamentally different relationship with the lion than that of her male counterparts in the lion-hero tradition. Instead of conquering the lion, the lion-heroine sources her power by attuning with it and forging a working alliance. In telling my own story, this notion of befriending the lion and attuning to its power has informed my handling of the dragon within.

The heroine's relationship with the darkness is another important deviation from the hero's path. For the heroine, the descent into the abyss is, in fact, an important way station. It is a womb-space of gestation and preparation for rebirth. She undergoes profound change in the fecund darkness, much like the larva in the cocoon before it emerges as the colorful butterfly. When the heroine reaches the abyss, she knows instinctively that this is the heart of a sacred journey, and she shouldn't move too quickly through it. The heroine's abyss is a place of surrender rather than action. It is a place of deep dreaming, where she begins to see herself and her world with new eyes; it is a place of becoming, where she gets to change her story if she feels like it. Here she retrieves her feminine nature, the part of her that has been severed and silenced by trying to fit in and succeed in a masculine world. In the darkness, she listens deeply to her feminine self and reclaims her true feelings, intuition, creativity, and dreams her life anew—a healing dream for herself and the world. Above all, her dream is not only for herself but for what she might contribute to the collective awakening. This healing dream is the real treasure and the heroine's true quest.

---

3 Linda Tucker, *Mystery of the White Lions: Children of the Sun God* (Hay House, Inc., 2010).

Returning to the known world, transformation and awakening are the gifts the Goddess bestows on the heroine. Whatever transpired along the way, she cannot go back to her old life or old way of being. Clear-seeing, she can no longer sleep-walk through her days. More alert now, her time in the dark has rekindled her interest in feminine ways of knowing. This new thread of inquiry helps her to navigate the journey onward. These initiatory gifts are the gold she passes on to others.

On my own journey as a healer, I went through this archetypal cycle many times, in major circles and minor loops. My gifts from the Goddess were healing hands and the ability to walk between worlds—what I have called the surface-world and soul-world—and be a bridge for others. The art of healing is the gift I have endeavored to pass on to others.

Healers have come a long way since the days of witch-burning in the Middle Ages when they were branded as witches and persecuted for sharing their gifts. In the twenty-first century, healers of all persuasions are stepping into the light. Not only are healers increasingly sought after for their varied offerings, but energy medicine is recognized as an important therapy in the rapidly growing field of integrative medicine. Coined in the late eighties, energy medicine is defined as "energetic or informational interaction with a biological system to bring back homeostasis in the organism."[4] Quantum healing is one of many modalities that fall within this broad definition of energy medicine. Even if not yet fully part of the mainstream, quantum healing is backed up by science. Quantum physics explains what mystics and healers have intuitively known for eons—that everything is energy and initiating change at the energetic level creates change in the visible world of matter, flesh and bone, and even in the less visible fields of heart and soul.

As much as it can be explained by science, healing remains an art. The art is in coaxing stagnant, sometimes frozen, energy to flow. Trawling the energetic body's murky pools and stagnant wells to get the inner waters flowing like a river of light through the body, modern healers dissolve, transmute, and channel energy in a fundamentally unique way

---

4 Sai Shradha, *Importance of Energy Medicine*, Alternative and Integrative Medicine, Volume 10, 2021.

with each client. Ultimately, healing is an alchemical process working with the base elements of stagnant or dense energy and channeling high-vibrational light to forge a new synthesis while guiding those that seek it to the deep well of wisdom within—their spiritual gold.

This process is not a straight line but a deepening spiral. One of the most ancient symbols, the spiral represents the journey inward. When we go within and are prepared to do the distance, we tap into our innate wisdom and wholeness.

When I started working as a professional healer, I approached the job as if I had to solve all the problems that each client brought to my healing room. While miracles abound in the healing space, and I have witnessed many almost instant *cures*, healing is not so much about providing a cure as it is facilitating a journey back to self and wholeness.

Wholeness does not mean perfection. One way of understanding wholeness is integrity of being. Integrity means that all parts—mind, body, and spirit—are integrated and work harmoniously in unison. We have lost much of our innate wholeness in our rational western society. We operate from our heads, cut off from our hearts, disconnected from our bodies, and very often alienated from our souls. This cut-off state of being reflects a deeper malaise in our modern world, where we have been separated from our instinctual natures, from Source, and from the heartbeat of Mother Earth. And so, we find ourselves in a spiritual wilderness.

The goal of healing is to return from the wilderness to a place of deeper connection with our bodies, our souls, each other, and with Gaia herself. Through connection, we create community in the very real sense of the word—a unified body of individuals, groups, or species. This inner unity is the very basis of emergent Oneness consciousness, for how can we hope to be in harmony with our world if we are cut off from ourselves? The art of healing is to hold space for inner transformation and a return to wholeness.

To illustrate my work as a quantum healer, the book includes case studies and short anecdotes based on my work with clients over the last fifteen years. These case studies highlight a range of typical issues and the energy work that supported my clients to heal, transform, and find their version of wholeness. Through these real-life stories, I share unique insights into the world of energy with its special rules and mysteries.

Although I have used the subjective "I" as my point of reference when discussing the healing work, a more accurate understanding of how healing works is that the healer is a channel for healing energies. It is an intricate co-creative dance between the channel, the spirit guides who relay important information, and the recipient of healing energies. The recipient is as important as the healer to the healing process, and their availability to receive healing energies greatly influences outcomes. Time and again, I witnessed the most powerful results when my client believed in the power of energy work and engaged with their healing journey as a process rather than a quick-fix cure. In the end, the healer's most important role is to bear witness to this process—with great respect, compassion, tenderness, and encouragement.

That said, my role as a healer required dedication and skill to harness the available energies. It was undoubtedly a steep learning curve that called for constant refining and reflection. Everything I learned about working with energy is conveyed through the case studies and my reflections on them.

At the end of each chapter, you will find the Dragon's Gold—a summary of the lessons and insights gleaned through the healing work with clients. Every client was a teacher. While I might have helped my clients, they pushed me to grow and rise to the challenge of new knowledge frontiers. It was an inspiring dance, and the dragon a demanding choreographer.

Even in the writing of this book, the dragon kept me on my toes. Quite by chance, I wrote part of it at the foot of the Dragonridge mountains in the Western Cape, where the shape of the dragon on the ridge was a constant reminder of my faithful companion. The dragon, in this manifestation, demanded truth. Writing a memoir is a tracking exercise, following memories this way and that, tracing multiple storylines across time, letting some things go and others not, weaving the narrative threads until they yield a version of the truth. In the end, memory informs identity and reveals the substance that remains after all the paring down. This was an often-uncomfortable process! It forced me to look in the mirror, confronting every choice, every perceived mistake, the wrong turns, the detours, and the things that were not within my control yet had a life-changing impact. Neatly laid out in narrative form, my path appears coherent, but it hides the *what ifs*, the *should haves*, the regrets, and the paths not taken. There was both joy and grief in confronting these voices and other possibilities. And yet, writing about my life and encountering the dragon once more brought a deep acceptance of the imperfect path. The act of writing itself was a profoundly transformational process which has shaped my imperfect path in magical ways. My heartfelt wish is that my story inspires yours.

I wrote *No Gold Without the Dragon* for everyone but especially for those facing their dragons, diving into the muddy waters of transformation, scouring the depths for their treasures, and returning with their gifts— whatever they may be. Your offering to the world is so necessary right now.

My offering is the most authentic version of my story, with its many imperfections and the treasures that have prevailed. Now I place it in your hands in the hopes that you find courage to answer your soul's call and inspiration to walk your unique path of heart.

1

AWAKENING
1244 – 1999

[The heroine's] task is to take the sword of her truth, find the sound of her voice, and choose the path of her destiny. Thus, she will find the treasure of her seeking.

– Maureen Murdock, author of *The Heroine's Journey*

When I died, I found myself flying through the air like a bird. It's probably more accurate to say that I died when I hit the ground after a precipitous fall, but I'd left my body long before impact. Initially, it was very much like one of those flying dreams—the ones where you soar through the night sky, rejoicing in the liberation from form and density, before waking up with fleeting regret that the ability to fly was, after all, just a dream. Only this time, it wasn't a dream.

After the long siege at the Château de Montségur, we were forced to surrender. During the truce, our captors delivered their ungodly surrender terms—renounce our Cathar faith or perish in the flames of their punitive bonfire. For weeks, we had been watching the construction of a rough wooden pyre in the field below the pog and knew what was coming. Every living soul in the fortress stronghold—and there were hundreds who had sought shelter by then—had to make a life-and-death choice. Some souls chose life and renounced their faith, but most chose the Inquisition's fire. I was among those who leapt off the northern ramparts rather than surrender my soul to anyone other than my Creator.

Untethered from my body during the freefall into nothing but air, my entry into spirit world was quite abrupt. Still, the exact moment of death was imprecise. It was like flowing from solid to liquid to ether, transitioning from one state to another in little leaps and sighs, surrendering to a more amorphous state of being, allowing the untethering its natural course. It took some getting used to an entirely new medium—Ether, not Earth.

In this realm, there was no gravity, and no need for it, as lightness is the enduring substance of spirit, and I understood, for the first time, that we are indeed made of light, as the teachings had suggested. Being pure light was exhilarating and disorientating all at once. Almost instantly, other light beings gathered around me, welcoming me with their hearts; that's the best way to describe it. There were no words in this medium, but I could feel waves of love enveloping me, putting me at ease as I oriented myself to my etheric home.

In the first moments of transition, time appeared to stand still—perhaps a subjective pause as my spirit slipped from one world to another—but then it seemed to collapse and bend in the most astonishing ways. One moment, I was reliving my short life; the next I was racing into other times—whether past or future, I cannot say—multiple worlds appearing in swirling images around me, as if I were already *inside* them. And I quickly realized I could choose what world to conjure up simply by *thinking* it!

Equally thrilling was the discovery that I could propel myself—rapidly—using thought alone to initiate movement, my spirit tethered to consciousness, if not to my physical body. I can't deny there was a pull to go back, a desire to return to the comfort of flesh and bone and beating heart. But my flesh and bones were a bloody heap on the grassy slopes far below the château wall. I resisted the urge to go any closer, my limbs quite obviously at awkward angles, my neck arching backward, unnaturally so. It was too late to go back. I'd made the choice when I jumped. This was not one of those near-death experiences where I was going to wake up in my body after a prolonged coma with life-changing insights and alluring tales about the afterlife.

I died alongside my compatriots. We'd made sure of that.

I didn't regret my choice then, and I'm not ashamed of it now. It was for a noble cause. At Montségur, we were in possession of a most sacred relic, none other than the Holy Book believed to be written by our beloved Mary and guarded with the utmost secrecy for centuries. In the final days of the siege, we had successfully spirited this holy treasure into safe keeping and had no more business with the affairs of the world. In any event, history would be the judge of our actions. Some might think that dying at twenty-one is a tragic waste of a young life, but I could surrender to death with a peaceful heart. I'd completed my soul assignment and was ready to move forward into the pulsing bright light and beyond.

That was nearly eight hundred years ago! In my current lifetime, I would again face death at the age of twenty-one, but this time I wasn't ready to die so young. This time, my life path was very different. At twenty-one, I was still in a slumber and didn't have a clue why I was here again. It would take a life-changing wake-up call to jolt my memory.

After the car crash that nearly killed me, my first spirit guide appeared. She gave me a message that opened the floodgates of memory and initiated my journey as a healer. As best I can recall, this is what she said:

> Your purpose is to heal yourself and others. Find the veins of gold, the treasure deep within you, and you'll find your path.

Despite the heads-up, it took me a long time to find my way. First, I would enter the hallways of remembrance and slow-burning fires of transformation.

This is my story.

WAKE-UP CALL IN THE MIDDLE OF NOWHERE

When I was twenty-one, I was given a stark choice—live or die. It was an event that changed my destiny.

I was in my final year of university, and like many of my contemporaries, I had no idea where I was headed. Despite an active student life at the height of the anti-apartheid struggle in the eighties in South Africa, I felt alternately disaffected and disengaged. I was going through the motions of what was expected of me, getting a university degree, being involved in student life (politics and parties), and playing in the city orchestra. A richly textured life of privilege, right? But, despite appearances, something vital was missing. I didn't know what that missing piece was until death came calling.

On an ordinary Friday afternoon, on a remote stretch of road in rural South Africa, the Universe threw me a curveball, which I later came to believe was simultaneously life threatening, life changing, and, in the final analysis, a lifeline.

The curveball was a serious car accident that I miraculously survived. After a beach holiday with my boyfriend Mike and his family, I was traveling home with his older sister Amber. Amber was driving, and I was in the front passenger seat. We were in an upbeat mood, singing along to Rodriguez's iconic album, Cold Fact. Growing up in South Africa, Cold Fact, with its anti-establishment lyrics, was the soundtrack of our youth. Suddenly, a voice in my head cut through the lyrics, instructing me to take my seat belt off. Believe me, I wasn't in the habit of hearing voices, much less listening to them, but this voice was so clear and urgent that I found myself following the curious instruction. Instinctively, I stopped singing and scanned the road ahead for any sign of danger. I didn't see anything at first, but then my attention was drawn to a cloud of dust billowing up ahead of us to the left of the main road. Looking more closely, I saw a white pick-up truck hurtling along a dirt side road toward the main road. Somehow, I knew it wasn't going to stop. I yelled at Amber to slow down, but it was too late to avoid the inevitable. Our car and the oncoming truck collided at nearly full speed in a tangled maelstrom of screeching tires, crunching metal, and breaking glass until everything and everybody came to an eerie standstill.

On impact, I was thrown into the windscreen and then flung back into the front seat when the car went into a seemingly slow-motion tumble down the highway. I could hear, rather than feel, my head hitting the roof again and again before losing consciousness. The next thing I remember, I was hovering above the wreckage. I was not in my body below, and I could see the car lying upside down in the middle of the road.

To this day, I remember my first thought. *Is this what it's like to be dead?*

At first, I felt as if I were drifting into nothingness. But then, gradually, like eyes adjusting to the darkness, I began to comprehend this new experience. I felt weightless and expansive as if I were suddenly much larger. I wasn't inside my body anymore, but I still felt connected to my sense of self and everything around me. It was light, yet not bright. It was very quiet, yet not silent. I was aware of a faint hum, almost like music, as if the ether I was floating in was alive in some way. Time seemed to have stopped as if I were suspended in an alternate reality where ordinary rules like gravity and linear time didn't apply. I drifted further into this spacious timelessness and the deepest sense of inner peace imaginable. The only word that comes close to describing what I felt is bliss. And I wanted to stay there!

At some point, I felt a presence with me, and that same clear voice I heard just before the crash told me that I had a choice. I could stay and travel further into the light or go back into my body and carry on with my life. The Voice explained that all I had to do was decide, then "think my choice," and whatever I had decided to do would happen. For a moment, I hesitated, wanting to drift in this blissful state forever, but then an unbidden thought arose, *I haven't finished what I came to do; I must go back!*

Even though I had no idea what I had yet to finish, the decision was made, and almost instantly, I felt as if I were spiraling backward, and then with a jolt, I regained consciousness in my body. The assault of ordinary reality on my barely conscious senses was a shock. Amber was screaming and trying to pull me out of the car. I was trapped between the front passenger seat and the crumpled hood. With Amber's help, I managed to wriggle out through the driver's side door. Blood was pouring from my head, drenching us both. We stumbled to the side of the road, where I collapsed. It would be months before I could walk without the help of crutches. Later, the people who stopped to help us said there was so much blood it looked like an apocalyptic nightmare.

We were taken to a rural clinic in the Transkei for emergency treatment. The clinic had run out of anesthetics and painkillers, and the initial procedures to stop the bleeding and close the open wounds were excruciatingly painful. I had sustained head injuries, including a huge gash on the crown of my head and a cracked cheekbone, my hands were a bloody mess of glass-filled cuts, and my left knee was shattered. I also had a cracked pelvis, but this was only detected much later. Several medics worked simultaneously to dress and close the wounds. Despite slipping in and out of consciousness, I was aware of the incredible kindness of the medical staff doing their utmost to mitigate the limitations of rural medicine. While shaving some of my hair off, one of the medics apologized for having to inflict temporary baldness, remarking that the wound on the crown of my head was the shape of a cross. Odd how memory sifts the fragments of trauma. I was also aware of the being with the Voice next to the bed, her soft whisperings keeping me tethered to the world around me. I briefly saw her face and shiny black hair and wondered if she was an angel here to fetch me back from the world I'd chosen. Then everything went dark.

While recovering from my injuries, I had a lot of time to think. Through the fog in my head, I was trying to figure out what I had experienced in those moments immediately following the crash. Was it a near-death experience or something else? Where exactly had I been? Had I made the right choice to leave that blissful space? Had I imagined a spirit guide beside me in the clinic? I couldn't stop thinking about the inner voice that said I had not finished what I came to do. What could be so important it was worth the choice to live? What was the unfinished purpose that lay ahead? Eventually, in my fuzzy state of mind, these repetitive thoughts petered out in a rabbit hole of more unanswerable questions. The spirit guide, who had briefly appeared by my bedside, seemed to have vanished, yet the other-worldly feeling and the questions lingered.

These were big questions, and in my early twenties, I didn't have any answers, nor did I have a spiritual paradigm to assist my thinking. Our paradigms have changed so much since the eighties. Gradually the questions faded as I focused on picking up the pieces of my life in a battered body with head injuries that left me feeling slow and prone to severe headaches for months on end. My relationship with Mike faded too. I was in my final year of university in Pietermaritzburg, and he was working in Port Elizabeth (now Gqeberha) on the other side of the country. It was just too complicated. I limped, quite literally, to the finish line of my English literature degree, pushing through headaches, cloudy thinking, and self-doubt to get there.

Painful as it was, I had awakened to my soul life. There was no going back.

GLIMPSE OF ETERNAL LIFE

Before writing my final exams, I saw Mike for the last time. When we said goodbye, I hugged him close and said, "I won't see you again." I knew this was true but was shocked that I knew it. A few weeks later, Mike was killed in a car crash. He was twenty-five years old.

There are no words adequate to describe a shock like this. When I heard the news, I collapsed on the pathway outside my student house. On top of my grief, I felt it should have been me and that somehow, my choice to come back had affected Mike's fate. Against the odds, I had ended up on this side, and he'd ended up on the other side.

I wrote my finals in a haze of grief and insistent questions about life and death. Soon afterward, Mike appeared in a vivid dream. He told me that his soul had lived on past death. Taking me by the hand, he showed me what it was like to be a discarnate soul in a different dimensional reality. He was happy; that much was clear. I woke up feeling deeply at peace. It was thoughtful of him to give me a little glimpse of life after death. More than anything, this dreamtime encounter with Mike's spirit helped me to move on and live my life. With my studies finished, it was time for the real world.

PARANORMAL GAP YEAR

My entry into the real world started with two more rounds of surgery on my leg. Barely a month after casting off my crutches, I set off with my best friend Lee to travel around Europe. My injured leg was still weak, but I was determined to have a normal gap year experience. I had already squandered three months of my gap year recovering from surgery, and I was eager to join the legions of other young graduates heading to Europe and make the most of the remaining nine months of the year.

But nothing about my gap year was normal. While my contemporaries were exploring the world and having fun, my gap year was more like a crash course in the paranormal. While working as an au pair near Paris, I was plagued by disturbingly accurate precognitive dreams. In London, on my long commute to and from a waitressing job at St Katherine's Dock near the Tower of London, I witnessed numerous car, motorbike, and bicycle accidents *before* they happened. In Barcelona, a sudden premonition helped me narrowly avoid being blown up by a Basque bomb. During 1987, the Basque separatist movement was very active, and there were many bombing incidents in Spain, particularly in and around Barcelona. Seconds before the bomb exploded, an invisible force propelled me to the other side of the road, and I dragged my bewildered traveling companion with me. Even so, the force of the bomb blast threw us to the ground, but at least we were unharmed. The side of the road where we had just been walking was a pile of smoking rubble.

There were many other less dramatic experiences. Sometimes my new skill was useful, but it didn't win me any friends. Shaken by the bombing, my transient travel buddy in Spain accused me of *causing* bad things to happen—this after I had pretty much saved her life—and left the next day. I learned to keep quiet about the things I saw and only take action in a life-threatening emergency. As the months went by, the onslaught of psychic information intensified. It was like having extrasensory antennae that hummed and whirred day and night. I was still dealing with residual anxiety from the car crash, and I was desperate for some relief. Back in France, on my way to a late summer job restoring an old farmhouse in the Dordogne, I had a complete meltdown. I had just seen yet another gruesome accident before it happened—this seemed to be my specialty, and I'd had enough. The South of France is strewn with beautiful medieval churches and abbeys. Taking refuge in a small stone church, I dropped to my knees, begging God, Jesus, Mary, the Holy Spirit—or whoever oversees these sorts of things—to take *the sight* away. "Please, make this stop!" I cried out into the dim silence. There was nothing measured about my request. I sobbed at the foot of the marble Madonna until, gradually, relief settled over me like a comforting blanket.

Miraculously, my petition to those Above worked. The premonitions stopped, and the unwanted clairvoyance waned. For many years, my overactive psychic senses quieted down to a manageable whisper until I was ready to turn the volume back up. But I had a long road to walk first.

POLITICS VERSUS SPIRITUALITY

When I returned to South Africa at the end of my gap year, I did my best to forget my brush with the paranormal. I was not ready for it. I immersed myself in a new job as a junior reporter at The Natal Witness in Pietermaritzburg and a new romantic relationship. I met Patrick at university, but at the time, neither of us was ready for a relationship. After nearly a year of traveling, I threw myself into his arms, and with little serious thought, we embarked on a long-term partnership that lasted nearly fifteen years. I thought he was my soulmate but learned the hard way that even soulmates aren't forever.

From the start, I knew that Patrick was the one. The first time I saw him was at a student council meeting on campus. He was dressed in fencing attire and looked somewhat medieval. Before the meeting started, he picked up his fencing sword and started jousting with a friend. For a brief translucent moment, I saw Patrick in a different time, wielding a sword on an ancient battlefield. With a jolt, like a door closing, the scene vanished, but I had seen enough to know that I knew this man from another life. A soft inner voice said, "We will be together in this life too." This fleeting parting of the veils quickly faded amid the chatter and laughter in the room, almost as if it had never happened.

The stranger thing about this experience was how quickly I pushed it out of my mind. I didn't make any effort to meet Patrick properly or even find out who he was, which would have been easy on such a small campus. But I had such a deep knowing that we would meet again that it didn't need any action on my part. In fact, I quickly forgot about this sword-wielding man until we bumped into each other again shortly before I left for my gap year.

When I returned from my travels, we dived into togetherness and wove our fates together. Our life in KwaZulu-Natal was shaped by the politics of the day. We were part of what was called the White Left and, to varying degrees, were involved with the recently formed United Democratic Front (UDF), which was closely aligned with the underground liberation movement, the then-banned African National Congress (ANC). Patrick was an active branch member of the UDF and took part in one of the secret missions to Lusaka to meet with the ANC leadership in exile. I played a more peripheral role, showing up at marches and protests when required. Our friendships and conversations were defined by politics and secrecy, and my nascent spiritual awakening went further underground. This was no time for such bourgeois indulgence!

My job as a newspaper reporter exposed me to more trauma; the winds of change were howling as the country lurched toward democracy. In covering local events, I was caught up in the increasingly violent power struggle between the ANC and Inkatha, which saw civil war sweeping through KwaZulu-Natal. I saw death more times than I care to recall. It was a turbulent time.

SPIRITUAL REFUGE

I found refuge at the Buddhist Retreat Centre near Ixopo, where I discovered Buddhist teachings and learned to meditate. Perched on a ridge above an expansive valley, the retreat center looks out over the iconic green hills of KwaZulu-Natal. In those days, the center was very rustic. Retreatants slept in a monastic-style dormitory, which was freezing cold in winter. We awoke to the sound of a gong at dawn and weaved our way to the equally cold meditation room, which was light and airy with floor-to-ceiling windows and breathtaking views of the lush valley below.

I spent many hours in this room imbibing the teachings of a Tibetan Buddhist lineage that emphasized compassion as its core tenet. I learned about the Four Noble Truths and the Eightfold path, which are fundamental teachings at the heart of Buddhism. My experience of Buddhism was that it is more of an attitude rather than a religion, a way of experiencing the world, rather than a rigid belief system. This appealed to my Libran nature, and I soaked up the teachings like a sponge. My meditation practice quickly became a daily anchor and has since been a touchstone throughout my life.

Weekends of contemplative silence at this beautiful sanctuary whet my spiritual appetite. Inspired by the teachings and the people who lived at the center, I kept going back for more. I was especially fascinated by Jane, a young novice who lived at the center. She had long gold-blonde hair that tumbled down to her hips, making her look like a goddess. In her late twenties, Jane wasn't much older than me, but she had given up worldly pursuits and chosen the seclusion of living at this off-the-beaten-track center. Jane was positively serene. I fantasized about following this same path, leaving the world, and becoming a true seeker. But I was twenty-three, and the world beyond the center was a compelling call. No doubt I was addicted to real-world drama. Besides, I had too much inner turmoil. I wasn't in the least bit like Jane, really, though I wished I was.

On one of these weekends, I met Rachel, a young Jewish woman who had become a devout Buddhist. Just a few years older than me, she was on a clearly demarcated spiritual path. Rachel got up at four o'clock every morning to meditate and pray. She explained that this was the time of day when the energy was pure, and the veils between worlds were thinnest. Unlike Rachel, this thinning of the veils wasn't tangible enough to compel me to get up before the myna birds. Clearly, I lacked something in the commitment department. Nevertheless, Rachel and I struck up a friendship. She taught me that you could walk a spiritual path without choosing a life of seclusion.

Despite these nascent spiritual aspirations, my life was too turbulent to be like either Jane or Rachel. I was torn between political journalism and a spiritual path, and there didn't seem to be a middle way. Evidently, one part of me was happy enough; I showed up as a journalist, a vocal feminist, and the partner of a political activist. On occasion, I taught seminars on gender politics to first-year students at the University of Natal. Although all of this was fun, it didn't feed my soul. I felt like an outsider, an observer of my own life, and I was restless.

Still haunted by my experience on the other side, I had an urgent sense of purpose but didn't know where to start. Why had I chosen to come back into my body if I was going to be so aimless in my pursuits? Shouldn't I be getting on with it? Apart from Rachel, I had no one to talk to about my choice to come back or the ensuing psychic avalanche during my Paranormal Gap Year. I was hungry for spiritual knowledge. This was long before the advent of the Internet or Google, and South Africa was an isolated country in the grips of its own all-consuming trauma. I scoured second-hand bookshops for esoteric texts but found little to satisfy my soul hunger. This was also well before the explosion of spiritual books that line today's bookshops, and my undercover quest was rather haphazard.

And then the Universe intervened with an unexpected invitation to leave South Africa and take my quest further afield.

FORK IN THE ROAD

Three years after returning to South Africa, I was headed back to London with a little push from fate or, to be more precise, from the

Chapter 1 | Awakening

South African Defense Force (SADF). In those days, white men over the age of eighteen faced two years of compulsory military conscription. As soon as young men finished school, or tertiary education, their fate was determined by an increasingly aggressive and desperate apartheid government. Many young conscripts were sent to Namibia or Angola to fight in the controversial border wars with neighboring states. In an even more controversial development, army troops were being deployed in the so-called townships to quell protests and control an increasingly angry populace.

In politically conscious circles, there was widespread objection to conscripts being forced to take up arms against their fellow citizens. Evading conscription was the topic of the day. Tertiary education was a legitimate alternative, but after that, the only feasible option was to leave the country. Many of our friends were heading to England. Some had British passports or ancestral visas, and a handful received political asylum. A brave few in our political circles had chosen the path of conscientious objection. Being a conscientious objector meant making a formal stand against conscription and facing a six-year prison sentence, the penalty for refusing to comply with compulsory military service. Patrick was weighing his options. He had just completed two years as an articled clerk at a law firm in Durban, so his formal studies were over. When the next military call-up came, he would have to make a tough choice—go to the army, go to prison, or flee the country. Only Hobson would have been happy with that line up.

As it turned out, luck was on Patrick's side. Just before the next military call-up, his law firm offered him a job at their London office, and the day before he was due to report for military training, he was on a plane out of the country. He'd had a lucky escape, but he wouldn't be able to return to South Africa until compulsory conscription was abolished just before the first democratic elections in 1994.

Once again, life had thrown me a curveball. I had a big choice to make as well, though this time with none of the advantages of inter-dimensional lucidity. Was I going to take my chances and join Patrick in London or say goodbye to the life we had envisioned together? I was happy in Durban and had an exciting job as a sub-editor at The New African, a left-wing start-up newspaper that offered a daring alternative to the mainstream news. The New African's downtown office was a drop-in meeting place for activists and intellectuals, and the newsroom buzzed with intense debates. As a sub-editor, my work consisted of tidying up hurried copy and outsmarting the strict censorship laws that controlled the South African press. In this exhilarating environment, I felt part of the throbbing pulse of rapid change in the country and was reluctant to throw it all away to follow my heart. But a few months later, shortly after Nelson Mandela was released from prison, I found myself once again on a plane bound for Europe.

This time I stayed for nearly ten years.

THE LONDON YEARS

The first year in London was a blur of finding our feet, trying to find an affordable place to live, and for me, an endless round of temporary residence and work permit applications. Daily life was focused on survival in a city where we had no history and none of the advantages of social networks. Our saving grace was a large community of exiled South Africans, some of whom had been part of our friendship circle at university. We clung together like refugees on a flimsy life raft. A few, like Patrick, had good jobs, but most, like me, were picking up illegal morsels in a depressed job market.

Thanks to a major slump in the housing market, we managed to get 100% financing on a mortgage bond to buy a flat in Islington. Considering we had zero savings, this was a small miracle. Relieved to have a home, we moved into our two-up, two-down Victorian semi-detached terrace house with a few suitcases and two chairs. How odd that I became a homeowner long before I became a citizen. With this scanty semblance of roots, we set about becoming Londoners.

Freed from politics, we threw ourselves into exploring London's thriving cultural life—music, theater, art galleries, famous writers giving readings, and the Indie film scene. One of my favorite haunts was the Renoir Cinema, where I developed a lasting love for French movies. I dived into bookshops with a ferocious hunger; for my South

African eyes, the well-stocked bookshelves were like candy for the soul. But despite the city's exciting distractions, I hit rock bottom within a year and fell into a major depression. Far from home and unable to find meaningful work, I felt out of place in this vast city. The initial appearance of a familiar culture soon wore off to reveal a cultural gap far wider than I could cross in just one year. I felt totally lost. This was a sure sign that I had wandered off my soul path and had no idea how to find my way back.

DARK NIGHT OF THE SOUL, ROUND ONE

So began two years of soul-searching, during which depression stalked me like the black dog in Paulo Coelho's novel, *The Pilgrimage*. London's grey skies mirrored my mood. I wandered the streets trying to recapture the magic of my early love affair with the city. I was really trying to find myself again. Instead, wherever I turned, there was the black dog, like a hungry shadow. By nature, the black dog was tenacious. When I left my body at twenty-one, I had seen the light; now, it felt as if I had descended into the darkness. This change of direction was utterly disorienting. Sometimes, I felt as if I were drowning. To soothe myself, I wrote poems about surfacing from the watery depths.

Little did I know then that this was the first of three dark nights of the soul I would encounter on my path. What I learned is that a dark night of the soul is a kind of initiation for an inner journey. Women, especially, must travel inwards to find their true nature, and often it takes a transformational experience to prompt the inner quest. For most of us, at least once in our lives, and perhaps more, into the darkness we must go, foraging in the fecund ground of our being, gathering ourselves for the journey back into the light. This is the kind of journey that is sourced from the depths of untamed instinct. As everyone who has experienced this knows, when you are going through this dark night story, it sucks the life out of you. Nothing seems to help. When you are in a true dark night of the soul, it feels as if the soul itself has fled.

There are many ways to call the soul closer—meditation, prayer, painting, writing, dancing, singing, ritual, solitude; I tried them all.

But in the darkest night, nothing seems to work. You just have to wait until the dark night passes. When the moon is covered by thick clouds, the night is pitch dark, and it doesn't help to beg for moonlight. There is nothing for it, but to trust that come dawn, the light will seep back again.

At twenty-six, I didn't yet have a map to find my way through the deep interior of this depression. Later, I understood that it's best to embrace the darkness and stop calling for the light. At such liminal times, it is important—no, essential—to go beyond the surface waters of your life and dive deep. In the process, you may even learn how to breathe underwater, which is a useful skill. Everything you need is within you, but a bit of dredging might be required. And when you've done all the dredging and scouring you're capable of, it's just as important to surface again.

As you traverse the dark night, help will appear in many guises. During my first dark night transit, help eventually came in the form of a vivid dream. In the dream, a large golden Buddha appeared in front of me. It was shimmering gold. Lighting up even more brightly, with almost electric intensity, the golden Buddha spoke to me. "This is your path," it said.

I woke with a start. It was so clearly a message, yet, I wondered, *what is my path?* I was reminded of my choice to return to my body and finish what I came to do. But, despite my spirit guide's message at the time, I hadn't made much headway on this front. Healing myself, let alone others, seemed an impossible task. Was Buddhism the treasure I was seeking? The spiritual world seemed so far from where I had landed—a journalist with a derailed career, foraging for bits of work in a foreign country in the middle of a recession. My life was a sorry mess.

Curious about the golden Buddha and desperate for clues, I did some research. Over 300 years ago, the Burmese army planned an invasion of Thailand (then Siam). Siamese monks were in possession of a rare treasure—a solid gold Buddha—and decided to cover it in thick clay to protect it from being plundered by the invading army. The Burmese invaders were fooled and, thinking it worthless, left it in one piece. The golden Buddha's secret was lost with the passing of time. For over 250 years, it existed only as a clay Buddha until its secret was revealed in the mid-1950s when the five-ton artifact was being moved to a new location. The clay began to crack, and the gold hidden beneath the clay began to peek through. The attending Thai monks chiseled away the clay until the solid gold Buddha was fully restored and shone once again in its full glory.

I loved this story and wondered how to apply it to my own life. I considered that the golden Buddha was pointing me toward the light within me that lay beneath the thick clay covering my soul: a golden light wanting to shine through that had been covered over by years of trauma, turbulence, and distraction—and, more recently, was mired in gloomy depression. My task was to find the cracks, chisel away at the clay, and get to the gold within. But how?

I decided I needed help. *Was I the only twenty-five-year-old who wasn't on a fun-filled round of partying?* Feeling like a failure, I found a therapist who specialized in a somatic therapy called psychosynthesis. I didn't know anything about psychosynthesis, but when I saw Rose's business card, with her blue rose logo, at the local health shop in Islington, it jumped out at me. By then, I had learned that when something lit up or glowed, like the Buddha in the dream, my soul was trying to get my attention.

I was reminded of a childhood game I played when I was learning to read. Every Saturday, my family would pile into our old Kombi mini-van and drive down to the coast. We lived in Grahamstown (now called Makhanda), which was a hop, skip, and a jump to any number of Eastern Cape beaches. Our favorite destination was Kleinemonde, which means Little Mouths, named for the two river mouths and tidal lagoons separated by a few miles of deserted beach and voluptuous sand dunes. It was a kid's paradise. My older brothers and I were let loose on this stretch of beach while my little brother played in the lagoon under my mother's watchful eye. The three of us were free to roam for miles, exploring rock pools, picking up shells, sliding down sand dunes, and baking in the hot sun. Those were halcyon days, and I'm eternally grateful for the unfettered freedom of my early childhood, which primed me for wildness. The taste of freedom is always close to the surface, a visceral mix of salt water and sunburn. When we got home, my mother ran a bath infused with rooibos tea, and one by one, we were plunged into the red-brown brew to draw out the heat.

It was a half-hour drive to Kleinemonde, through town, onto the highway, and then a long gravel road down to the coast. Driving through town, I used to speed read every single signpost, billboard, street name, or shop sign we passed. The challenge was to read every word in English and Afrikaans—the two official languages at that time. If there were too many signposts, I would focus on the one that jumped out at me. I was an obsessive sign reader. At twenty-six, the language might have changed, but the principle of eye-catching signs was exactly the same.

I called Rose without hesitation. It was one of the best decisions I've ever made. For the next two years, I saw Rose every week. With her help, I set about chiseling away the clay and finding myself again. As it turned out, I hadn't needed to look any further than my own body to find myself. After the car crash, I hadn't fully come back into my body, preferring to float just outside of it. To heal, I needed to reconnect with my soul's choice to continue with my life, and this meant, first and foremost, coming fully back into my body. With Rose leading the way, I worked through the trauma from the car crash and the resultant anxiety. I learned to listen to my body and pay attention to my feelings. Inevitably this process led me back to childhood, and I was able to lick clean some of my early wounds. It came as something of a revelation that I had suffered so much trauma in such a short time on the planet.

From the time of the car crash, my soul had been trying to wake me up to my path. Tough as it was, this period of my life was a blessing. Much later, I realized that had I not made the choice to heal in London, my path would have changed irrevocably at this point, and my soul mission would not have been possible.

SPIRITUAL ALLIES

Another source of help during this period was my first real English friend. Clare was the same age as me, but I came to regard her as

Chapter 1 | Awakening

a teacher on my path. Teachers come in many guises; it's tempting to look for the one guru, the uber teacher who will show you the way, but it doesn't work like this, and you run the risk of missing the many brilliant teachers who show up in your life—some for a moment, some for a season. These are our spiritual allies.

Clare was one of these precious gems. Her long blonde hair reminded me of Jane from the Buddhist Retreat Centre in Ixopo, although she was less serene than the nobly silent Jane. Clare was more like an effervescent light. She introduced me to organic vegetables and London's alternative health scene. I was an instant convert to both.

When I met Clare, she had just embarked on a Traditional Chinese Medicine (TCM) degree course. She needed a guinea pig for her acupuncture case studies. I jumped at the offer. Our sessions morphed into long discussions about energy and the most effective tools for transformation. Like me, Clare was a seeker. I joined her on a crusade to try out every healing modality for a true fit. While Clare pursued her formal studies, I became a workshop junkie. My spare time was full to the brim with weekend and evening courses on Shiatsu, Reflexology, Aromatherapy, Reiki, and countless other modalities. I attended talks and festivals in perpetual hope that my spirit guide would take me firmly by the hand and show me what to do.

It is a perplexing thing to have crystal clarity in one incandescent moment of your life, followed by clairvoyance—and then radio silence. But I knew, in my heart, that I was the one who had blocked the channels of communication with my begging and pleading to be released from what at the time felt like the torment of an unwelcome gift. It was perfectly clear how this awkward silence had come about. I had chosen the slow road and had to be patient.

Clare, on the other hand, was on the fast track. She completed her TCM and Acupuncture training at lightning speed and dove into Osteopathy. After graduating, she made a name for herself as North London's best osteopath and helped thousands of people on their journeys. We didn't know it then, of course, but Clare had much less time than me, and perhaps this is why she hurried along her path. A shining light, Clare passed away in 2014, just shy of fifty.

My perpetual seeking took me to many spiritual festivals. At the annual Mind Body Spirit Festival at the College of Psychic Studies in London, I attended a past life regression workshop with Denise Linn, an internationally renowned spiritual teacher and author. Having read one of her books, I was excited to meet her. Past life regression was new territory for me. After an introductory talk, we broke into small groups for a guided regression to find our life purpose. As Denise guided us into deep relaxation, I found myself quickly slipping into trance, very different from the kind of rising upward out of my body I had experienced after the car accident; this was a dropping down, a freefall into a deep well of memory within.

When I came back from the depths of my inner world, I knew without a doubt that my purpose was to *heal myself and others*. During the past life journey, I heard the very same words that my spirit guide had uttered after the car crash. When we shared our purpose in the group, I felt very shy. I was by far the youngest in this circle of women, and it felt exceedingly arrogant to be declaring that I was a healer.

Perhaps seeing my discomfort, an elderly woman next to me leaned over and whispered, "start with yourself, and you'll learn everything you need to know about helping others."

These were prophetic words indeed. I might not have had a map yet, but I left Denise Linn's past life workshop with a renewed sense of purpose. The tenacious dog glared at me from the shadows and slunk away. I threw myself into *Project Healing* with renewed vigor and conviction. With Rose at my side, I embraced the Wounded Healer archetype as if I had invented it. Everything I did was geared toward healing myself or learning about healing. My mantra on homesick days, and there were many, was *London is my place of healing.*

Chapter 1 | Awakening

GIFT AWAKENING: HEALING HANDS

Taking the first tentative step to healing others, I qualified as a massage therapist and started my own portable business. Following Rose's example, I had my first business cards printed and put the word out at local health centers. In no time at all, I had a few clients in North London. Getting to my clients meant lugging my fold-up massage table and box of tricks—massage oil, essential oils, music—across London in snail-pace traffic. It was a time-consuming endeavor, but I threw myself into it with zeal and soaked up the experience. I also had a part-time job as a copy editor at an advertising company. After my days as a reporter in war-torn KwaZulu-Natal, copy-editing was deathly dull, but it paid the bills. My massage venture added a splash of color to an otherwise monochrome existence.

Just as business was taking off, the company offered me a job as an on-site massage therapist as part of its staff wellness program. Back in the early nineties, there were virtually no staff wellness programs, and very few companies were even aware of this concept. Being in the right place at the right time, I grabbed the opportunity with both hands. My tiny treatment room, which I shared with another therapist, was like a railway station. Each treatment was ten minutes. There were a lot of *bums on seats* in a day, and the learning curve was steep and rapid.

Looking back, it was the best preparation I could have had. Massaging scores of people every day, I discovered that I could sense what was happening in someone's body just by touching them. I learned to feel into the hidden layers with my hands, which often surfaced emotions or memories for my clients. Everyone wanted to talk. Our railway junction was a hubbub of noisy chatter. I noticed that some people drained my energy, and others recharged me. Having no idea then how to protect my energy field, I was constantly exhausted. But I was happy. This fact sneaked up on me as something of a surprise.

It was like a soul hallelujah; I was back on track with my mission. The black dog had vanished too. I know now that when I rejected the first soul call in that little French church, something got buried that day. That was the price I paid for relief. In answer to my prayers, I gained a temporary reprieve from the psychic flood but suffered a more serious severance from the soul. Was the cross-shaped wound on the crown of my head an ominous forewarning of the spiritual wound I would inflict on myself? Depression is a soul's call to reconnect with the exigencies of the soul. This experience in London helped me understand depression from a spiritual perspective and equipped me to help many clients in the years to come. It also helped me to stay on course when the black dog returned.

One of the perks of my new job was that every month I got a free treatment of my choice to balance my energy. With the whole of London on my doorstep, I continued with the task of healing myself and sampled every single alternative modality on offer. My personal healing journey was being paid for, and, at the same time, I was on a quest to find my training path. Despite ample exposure to a growing variety of options, nothing grabbed me. Either I was missing what was right in front of my nose, or it wasn't yet time.

In fact, three significant events had to happen first.

KEEPER OF THE KEYS

The first significant event was a visit from Patrick's flamboyant mother, Chatelaine, which just happens to mean *keeper of the keys*. No one wants their partner's mother to hold the keys, and so it was with some trepidation that I welcomed her to our tiny Victorian semi, with as much grace as I could muster and stern resolve to give her a good time. Chatelaine's plan was to use our home as a base for her travels. "Six weeks of popping in and out," she said. In the end, it was far more popping in than out.

When she arrived, Chatelaine wasted no time in getting on with her mission. Our tidy home was quickly transformed into a chaotic base camp. Maps were laid out on the lounge floor, pencils, red pens, stickers, brochures, and a slew of assorted books and videos were scattered around. Somewhat aghast at the colorful chaos, I watched from the sidelines as Chatelaine set about decorating her maps with stickers and red lines— Stonehenge, Avebury, Glastonbury, Tintagel,

Findhorn; the stickers proliferated on her map. She wanted to travel the length and breadth of England and Scotland to visit every one of these sacred places.

As she chattered away, it dawned on me that she wanted me to go with her. This was not my plan at all, but she was so enthusiastic about her ideas that it was hard to say no. Frankly, I don't recall saying yes, either, but that didn't deter Chatelaine. She thrust some spiritual books in my direction and instructed me to get reading. Ah, she knew my weak point, this wily key-keeper. I succumbed to my love of books and, as her would-be traveling companion, quickly got with the program.

Mercifully, this preparation phase was short-lived. Chatelaine did everything quickly and enthusiastically, in equal measure. Despite my reservations, I was swept up in her joie de vivre and decided the best approach in this situation was the path of least resistance. And so, without giving it too much thought, I took some time off work and became Chatelaine's unwitting companion on a pilgrimage to England's sacred sites.

Our first foray was to the southwest of England to visit Glastonbury, Stonehenge, and Avebury. Chatelaine was dressed for the occasion in a flowing ensemble of purple and blue. My regular London attire—faded black jeans, tee-shirt *probably black*, and Doc Marten boots—was positively dour in comparison. I ignored Chatelaine's disapproving glances and focused on getting us through the London traffic. In normal circumstances, Chatelaine talked constantly in a kind of stream of consciousness. Heading south on the M1, she seemed to gather pace, regaling me with information about our sacred itinerary and all manner of spiritual revelations. While I found the delivery overwhelming, I was intrigued by the message. By the time we got to Glastonbury, I was well versed in the myths of Avalon and very ready to climb the Tor.

When we arrived, Chatelaine said we had to visit the Chalice Well first. After the long drive, I was restless, but she insisted that we had to tune into the energy at the well. While Chatelaine quieted down in the shade, I splashed around in the shallows of the Vesica Pisces pond. We walked up the Tor in blissful silence, save for one or two gasps from Chatelaine at the breathtaking views over the patchwork countryside. At the top, we lay in the grass, and before long, we both dozed off in the warm July sun. It was like sinking into a deep well of peace.

After a few lazy hours on the Tor, we went back to Glastonbury and wandered through the village. Revived, Chatelaine chatted exuberantly with everyone we met. As an introvert, I hung back rather than getting dragged into every conversation. While Chatelaine spread her good cheer, I browsed through the many New Age shops. Some felt creepy and spat me out the door. I decided to listen to this sixth sense—*my shop vibes*—and only linger to browse when I felt comfortable in the energy.

It was in one of these good-vibe shops that I bought my first crystal pendant, a clear quartz on a silver chain. The shop owner was a New Age type, dressed in swirling skirts, a purple tunic, dangling earrings, big eighties- style hair, and an even bigger smile. Her crystal shop was more of the same—purples, blues, greens, feathers, and all manner of dangling things hanging from the ceiling. The shop smelled of incense and sage, and I was quite happy lingering for a while. I realized it was the shop owner's calm energy that gave it the *good vibe* I was enjoying.

When I paid for my crystal, she took my hands, glanced at the scars, then looked at me intently with twinkling blue eyes and said, "You too, dear. You're one of us. Look after your hands."

On our way to Stonehenge a few days later, we stopped in Bath to visit the Roman baths. Quite by chance, we passed a bookshop with Barbara Brennan's *Hands of Light* in the window display. Primed by the crystal shop owner's comments the day before, I bought a copy without even looking at the contents. This enlightening book was to become my bible for many years to come.

At Stonehenge, we joined the busloads of tourists viewing the Neolithic stone circle. I knew this had been a magical place in Druid times. Some said it was one of the great inter-dimensional portals. Try as I might, I couldn't feel anything and left feeling rather disappointed. With the long summer evening ahead of us, we went on to the less-frequented Avebury Stone Circle in Wiltshire.

Avebury is the largest megalithic stone circle in the world, but in those days, it was not as well known as Stonehenge, which is the more architecturally sophisticated of the two sites. Avebury consists of three stone circles with a large henge (embankment with a ditch) around it. Dating from prehistoric times, Avebury's original purpose is unknown, but it has been used for Solstice ceremonies and other pagan rituals since Druid times. There were fewer people at Avebury, and in those days, the site wasn't even cordoned off. We wandered among the standing stones at our leisure. This was a completely different experience, and the energy felt alive. Chatelaine was positively glowing. Leaving her be, I lay against a grassy bank in the outer ring, soaking up the energy and feeling, at last, that here was something sacred.

While daydreaming in the henge, an earlier experience came flooding into my memory. When I was fourteen, my family spent a year in Dorset while my academic father was on sabbatical. His research into Roman Britain and my mother's mission to visit every church and assorted sacred site led us on a merry dance around the south of England. Every weekend my younger brother and I were expected to take part in these educational outings. By the end of the year, we had visited every historical and sacred site within striking distance, which is to say, most of the south of England.

At fourteen, I was largely disinterested, but the repeated exposure to sacred sites rubbed off. Despite my teenage indifference, my mother's imploring to *feel the special energy* undoubtedly sensitized me in some primal way. Later, I realized that this, too, was a significant initiation.

THE SOIL OF MY CHILDHOOD

Here I should say a little about my parents and their role in my spiritual development. Between the two of them, I grew up in the rich humus of the mythical and the sacred.

My father was a professor of Classics, well-versed in obscure languages such as Assyrian Babylonian, Latin, and Ancient Greek. Our bookshelves overflowed with volumes on mythology and ancient civilizations. As a child who loved reading, this was an exciting treasure house of discovery. I was especially captivated by Egypt. At the age of eight, I was obsessed with learning hieroglyphics and mapping the lineages of Egyptian kings and queens. My father's gift to me was this love of language and history.

My mother was a math teacher and devout Christian. She was well-versed in the gospel and believed in the power of prayer. Naturally, I read the New Testament from cover to cover, but this captivated me less than other mythological texts. My mother's lodestar felt off to me. For reasons I couldn't articulate as a child, I didn't buy the Bible's version of truth. My mother and I had fierce arguments about *truth* versus *knowing* throughout my childhood. This didn't make for an easy relationship, but I cut my metaphysical teeth at a very young age. My mother's gift to me was this spiritual grinding stone and a deeply ingrained sense of the sacred.

With two pedagogical parents, extra-curricular education happened by osmosis. This bonus teaching culminated during our family's sabbatical year in Dorset—not that I appreciated it then. Like most teenagers, I probably missed most of the luminosity on our travels. I remember my mother's exasperation when her disinterested daughter slouched against yet another dolmen, oblivious to its sacred significance. "Don't be so profane," she'd say, imploring me to show more reverence.

I couldn't really blame her. Evidently, I was going through some teenage stuff. As an Indigo child, school was a trial at the best of times, but that year was plain tough sledding. Being thrown into a rough, comprehensive high school in rural Dorset was a culture shock, to put it mildly. For the first month, I hardly understood a word my classmates said in their broad Dorset drawl, and they didn't understand me until I adjusted my accent. The kids thought I was an exotic oddity. Not fitting in is every teenager's nightmare. Being ostracized is even worse. The teachers did a good job of that. This was 1979, the height of sanctions

Chapter 1 | Awakening

against apartheid South Africa. In the wake of the Soweto riots in 1976, South Africa was a pariah state, and I was its hapless representative. The summer holidays couldn't come fast enough!

That summer, my family stayed with friends on a Hebridean island called Mull on the west coast of Scotland. It was here in the remote Scottish wilds that I came to terms with my Celtic name. I had never much liked the name Heather until my mother pointed out this hardy wildflower in situ. "This is the wild heart of your name," she said, making a sweeping gesture toward the rugged landscape.

My mother loved the Hebrides. On one of the only sunny days of our holiday, she announced an expedition to a thirteenth century abbey on the even more remote Isle of Iona. Weather permitting, we'd visit Fingal's Cave on the uninhabited islet of Staffa on the way. She was in seventh heaven when we docked at the storm-battered islet and took great delight in the sheer improbability of being able to go inside Fingal's Cave on one of just four days of the year when the weather permits entry. Even the teenage version of me was stirred by the magic of Fingal's Cave, which, by the way, inspired Mendelssohn's Hebrides Overture, so it was no small magic. "This is a luminous moment," my mother said with a knowing look. "It can't be just coincidence."

What she meant was that she had prayed for this to happen. Coincidence or not, Fingal's Cave primed me for my first real mystical experience. Later that day, when we visited the abbey on Iona, my body started to tingle. I felt slightly faint, and then a tug, an unmistakable pulling toward something else. For a moment, everything around me faded. I was vaguely aware of the sea of visitors around me, but there was no movement. Everything was frozen, in a kind of time paralysis. I stood dead still, too, as if moving would break the spell. The déjà vu feeling that washed over me then was so strong, not even the most prosaic of teenagers could ignore it. Soon enough, my mother called me to join the tour, and I snapped back to the present.

At fourteen, I had no frame of reference for what happened in the abbey. I had heard of déjà vu but didn't know how I could possibly have been on Iona before. Liberated from my mother's educational tour, I spent the rest of the day exploring the island on my own. With its grassy hills, turquoise waters, and beaches of colorful pebbles, Iona had a magical air. On a far north beach, I collected glittering stones while the wind whined. What I remember most clearly is the light on Iona; it was muted yet vibrant, with a quality I've never seen anywhere else. The surreal landscape mirrored my experience in the abbey as if some long-forgotten part of myself was trying to reach me through the mists of time.

SACRED SITES REVISITED

Visiting Avebury with Chatelaine opened a portal to this earlier experience on Iona and awakened something deep inside me. At fourteen, I wasn't aware that I was being attuned. Now, exactly fourteen years later, at Avebury, I was far more aware of the sacred energies and was curious to find out more.

When we returned to London a few days later, I was more receptive to Chatelaine's chatter. Over the next few weeks and a second foray to visit the crop circles in Wiltshire, we engaged in an ongoing spiritual conversation. While I was learning about people's energetic bodies at work, Chatelaine was exploring the Earth's energetic body. We had a lively exchange.

In her galloping style, Chatelaine told me about the Earth's chakras, the ley lines, and the sacred sites around the world. I followed as best I could. Like our own bodies, the Earth has energy centers and pathways. The Earth's body has seven major chakras and four spinner wheels, or vortices, which are as powerful as the chakras. The heart chakra is situated at Glastonbury. The Earth element spinner wheel is under Table Mountain in Cape Town. These chakras and wheels are planetary gateways, connected by the Earth's ley lines, which crisscross the globe. The ley lines are like the Earth's veins, Chatelaine explained. Like vast underground rivers of light, they carry the lifeblood of the Universe.

The sacred sites are like nodes on this light grid. Many early monolithic sites were deliberately built on the Earth's energy points, and they connect to each other through the grid of ley lines. Some of the earliest sites, like Stonehenge and Machu Picchu, are considered inter-dimensional portals to other places in the Cosmos. These nodes are highly charged points where people have worshipped or conducted sacred ceremonies over centuries. Charged with a high vibration, sacred places are like gateways to higher consciousness, connection points with the soul, and bring a sense of deep peace, as I had experienced on the Glastonbury Tor. The charged energy is encoded in the rocks, the land, and the Earth itself. This is the reason that, through the ages, people have made pilgrimages to sacred sites to receive the energy, experience the magic, and unlock the parts of themselves that get obscured by our material lives.

Much later, I learned that sacred sites are considered to be portals for spiritual awakening. This is exactly what I experienced on Iona as a teenager and at Avebury with Chatelaine. In the intervening years, I had taken the first tentative steps on my spiritual path at the Buddhist Retreat Centre in Ixopo, which is situated on a powerful node known as the southeast Earth chakra, located at thirty degrees south and thirty degrees east. When we enter these sacred places, we cross a liminal threshold, consciously or not, into a field of energy that is attuned to higher dimensional consciousness.

Every site is different and will capture the sound frequency from the Earth at that point on the grid and then act as an amplifier for that frequency. This is what we feel when we enter these magical places. Just being at a sacred site, we are imprinted with its energy. Our cells will resonate with the vibration, and we may be transported into a state of higher awareness or connection. In the past, indigenous peoples, like the Celtic Druids or the Incas in South America, consciously used these places to access the mystical and the divine. As we became locked into third-dimensional consciousness, we lost our connection with these power points, and, sadly, the sheer volume of tourists at places like Stonehenge and Machu Picchu is slowly dimming the energetic field.

After Chatelaine's visit, I devoured the books she gave me. Everything else faded into the background as I immersed myself in spiritual waters. I reflected on my experiences at England and Scotland's sacred sites at age fourteen and now again at twenty-eight. Tasting the mystery as a rebellious teenager had gently awakened me to the unseen, energetic dimension. The déjà-vu experience on Iona connected me with my soul's journey, reminding me that I had walked the Earth before this life. At fourteen, that was a revelation. Although I didn't know it as a teenager, being in the energetic field of so many sacred sites throughout that year was the start of a process of attunement to higher energies. This was the groundwork for my soul mission.

My recent experiences with Chatelaine had shaken me awake again. It could hardly escape my notice that my *awakenings* had come in seven-year cycles. At fourteen, on Iona, I had a taste of the mystery, and at twenty-one, I was immersed in the mystery of my car crash experience. Now at twenty-eight, I had been reminded to get back onto the mystic's path. This time, it was Chatelaine—*keeper of the keys*—who handed me the spiritual keys. It was up to me to open the doorway and step across the threshold into the soul-world.

At last, I was on a more conscious spiritual path.

MY FIRST SON ARRIVES

The second significant event was the birth of my first child, Luca, in 1994. Before I got pregnant, I had a vivid dream about a little blonde boy. In the dream, the little boy gets bigger and, literally, grows up as he toddles and then strides from one side of the lawn to the other.

I wasn't planning to have children just yet; still, I had a sense that the dream foretold events not yet privy to my conscious mind. So, when out of the blue, I started craving oranges and pork sausages—a mysterious impulse for a vegetarian, it wasn't really a surprise to discover I was pregnant. Despite my inner knowing, I remember the intense rush of feelings when I saw the blue stripe slowly forming across the home pregnancy test strip—first disbelief, then a warm glow that infused my heart. I wanted to shout and sing! At the same time, I wanted to keep this precious secret all to myself, so I could fully savor every little magical nuance of this new life growing inside me.

Chapter 1 | Awakening

Luca's arrival was a major turning point in my life. Nothing could have prepared me for motherhood. There was no warning about the freefall into love. The first glimpse of my baby as he arrived in the world, wide-eyed and startled after a grueling birth, took my breath away. It was on Day Three that I fell headlong in love. I remember the exact moment. The doors of my heart flew open, and the love flowed out like a river that had burst its banks, sweeping me with it. It was a visceral thing. It was the kind of love that changed me from the very inside out. This little soul had given me the gift of unconditional love.

As much as motherhood opened my heart, it also threw up new challenges. Those early baby years are tough sledding for any couple. The couples that survive are the ones that stay connected, not just as parents but as friends and lovers. In challenging circumstances, we had our work cut out for us.

When Luca was born, I gave up my massage job and threw in my lot with Patrick's fledgling environmental law start-up. With me juggling a new baby and work, this arrangement worked well for our family, but there was a looming shadow. Patrick's traveling schedule meant that we were apart for frequent extended periods. Our solution to this problem was to accompany Patrick on as many trips as possible, and so we tagged along to South America, Southeast Asia, Europe, and, of course, South Africa. By the time Luca was two years old, he had sampled rainforests, tropical beaches, and coincidentally, or perhaps not, an impressive number of sacred sites on four continents.

In the beginning, it was exciting to explore new countries and exotic cultures. Inevitably, we stumbled on many sacred sites on our erratic path—Malta's megalithic temples, Malaysia's Batu Caves, the standing stones in Brittany, the list goes on. As if by magnetic pull, they seemed to pop up wherever we went. They were a constant reminder not to lose sight of my spiritual path. I always left these sacred places feeling recharged. Nonetheless, caring for a young child in a foreign environment while Patrick was working around the clock was demanding. Without friends and support groups, I was lonely.

When Luca turned two and started nursery school, we stopped tagging along with Patrick. Luca needed a routine and stability. I needed home and friends. While this was a good decision, the shared space we had forged on our travels began to shrink. As Patrick continued with his relentless travel schedule, our daily experiences diverged. By force of circumstance, for much of the time we inhabited different worlds with different priorities. While Patrick was on his missions, I was left holding the baby, literally.

During Patrick's absences, I was also managing the office, which now had three employees and itinerant contract lawyers. This was what I was good at, keeping the home fires burning. But it was a very lonely vigil. What kept me going was my beautiful baby, who I loved more than I thought was possible. I threw myself into motherhood. I could at least do this well, even though I was less successful on the relationship front.

The exigencies of this period pushed me further into my inner world. In my search for an anchor and perspective, I dove further into meditation and spiritual reading. Patrick, on the other hand, continued with field trips to assorted developing countries to keep the consultancy business afloat. As our paths diverged, our increasingly strained communication centered around the business and Patrick's next field trip. Our emotional landscape was shrinking, and my resentment grew apace. We were on dangerous ground.

Justified or not, resentment is never a good thing. It pushed Patrick even further away. I was hurting, he was hurting, and we both did things that made it worse. We also had good times, moments when the sunshine broke through the clouds. One of those sunrays was that I was pregnant again. The desert landscape was suddenly greener. The distance between us narrowed. With a second child on the way, we discussed Patrick traveling less. For a while, things were better. I was hopeful.

MY YOUNGEST SON ARRIVES

This was the backdrop for the third significant event, the birth of my youngest child, Liam. Liam was two weeks late, and much to my disappointment, he had to be induced. While I settled into the hospital birthing room, Patrick received a phone call from our five-year-old niece, Kayla. She told him she'd had a dream that a little boy called Liam was coming. At the time, we didn't know whether our baby was a boy or a girl. In the flurry of a very quick birth, Patrick didn't tell me about Kayla's dream. After holding my new baby boy, I went to the bathroom to clean up. While I was lying in the bath, a sudden rush of wind flowed right through me, whispering the name Liam. Startled, I turned around, half-expecting to see someone standing behind me, but the bathroom door was closed. There was no one there. Then I heard my grandmother's voice and understood that she was the wind. She told me this would be my last child and proceeded to assign me a spiritual task. Listening intently, I got the memo that I was to clear the ancestral pattern of abuse on my mother's side, which started with my great-grandmother, Sarah. In my post-birth stupor, this was very confusing, especially because, as far as I knew, Grandma Olivia was still alive and well in South Africa.

When Patrick and I swapped stories, there was little doubt about our new baby's name. Liam had been announced in no uncertain terms. When I got home from the hospital, my mother told me that Grandma Olivia had passed a few days before. She hadn't told me because she didn't want to upset me just before Liam's birth.

With a new baby and a three-year-old to care for, my late grandmother's message quickly slipped into the far recesses of my mind. As my heart swelled to make room for this new little being, life was happily busy. It's an incredible thing, the heart. As any mother will know, you think you can never love another child as much as the one you already have, that there cannot possibly be more space in an already full heart, and then this crazy thing happens—your heart just gets bigger. It adjusts like the ocean. It's limitless. There is no sharing or dividing or compromising, just more space and love, like a bottomless well.

The week before Liam arrived, I was painfully aware that it was the last time Luca would have my undivided love, the last time he would be an only child. I spent three days in conscious presence with him, allowing myself to feel completely how much I loved this little being and giving him my full attention. It was a precious time, but the impulse came from a misperception that there would be less love for him with a sibling around. When Liam was born, I laughed at how little I knew about love.

Falling in love is really an opening of the heart. It's when we drop into that deep well of love that is already within us. It's what happens when we stop judging and see someone with the eyes of the heart. It is that small miracle when we allow ourselves and another to dip into unity consciousness. Fresh from the inner waters, babies are still immersed in unity consciousness, and so it is little wonder that the doors of the heart are easily flung wide open. Wide-open hearts are also vulnerable. When baby Liam was three weeks old, Patrick had to go off on a three-week field trip. Enamored as I was with our new baby, I wasn't yet through the six-week woods, which, as every new parent knows, is a physical test of endurance. This time, I also had a very active three-year-old to look after. In London, I had no family support or hired help, so my mother came from South Africa to help me. After her fleeting visit, the recent spark of hope dimmed. When Patrick returned, the distance between us seemed to take more effort to traverse. Despite our best efforts, things were going to get a lot worse before there was some sort of light at the end of the tunnel.

The newborn woods with Liam proved to be thick and tangled. I needed a sword to cut my way through. Our new baby was ill. To make it worse, no one knew what was wrong with him. He was unmistakably yellow and covered in rashes. Liam was allergic to everything, including, in the end, breastmilk. He was given the loose diagnosis of "prolonged jaundice, *cause unknown*." It was the cause unknown that made my heart pound. This is what doctors tell you when they don't know what's going on. Throughout his first year, Liam was monitored by a top research team at one of London's hospitals. Being monitored meant fortnightly check-ups at the hospital and blood tests for a list of terrifying diseases with unpronounceable names. Between visits was a nail-biting round of researching said unheard-of diseases and waiting for the results. This translated into nine months of sitting on the precipice of wanting a diagnosis yet not being able to face one. I braced myself for the worst.

Chapter 1 | Awakening

After a few months, I stopped researching dread diseases and started exploring holistic medicine. When Liam was nine-months old, I found an amazing homeopath within walking distance from my home. In London, that was like striking gold. This amazing medicine woman prescribed some remedies, and Liam's rashes cleared up within days. By the time he reached his first birthday, Liam appeared to be in good health. I didn't have a diagnosis, but I stopped going to the hospital. Medical science had given me nothing but unanswered questions and an unhealthy dose of fear.

With the help of the homeopath and gut instinct, I muddled through Liam's babyhood as best I could. His illness was an important teacher. Gradually cold terror loosened its grip on my heart. He was doing well! I clung to this narrative, especially on the bad days. Liam was often a sickly yellow, and he didn't have the energy of other toddlers. But he was meeting his milestones, and I just had to trust that we would find our way through the woods.

HOMECOMING

While this was going on, Patrick and I decided to return to South Africa. This was the culmination of a long-running debate. Anyone who has lived in exile circles will know that there is an unresolved disquiet in the exile's heart and that going home is the background track in every conversation. Even those who pledged to stay in England kept a foot in both worlds. We were tired of sitting on the fence and wanted some sort of resolution.

When Luca was a baby, I had taken him to meet his family in South Africa. In Cape Town, I was filled with a curious joy—the kind of joy that bubbles up to the surface when the soul is singing.

When I visited my parents in Durban, I announced, "We're going to live in Cape Town!"

The words flew out of my mouth before I even had the thought, and in that lucid moment, I knew it was true. My soul wanted to be in Cape Town, and that was that. It was only a matter of time. The decision to leave London came nearly five years after the soul-singing moment. Our circle of friends in London thought we were crazy to go back to South Africa. The consensus seemed to be that we were being irresponsible in dragging two young children into an uncertain future. Some of our close friends were angry as if our decision to return were a personal affront. We ignored the chorus and packed our bags. It's hard to ignore a soul's call.

On the inside, I was less certain about our decision. Five years later, could I still trust this distant soul song? Packing up our beautiful Victorian flat, home for nearly a decade, I was filled with sadness and uncertainty. Cramming our worldly belongings into a storage container and two suitcases felt like sheer madness. I was wavering, to put it mildly. On the overnight flight to Cape Town, I was too exhausted to feel anything.

As we settled down for the long night ahead of us, Luca observed, "You can't sleep backward." Out of the mouths of babes. There was no going back.

Arriving back in South Africa after nearly ten years away was a homecoming in many ways, yet we were returning to a different country. Since 1994, South Africa had lurched into the democratic era, narrowly avoiding civil war, and had morphed into the hopeful Rainbow Nation. The heady days of early democracy were in full swing; transformation was the buzzword on everyone's lips. It was an exciting time to be returning home.

Our first day in Cape Town was a breezy spring day in September 1999. We drove into the city, rounded the curve of Nelson Mandela Boulevard, and caught our first glimpse of Table Bay. Lion's Head and the Sentinel loomed ahead of us. I burst into tears and couldn't stop crying as ten years' worth of pent-up homesickness poured out of me. In that moment, I knew that no matter what happened in this tempestuous beloved country, wild horses wouldn't drag me away again.

I was home!

DRAGON'S GOLD
Wisdom teachings from Chapter One

- A dark night of the soul is an initiation into the soul world and an important teacher. When the dark night arrives, don't shy away from it. Embrace the darkness and seek your treasure. It will irrevocably change your trajectory and set you on a higher, soul-aligned path.

- Learn to read the signs that light up your path. When something jumps out at you or glows brightly, makes your skin tingle, or opens your heart with excitement, joy, or tears, pay attention. Get to know the language of your intuition, and you will never lose your way. It is a trustworthy compass.

- Teachers come in many guises. It's tempting to look for a guru to show you the way, but in seeking a savior, you run the risk of missing the many helpers and mentors who will show up on your path, some for just a moment, others for a season, and a rare few for a lifetime. These are your spiritual allies, and they may well hold the key to your next soul-led step. It's up to you to receive the key and unlock the door.

- Sacred sites are highly charged places considered to be portals for spiritual awakening. Many early monolithic stone circles and temples were strategically built on the Earth's energy points and are connected through the grid of ley lines. Some of these sites are considered to be inter-dimensional portals to other places in the Cosmos. Charged with a high vibration, sacred sites are gateways to higher consciousness and connection points with the Cosmos. The charged energy is encoded in the rocks, the land, and the Earth itself. Just being in these special places can attune your energy to a higher frequency and bring a deep sense of peace.

2

DRAGON FIRE
2000 – 2005

Why do dragons hoard gold? Because the things you most need are always to be found where you least want to look.

– Jordan Peterson, "Slaying the Dragon Within Us" podcast

This is the chapter of my life I don't want to revisit, the place I least want to look. It is true that time heals, but some wounds leave an indelible mark that never goes away, not completely. It is twenty years since Patrick and I separated, and the imprint of sadness persists, evident in the tears that sometimes well up at unexpected moments. But this chapter of my life was the fork in the road that ultimately took me in the direction of my soul's calling, and for that, I am truly grateful.

Coming back to the New South Africa after ten years out of the country, I was awash with the excitement of being part of the Rainbow Nation. Relieved to be home, I quickly put down roots in Cape Town. Living at the foot of Table Mountain gave me an even deeper sense of home. A towering presence in the middle of the city, the mountain is a major energy node known as the Earth element spinner wheel, which is a grounding force for the whole planet. Here I was wired to the Earth's sacred grid, a subtle yet reassuring refuge.

On known ground again and feeling more like myself, I slowly began to acknowledge how unhappy I was with my relationship. It was like I was finally letting myself in on my own tightly wrapped secret, which had been hidden away in the quiet desperation of the last few years in London. I had pretended not to notice how lonely I was and when this unwelcome feeling broke through the surface, I pushed it away. I could never act on it anyway; I just didn't have it in me to break up our family. So, I put on a convincingly brave face, determined to be grateful for what I had. *Isn't that what good mothers do—put their children and family first, even if they are dying inside?*

Again and again, I ignored the voices of disquiet, which were subtle nudges to seek a larger version of myself and to embrace my life purpose. If you ignore a soul's call, it will come again, usually with greater urgency and force. Sure enough, the call came again, not in the way I would have expected, but loud and clear all the same.

The dragon inside me that had been asleep for so long suddenly awoke with a surge of anger. While my dragon had many faces, it chose to show the face of anger first. It puffed fire through my veins and demanded to be heard. What should I do? Slay it like a hero in a mythical story? Tame it? Make it do my bidding? I decided to unleash the dragon and follow the energy. What a wild ride I was in for! Had I known then what was coming, would I have listened to the dragon's rumblings and so carelessly unleashed it? In all honesty, probably not.

The thing about dragons is that once unleashed from the depths of their hidden caverns, there is no tethering them, and they have an unstoppable tendency to cause mayhem. It is also true that dragons, if respectfully treated, hold the keys to wisdom. But that only comes after the destruction. No gold without the dragon, I'm afraid.

One of the greatest tests on our human journey, and opportunities for spiritual growth, lies in the arena of relationships—all our relationships, but particularly romantic partnerships. This is where we lay ourselves bare, with all our vulnerabilities, and hope to find unconditional love and acceptance. When we don't find what we are seeking, it is shattering, not only because there is a primal feeling of betrayal, but because, in this innermost temple of hope, it is a shattering of the illusion that we can meet our needs and find safety through an-Other.

From this perspective, the break-up of a long-term relationship, particularly when you share children, is one of the biggest initiations we can encounter. It is also one of the most powerful agents for soul growth and transformation. It is a resounding invitation to consciously reshape your life in ways that might not have been possible or accessible from within the consciousness of the old relationship. The problem with soul growth of this magnitude is that there is no bypassing the pain of it. You have to go through it, and make no mistake, the post-relationship transformation process is a grueling one, much like climbing a high mountain. When you're on the uphill climb, it's agony at times; you huff and puff, convinced you'll never make it, but when you reach the summit, the view is worth every moment of muscle-aching pain on the way up. It takes your breath away!

On the slow ascent, it really helps to detach from the personal embodiment of the Other, who seems to represent all that is *wrong*, and to see them instead as a reflection of what needs to shift within. Relationships are the great mirrors, the stark-truth reflections of the not-so-visible inner world. It is here in the deep, dark interior that you'll find healing and resolution. And if you are willing to regard the Reflective Other as a soul-in-service, you have every chance of alchemizing the internal landscape and becoming sovereign over all the old programming and patterns, replacing social programming with soul knowing. Gradually, eventually, the outer reflections will change too. This is the gold.

In the aftermath of my own relationship collapse, I knew in a theoretical sort of way that it was important to look for the higher perspective, but it would take years to reach higher ground. What was happening in the outer world was deeply confronting and painful, and it was a long, hard climb from the bottom of the mountain to the breathtaking summit.

After the car crash that woke me up to my soul's agenda, this was the second major initiation to get with my soul program. This is how I completed a disempowering cycle and found new ground.

FACING THE DRAGON

When my dragon woke up, my life crumbled around me with ferocious swiftness. Within two years of landing back in South Africa, my relationship with Patrick fell apart. That was probably not a coincidence. Back on home ground, I felt stronger and face the dragon I must. It was as if I'd stepped into the light and could no longer hide in the shadows of denial. The tightly sealed unhappiness I had dragged around in London couldn't be magicked away any longer. Swallowing my anger wasn't an option anymore.

During the years of exile from my home country, I had fallen into all the classic traps that naïve young women stumble into unwittingly. Somewhere along the relationship path, my intuition had come undone, and I had lost my way. I was normalizing what didn't feel right to me. I had given up on my hopes and dreams for what partnership could be, settling instead for unsatisfying scraps and morsels. When the dragon of anger made its presence known, I could no longer sleepwalk through my days pretending all was well. It was time to disentangle from this unhealthy entanglement and listen to my heart's knowing.

The breakdown of a relationship is a complex thing; the build-up to its ultimate demise can take years. It's not as if you wake up on a bad day and pack your bags on a whim. It isn't one single thing that happens, though there are defining moments. For me, there were many pivotal moments that culminated in the Big Decision, but this is not the place to dissect them. Separation is, by nature, messy; the unraveling, a painful struggle between two people who don't know how to cross the widening chasm and find each other again. Somewhere along the line, the narratives diverge too, and it's nearly impossible to find a way across this perceptual divide without deep listening and understanding. Few dissonant couples are capable of such acts of grace.

While I longed for a magical relationship fix, a clear pathway through the impasse, I've come to believe that despite the best of intentions, this is not possible if the soul is calling for a different path. The number one cause of relationships breaking down is that consciousness levels change: one person grows in a new direction, and for a thousand reasons, the other doesn't grow at the same pace or in the same direction. Unless both parties are moving in the same direction, in search of healing and growth, and can see beyond the nitty-gritty of the power struggle of who is right and who is wrong, who is to blame and who should change, an ending is almost inevitable.

This was another way of thinking about the continental drift I was experiencing. Despite my insight, I was powerless to stop the drift effect for the sake of fixed togetherness. In the absence of shared understanding and growth, I chose heartbreak over continued suffering.

A SPIRITUAL TEACHER APPEARS

My choice to end the relationship was spurred along by an insistent combination of inner and outer forces. No longer to be ignored, my inner dragon was perched at the cave entrance, puffing out warning plumes of smoke. It was itching to knock my house of cards to the ground. Equally persistent in trying to get my attention was a recurring dream about a striking woman with long dark hair and sky-blue eyes, running up a mountain and beckoning me to follow. Around this time, I attended a New Year's Eve ceremony in Hout Bay. As we gathered around the fire, a tall woman dressed in traditional African robes and headdress raised her arms and welcomed the group. With a shiver, I realized that this was the woman from my dreams. The instant I laid eyes on her, I knew that our destinies were intertwined. As it turned out, Frieda was to become one of the most important spiritual teachers on my path.

Frieda was a trained *sangoma*, a healer and diviner in the African tradition. African medicine—or *muti* as it's locally known—includes working with indigenous plant medicines and the spirit world, a unique combination of herbalist and healer. It is believed that one is called by the ancestors to become a *sangoma*, and only those who are called may go through the very rigorous formal training. Having received the ancestral calling, Frieda had trained as a *sangoma* in Swaziland and Botswana and then made her home on a beautiful tract of fynbos-covered land on the slopes of the Hout Bay mountains. At that time, there was a small cottage on the land and an even smaller *ndumbe* (African hut) where she kept her medicines and met with her clients.

Shortly after the New Year's Eve ceremony, I contacted Frieda and arranged a reading with the bones in her *ndumbe*. Throwing the bones is a traditional African divining technique. Much like a Tarot reader uses cards to do a reading, a *sangoma* throws an assortment of old bones, usually of birds and small animals, and then, with the help of the ancestors, interprets the patterns and symbols for their clients.

When I arrived, Frieda smudged me at the doorway with *impepho*—indigenous wild sage—and then invited me to come inside. We sat cross-legged on the floor, facing each other. The smell of *impepho* permeated the dimly lit hut, which was crammed with all manner of ceremonial paraphernalia: beaded sticks, feathered rattles, drums of assorted sizes. Glass jars filled with dried herbs, powders, and roots lined the walls. It was a lot to take in.

Frieda laid an animal skin on the floor, which was to be the tableau for the bone throwing. Before throwing the bones, she fixed me with her hawk-like gaze and asked me why I had come. Not wanting to give too much away, I stammered something about being at a crossroads and having to make a difficult decision. We chatted for a while, and Frieda exuded such warmth and compassion that I quickly relaxed in her otherworldly *ndumbe*. Without further ado, Frieda started praying to the ancestors—hers and mine and slipping into trance. Her hawk eyes no longer seeing me, she picked up a red velvet pouch, blew into it with long slow breaths, and then threw the bones onto the cloth, a sprawling oracle before us.

Peering at the bones and beyond, Frieda told me that my soul was dying a slow death. This wasn't exactly new to me, but it was shocking to hear it stated so plainly. Then she said, "If you stay where you are, you'll get ill. It is a path of darkness. If you go, you enter the fires of transformation. It won't be easy, but it is a path of light. Your choice."

As the bone reading progressed, Frieda hit upon many truths about my journey and the stark choice in front of me. She talked about answering the call of my soul and my *work with spirit*. She warned about ignoring the soul's call and the potential cost of continuing down a path of darkness. She called it the *victim path*. "You need to take back your power and walk," she said, looking up from the bone tableau to signal the end of the reading. The truth of her words hit me with startling force.

I left Frieda's *ndumbe* with an odd mix of emotions. My soul had been laid bare in that small hut. I felt raw and exposed yet liberated by the truth I'd been hiding from, reeling at the prospect of sweeping change yet curiously relieved by the affirmation of what must be done. I could no longer pretend to myself or anyone else. I hoped that the good mother in me had been listening!

This was the first of many visits to Frieda's *ndumbe*. For the next seven years, Frieda walked alongside me on an incredible journey of transformation.

HEEDING THE SOUL'S CALL

Despite the clear message from my first bone divination session with Frieda, it was a long time before I was ready to walk away. It took several painstaking months for my mind and heart to catch up with what my soul already knew. Besides, the unraveling of soul ties is no small thing.

The decision pressed in on me—stay or leave? The only thing harder than staying was leaving. Dragon or no dragon, I wasn't ready to shatter our known world. I looked at my boys in the playground and could not imagine inflicting pain on them. I kissed their trusting faces at bedtime and did not have the heart to shatter their certainties. I watched them playing in the garden of our beautiful home and couldn't bear to take this away from them.

While my mother's heart was resisting, willing to sacrifice everything for my children's well-being, my soul wouldn't rest. Night after night, I woke up sweating, the unleashed dragon blowing fire every which way. I'm a night-time processor, foraging in the liminal spaces between waking, sleep, and dreams for insight and guidance. I knew I had to go. I had to allow the too-good mother to die. But after every torrid night, I rallied again, resisting the too-good mother's demise. I was going to make this work, try harder, do my inner work, and somehow fix what was already broken. *Patience*, I told the dragon. *Wild patience, pretty please.* I wasn't ready for dragon-wrought destruction just yet.

One day, after about nine months of nightly tossing and bargaining with the dragon, I woke up with a blinding migraine. My body was on fire, and I couldn't move. My dear neighbor took the boys to school, and I called Frieda. She said that my body was showing me that I was not acting in alignment with my intentions. The panacea was to get in touch with my deepest intention and then find the courage to act on it. The migraine and fever would disappear when I was in integrity. She sounded so certain. Frieda was like this. She shot truth straight from the hip.

"Listen to your body," she said. "It holds the answer to your question."

"How can I possibly make this decision?" I whispered into the phone. "It's not just about my life. There are two little people with me. I can't drag them down this path."

"This is their journey, too," she said. "You can't know, in the bigger picture, what they need to learn and what's best for them. Staying in an unhappy partnership will have consequences too."

Her last sentence hit me hard. I felt like a rabbit caught in the headlights, paralyzed, not knowing which way to run. Every which way, there were consequences. Following Frieda's advice, I listened to my fiery body—the dragon—and contemplated the ceiling with blurry vision. My mind veered between staying and going, arguing back and forth. I am a Libra; decisions have never come easily. Every nuance had to be weighed and balanced on my Libran scales.

Chapter 2 | Dragon Fire

Finally, after three days, the storm in my pounding head abated, the dragon's breath subsided, and a very quiet voice grabbed my attention. It had been there all along. I just hadn't heard it because I was too busy trying to fix the relationship and worrying about my children. This quiet little voice had been drowned out by the chorus of much louder voices—family, close friends, and above all, the persistent views of the too-good mother. Everyone in the know had an opinion about what I should and shouldn't do. When I finally heard my inner voice beneath this external din, the message was simple, "You will die if you stay here." Evidently, it was me or her, the goody-two-shoes mother.

Three hellish days later, I made my choice. I was going to end this arid partnership. This was my deepest intention, and my soul wouldn't rest until I acted with integrity. The true meaning of integrity is that all parts of one's being are present and acting in unison. My many parts were clearly out of sync. I hoped my decision would remedy this sorry state of affairs. Just as Frieda predicted, when I finally arrived at a decision, the migraine disappeared, and I got up from my sick bed more clear-headed than I'd been for years.

That morning, while driving the boys to school, my soul made an appearance again. We were sitting in bumper-to-bumper traffic across the railway bridge, singing along to the boys' favorite CD of children's songs. They were happy to have me back from the dead. Despite what lay ahead, I was flooded with the intoxicating relief that clarity brings. Suddenly it got very bright and very quiet, as if all my senses had been reduced to one single point. I couldn't hear the music anymore. I was lifting right out of my body, ascending above the car into a place of weightless, soundless light. An angel wrapped soft wings around me, and I floated over the bridge engulfed in bliss. Looking down at myself at the steering wheel, I knew that all was well.

Just as suddenly, I was jerked back into my body. The car in front of us had stopped abruptly. With total calm, I braked just in time to avoid a collision. I was fully present and aware, not at all as if I had just slipped out of my body and hopped back in again. We had crossed the bridge, and a different song was playing. Time had indeed passed without me being physically present in it.

It was a visceral reminder of the out-of-body experience after the car crash in my twenties when I was given a choice to live or die. My soul was calling again, urging me to make another life-changing choice. This time the feeling of bliss was even more intense, as if I were being given a taste of the world of the soul. Being spontaneously transported into this blissful state seemed like a confirmation that I was on the right track. Yes, it would take courage, but with none of the accompanying trauma that had ensued after the car crash when I came back into a battered body and a bewildering psychic opening. If I had any lingering doubts about the small, quiet voice of my soul, this extraordinary experience crossing the bridge sealed the deal.

There are some moments in life that are defining. This was one of them. I had made the decision to leave my old life behind, and there was no going back.

CROSSING THE BRIDGE OF NO RETURN

Six weeks later, I packed my bags and moved into a Victorian cottage with the boys. After that soul-illuminating moment, I had no choice but to forge a new path. My greatest agony was that I had to drag my two young children with me. My spiritual teachers assured me that this was their journey, too, that at a soul level, my sons would benefit from my growth and transformation. Spiritual wisdom, perhaps, but as a mother, it was the toughest call I have ever had to make.

From then on, my life was defined by Before the Separation and After the Separation. Everyone says the first year is the toughest. It's like the first year of having a baby, only this time you're moving away from family rather than toward it. It's a different kind of tough. It's a tough filled with heartache rather than hope. I should have been well prepared to be single. But the reality of being alone in our rented cottage with two shaken children and the responsibility for all things adult, sent me reeling. And then came the aftershocks.

The first aftershock was the social fallout. When a long-term partnership breaks up, an intensely private struggle becomes instantly public. People are like vultures circling over a dead carcass, hoping for juicy titbits.

Suddenly everyone—from close friends to vague acquaintances—arrived to feast, but very few stayed long enough to hear the full story. Very quickly, judgments were made; sides were taken. I was dropped like a hot cake by more friends than I care to count. Among them were those who never once asked to hear my side of the story. I was simply erased.

The gossip mill spewed out so many variations of *my story*; it would have been laughable had I not been so enraged by the injustice of all the ill-informed, snap judgments. Fair or not, I had been exiled, which, in the end, proved to be my boon, but that was a long time coming. I already understood what it meant on a spiritual level to lose an old life and begin the new life of being who we are meant to be, but it was a painful road from old to new.

The social judgments unnerved me and rattled my good mother's cage. I picked apart my decision a thousand times: *Had I tried hard enough? Could we have fixed it? Should I have stayed for the sake of the children?* I circled around these questions obsessively. In the end, I kept coming back to one conclusion—our paths had diverged like two continents adrift, and the sheer force was beyond mere mortals to reverse. I had to let go of these incessant questions about the past and turn my attention to questions that would define my future, but in the grinding beginning, these more fruitful questions were elusive. The Victorian cottage period was shaped by more urgently pragmatic demands and a long stretch of grieving.

After the Separation, the days were governed by my routine with the children: breakfast, out the door and through the traffic to school; work or trying to find more freelance work; collect the kids from school. I spent late afternoons with the boys—sport, playdates, park. By the time we'd had supper, I was barely able to dredge up enough energy to read bedtime stories and finish my work once they'd gone to sleep. Most nights, we fell asleep in a tangle on my bed, books strewn around us. No matter how tired I was or how ragged my mothering became, bedtime stories were a non-negotiable part of the day. I wasn't going to let our evening story ritual slip.

Routine and ritual kept us anchored. We read through Roald Dahl books for Liam, and Harry Potter books for Luca, as if our lives depended on it, and in a way, it did. The normality we replicated in our cozy cottage was restorative. No matter how exhausted I was or how disoriented the boys were, this precious oasis held us in a comforting embrace at the end of every tough day.

Tough sledding doesn't quite capture what that first year after the Separation felt like. For all three of us, it was a challenging traverse through shadowlands, though different things became our own markers for the most painful aspects of tough.

For me, it was running the gauntlet of social judgment every day. At the school gate, there were friends who barely greeted me or looked the other way. There were others who were friendly but pointedly didn't invite me to social events. I pretended to be a duck and shook the ice off my back. *I know it's meant to be water off said duck's back, but it felt more like ice.* Luca bore the brunt of the social ice because many of his friends' parents didn't approve of his mother—a tough burden for a young boy to carry. He also missed his father.

For Liam, the post-Separation traverse required being prepared for all eventualities. He dressed himself for pre-school in several layers of clothing and took the rest of his wardrobe in two large shopping bags. The teacher made a second hook for him in the hallway, where the children hung up their school bags. She said being prepared was his way of coping with change. Despite her attentive kindness, bless her heart, it broke mine.

I can't possibly describe every facet of this toughness. It was like wading through mud, *twenty-four seven*, and I mean twenty-four seven, because as soon as the day was done and the boys were asleep, the night started. The nights were tough in a different way. I hardly slept, but at least it was quiet, and I had time to sift through my turbulent feelings. During the day, I was Stoic Mom, doing whatever it took to rebuild our lives. At night, I could collapse for a while and allow the tears to flow. In the quiet darkness, my heart broke open to the well of grief inside me. I lit candles to soothe myself and called in my

Chapter 2 | Dragon Fire

angels to surround me. My great-grandmother Isabella popped in, too, offering comfort and guidance in her ethereal way. In the sanctuary of the night, I had time to feel into the new life that awaited us and let the future-defining questions arise. I woke up exhausted, but at least I had the inner strength to face another day.

During that first year, I inhabited two worlds, the surface-world and the soul-world. In the surface-world, things appeared one way. This is where I dodged the social icebergs, earned an income, was a good-enough mother, and held it all together. In the soul-world, things appeared another way. Here, all the holding it together unraveled—it was raw, filled with shadows, doubts, and uncertainties, yet it was more real. This is when I went in search of soul truth and a deeper understanding of the forces guiding my new life. I was like the mythical Seal Woman who gathered up her seal skin at night and returned to the water. I have always liked water and felt safe in my soul-skin.

Wrapped in my soul-skin, there was a rising awareness, a very faint stirring at first, that the Separation was an initiation, a soul prompt to overhaul my inner template and all the programming that had kept me in a place of unhappiness. Slowly it dawned on me that I was free to forge a new inner template that would create a different type of relationship—with myself and others. This was the true and somewhat liberating purpose of this initiation.

With all the drama of the Separation, it was tempting to focus on the Other, but this was both a convenient distraction and a distortion of truth and not where the answers lay. Deeper understanding would be gained by taking a hard look at my relationship programming, the filters of my perspective, the sticky glue of my attachments, and the fears that had bound me in a relationship that, by the end, felt all wrong. Uncomfortable as it was, I had to look at what I believed, what I had been allowing, and what I myself was creating in my relationship field.

The harsh truth was that every relationship is, in part, our own projection. In the midst of a heart-breaking separation process, that is a tough one to accept. But if we consider that our creations are here to serve us, teach us, and ultimately heal us, then the acceptance comes more quickly. I just had to be willing to change my mindset and turn my attention from the external reflections to my internal world. Instead of blaming someone else, or the relationship, for this painful experience, I had to look within. It is here that I would make sense of the reflections and find the deeper answers I was searching for.

Before I could find answers, I had to change the questions I was asking and allow them to emerge in their own good time. When impatience tripped me up, I found hope and inspiration in Rainer Maria Rilke's wise words.

> *I beg you to have patience with everything unresolved in your heart and try to love the questions themselves as if they were locked rooms or books written in a foreign language. Don't search for the answers, which cannot be given to you now, because you would not be able to live them. And the point is to live everything. Live the questions now. Perhaps then, someday, far in the future, you will gradually, without even noticing it, live your way into the answer.*[5]

More patience.

AS WITHIN SO WITHOUT

This inner reorientation was infinitely more demanding than the outer world rebuilding. While my external reality was in turmoil, the state of my inner world was relentlessly tempestuous. During the long quiet nights, if they made an appearance at all, the elusive questions bounced off the walls, hung on the ceiling, and shape-shifted beyond my grasp.

Every night, I dove a little deeper, and very slowly, the questions took shape. It was as if the Seal Woman held the key to a more authentic inquiry. When I surfaced from the watery depths, the emergent questions flowed onto the pages of my bedside notebook:

> What is my relationship template?

---

5 Rainer Maria Rilke, *Letters to a Young Poet*, (USA: Vintage, 1984).

What are the disempowering beliefs that kept me in an unsatisfying partnership?

How had the status quo served me?

What was the gold to be mined from this painful experience?

What was the real nature of the change that my soul was calling for?

This abbreviated list was a long time in the making. It was even longer before coherent answers emerged, but even in the darkest hours of grief, at least I had some inkling of what most needed to shift. My relationship template, for example, was almost entirely based on romantic love programming; the conditioning I had received that there is only one true love and when you found that person—and followed them to the ends of the Earth, as I had done, quite literally—you'd live happily ever after. It turns out that there was far more to a love relationship than this fairy tale version. In spiritual circles, this is the equivalent of the one-soulmate trap. I would have to release that too.

More insidious and harder to root out were the beliefs encoded in this fanciful notion. What came to the fore, after thorough-going self-reflection, was not pretty. Despite having determinedly resisted marriage because I saw it as a patriarchal institution, it was an unpleasant surprise to discover that deep down, I was replicating many of the beliefs encoded in the very institution I had rejected. My old relationship template was simply riddled with them. As a young girl and teenager, I was my father's daughter and had been thoroughly, if inadvertently, programmed to seek approval from men. As a consequence, seeking to please men and putting their needs and happiness first was number one on the list. Related to this was putting my own career aspirations to the periphery of my vision. Far more injurious was doubting my intuition when it clashed with another's perspective and abandoning myself in the process.

Despite these gifts of insight, nothing seemed to quell my sadness in the first year after the Separation. Grieving is a deeply uncomfortable process, with its own mysterious rhythms, but if we truly want to heal, there are no shortcuts. Much as I wished to be rid of the heartache, I simply wasn't capable of bypassing it. It is not an exaggeration to say that I cried every single night of that first year. One Sunday morning, Liam crawled into my bed and looked up at me with big eyes. "There's been a flood in here," he said, knowing as children often do that his mother had been crying again.

Liam was too young for the Seal Woman story, and the part about her abandoning her children might have scared him. Instead, I enacted a wordless rendition of the fairy tale and took the boys to Kalk Bay harbor. Luca fished from the pier. Liam and I watched the seals playing next to the harbor quay. Afterward, we went to Kalkies and ate fresh-caught fish and chips.

INVITATION TO A NEW LIFE

In that first year, I drew strength from the soul-world, where I could dive deep, sifting through the ocean-bottom silt for nuggets of gold and gradually recalibrating my inner world. Though arduous at times, this nightly sifting process shored me up for the less inspirational, and often brutal, surface-world of doing, coping, surviving, and making decisions for our new life.

When I couldn't sift or figure things out, I read. Reading was my escape. Like comfort food for the night shift, there was a tower of books on my bedside table. My reading diet consisted of an elucidating mix of parenting and spiritual books: *Mom's House, Dad's House* by Isolina Ricci; *Spiritual Divorce* by Debbie Ford; *Living in the Light* by Shakti Gawain; *Letters to a Young Poet* by Rainer Maria Rilke, and on wakeful nights when the long hours stretched endlessly, Clarissa Pinkola Estés' *Women Who Run with the Wolves*. This was my soul food.

On top of the towering pile was *The Invitation* by Oriah Mountain Dreamer.[6] It starts with a poem, inviting the reader to explore a more meaningful life. This is an excerpt:

---

6   Oriah Mountain Dreamer, *The Invitation* (USA: HarperOne, 1994).

Chapter 2 | Dragon Fire

> *It doesn't interest me what planets are squaring your moon. I want to know if you have touched the center of your own sorrow, if you have been opened by life's betrayals, or have become shriveled and closed from fear of further pain.*
>
> *I want to know if you can sit with pain, mine or your own, without moving to hide it, or fade it, or fix it.*
>
> *I want to know if you can see beauty even when it is not pretty every day. And if you can source your own life from its presence.*
>
> *I want to know if you can live with failure, yours and mine, and still stand at the edge of the lake and shout to the silver of the full moon, "Yes."*
>
> *It doesn't interest me to know where you live or how much money you have. I want to know if you can get up after the night of grief and despair, weary and bruised to the bone, and do what needs to be done to feed the children.*

The Invitation spoke to the core of my heartache and struggle to find my way.

"Yes, Oriah, I can!" became my mantra. Yes, I have been opened by life's betrayals, and I'm not shrinking. I have touched the center of my sorrow, and I am sitting with it every night, like a nightly vigil to life's disappointments. The ancestors are my witness. And yes, I can get up after another night of grief and despair, bone-tired, and do what needs to be done to feed the children.

Inspired by Oriah's words, I decided to view my entire situation as an invitation to a life that is more nourishing than the survival version I had been living in London. I would dare to dream of meeting my heart's longing, even if I didn't know exactly what that was. And I would do my utmost to stand at the edge of that lake and shout Yes! to the silver moon.

I printed the poem and stuck it on my pinboard for the tough days. I had a smaller copy next to my bed for the tough nights. Re-reading it helped me feel steady. The highlighted excerpts were like bookmarks in unfamiliar territory, holding my place.

In the absence of clear answers to my emergent questions, I wrote lists to make sense of my new reality and help me transition from an old version of myself to a new one. They provided a map of sorts while I navigated further and further into unknown territory.

THINGS I KNOW

I am at rock bottom. It can only get better.

I can feed my children, get them to school and be present when they get home. This is a promising start.

I'm on the right path, even if I don't know the destination.

I can trust my intuition to show me the way.

I have everything I need within me to get through this.

I love my boys with every fiber of my being.

THINGS I DON'T KNOW

Whether I'll ever feel whole again.

How this journey will impact my children—irreparable damage or robust resilience.

Whether I'll get another freelance contract when this one ends.

Whether I'll have enough money for next month.

Whether I'll ever be able to afford our own home.

How to jump-start my aging car (a necessary survival skill).

THINGS TO RELEASE

The nuclear family fantasy.

My old relationship template.

Romantic love programming.

Victim consciousness.

Assorted toxins (blame, anger, resentment).

Social judgments and gossip (water off a duck's back).

Friends who blow hot and cold (depending on the prevailing social wind).

The list of *things to release* was a long-term undertaking. For now, I tried to focus on the *things I know*; these prolific lists kept me tethered in some inexplicable way. During this transition time, I sometimes felt as if I were two people: the woman who was struggling with the fallout of a painful separation, and the woman who was on a spiritual path, observing the grief-stricken straggler. My past self and future self; the one was being left behind, while the other had already transcended linear time and was calling me to move *through* time in a particular direction. If I didn't want to lose my way again, I would have to keep my ear to the ground of my inner being. After all the deep-diving, the word-maps kept me afloat.

My jazz band also kept me afloat. We rehearsed every Wednesday evening when the boys went to their dad's house. The ensemble of string instruments, an oboe, and a keyboard was my weekly reprieve. With little time to practice, my violin playing was ragged at best, but for those few hours, I could lose myself in the music and camaraderie of the band.

The oboe player, Jade, was a stalwart friend. A musician, a mythologist, and a Wiccan, she was a regular visitor at our cottage. On many evenings during that first cold winter, we sat at my fireplace and talked about the mythical underworld. Mostly we ignored the surface-world—that wasn't her thing. Jade taught me Wiccan principles and rituals. We worked with our chakras, and she made me laugh.

Jade said I was on a Heroine's Journey. Unlike the Hero's Journey, where the hero sets out on a quest to slay the dragon, among other things, and returns a man, in the Heroine's Journey, there is no dragon-slaying. Instead, the heroine sets out to befriend the dragon, tame the restless beast and source her power from the untapped depths within. While the hero journeys outward, seeking adventure, the Heroine's Journey is a descent into the darkness, going inward to seek her wild nature. On her quest, the heroine asks questions: What happened to my desire to write, to dance, to make music? Where is that voice of wild longing? What happened to my soul's call in the busy surface-world? The heroine's version of the archetypal journey gave me hope.

That first winter in our Victorian cottage, I was at rock bottom. But I reminded myself that this is where all spiritual journeys start—at the bottom. This is where truth springs forth—from the depths. I wanted to know the world of the soul and experience that weightless bliss again. This had become my quest, and even though the bliss zone seemed way out of reach, I knew I would find my way. Why else would I have been taken into that light realm, not once in my life, but twice? Still, there were some dragons to face. After the crushing grief during the winter months, the dragon of anger appeared again, this time with almost blinding force.

In the spring, my boys bought me a red spade for my birthday. We had a small back garden where I was planting herbs and flowers. This was my attempt at beauty—Oriah-style because the days were not yet pretty. The flowers were meant to add some color, the herbs some flavor. I'd always grown herbs—even in cold, grey London—and wasn't going to let a little impermanence stop me now. But with only a little hand trowel at my disposal, gardening of any sort was slow-going, and that red spade was one of the best gifts I've ever received. I yelped with delight when I unwrapped it. How did these two young children know? Somehow my boys intuitively understood the importance of our small backyard patch of earth. It melted my heart.

As it turned out, the red spade had another important function. Digging became my go-to assorted anger management strategy. On days when fury struck, I tackled the rocky wastelands in our small backyard and poured my anger into the Earth. The hard soil was my punchbag. I figured the Earth could handle it. No one else could, and I was grateful to Mother Earth for her forbearing.

Witnessing my children's struggles was far more difficult than managing my own. From a spiritual perspective, this was their journey too. They weren't just tagging along on my path. Their own struggles were the fires that would forge their characters and yield courage, resilience, and wisdom. At least I hoped so, but as a mother, I ached to spare them from the flames. The best I could do was protect them from dragon fire and give them as much stability as possible within the cauldron of change.

SMALL TRIUMPHS, SIMPLE PLEASURES

In that first year after the Separation, all my energy was focused on finding my feet and helping the boys find theirs. There were new rhythms that mostly centered around work, the school routine, and safeguarding my children's well-being.

During this transitional time, we finally got a diagnosis for Liam. I had noticed that his legs were covered in bruises, and he was often yellow. Alarmed, I had been surreptitiously researching leukemia; he had all the symptoms. Then one morning, he couldn't walk. I put all thoughts of paranoia aside and took him to the pediatrician. The soft-spoken doctor looked grave as he examined my child. He ordered blood tests for leukemia and a whole host of other dread diseases. Waiting for the results, the cold terror from Liam's babyhood sneaked back into my heart. My worst fears had finally caught up with me.

I nearly cried with relief when the results came back—it wasn't leukemia; the culprit all along was Gilbert's Syndrome. At last, we had something tangible to explain Liam's mystery symptoms; something to tell the teachers, who wondered, with raised eyebrows, why he had so many days off pre-school; something to tell the extended family, who dismissed my mother-gut concerns. Now blood test results and a bona fide specialist had confirmed that I wasn't mad; my gut was spot on. The prolonged jaundice had a name. We could work with this.

There is no treatment for Gilbert's Syndrome. It's a genetic condition caused by a missing or non-functioning enzyme in the liver that affects the metabolic or, to be precise, the methylation process. This explained the extreme ups and downs in Liam's energy and, of course, the yellow days. Instead of a treatment, we had a management plan: changing his diet, minimizing stress, and going with the flow of his energy. The doctor gave us permission to keep Liam at home when he woke up with yellow eyes and jelly legs. I could have leaped across his paper-submerged desk and kissed him! I restrained myself, instead thanking him profusely. I doubt he would have understood the extent of my gratitude.

Now we had a name for the wobbly times—Gilbert days—and a plan of sorts. Dietary changes? No problem. Minimize stress? I would just have to do my best in non-ideal circumstances. Go with the flow of his energy? We could do that. Together, we made friends with Gilbert, and in the process, Liam learned to listen to his body.

This was a small triumph at a time when everything else was still wobbly. There were other little triumphs and simple pleasures that anchored the three of us in our new life. I did my best to find joy in the simple pleasures, but this took time. For obvious reasons, my meditation practice went out the window. The only outlet was my jazz band. For the boys, their new life was divided between two homes. Every Wednesday evening and alternate weekends, they went to their dad's house. They loved that house. It was a tenuous connection with their old life while we took baby steps building our new life.

Our new life was settling into steadying rhythms and more peaceful reflections, the fortifying lull before the storm that was brewing. Sadly, the family home had to be sold, and at the same time, the lease for my safe-haven Victorian cottage expired. I had hoped to extend the lease period, but the landlord was returning from London and wanted his house back. All too soon, we were thrust into another round of turmoil, which pushed me to the limit of my resources, but in hindsight, this is when I got to test my newfound insights and very gradually reclaim power in the surface-world.

The day the family home was sold, Luca didn't talk. It was a Saturday. We lay on his bed for three hours, wrapped together in silence, the sadness a heavy blanket over us, knowing in our bones that there was no going back to the way things were. If we'd had any lingering fantasy of reuniting the family, this was the moment it sidled away forever. In the unspoken space between us, reality sank in good and proper.

With the sale of the family home and a mercifully swift financial settlement process, I received my share of the proceeds. This was something to be grateful for, and yet it was simply not enough to buy a whole house. Having recently moved into another short-term rental, I was longing to buy my own house and create a stable home for our reconfigured family. The inconvenient reality was that I couldn't do it without mortgage financing to bridge the substantial gap. My freelance work was going well, but without a permanent job, no bank would give me a mortgage bond. Meanwhile, house prices in Cape Town were skyrocketing, and my buying power was plummeting by the day. There was nothing suitable on the market in my price range, and when something appeared, it was snapped up within days. I was desperate for a home, but there were obstacles on every front.

Backed into a corner, I tried my hand at manifestation.

CALLING FOR HOME

Toward the end of 2004, I signed up for a vision quest. In many indigenous cultures, vision quests were undertaken by shamans to call for a vision that would offer guidance to their community. In our modern world, vision quests are more often individual undertakings—a space for reflection and extended solitude to surface the whispers of the soul. Above all, spending time alone in the wilderness is a way to face fears and find courage, and I needed all the courage I could muster to take the next big step and dream my home into being.

The vision quest was to be held at Nauma, a remote farm at the foot of the Anysberg mountains in the Little Karoo. The questers would spend three days and three nights alone in the wilderness and two integration days with the group at base camp. In the tradition of vision questing, we would be fasting during our solo time to bring forth the vision. Out in the wilderness, we would have just the barest essentials to cushion us from the elements—no food, no tent, no books, no distractions. Visions don't enter a busy mind or a troubled heart.

A month before we headed off into the Karoo wilderness, our group of five women met with our quest leader. At our first meeting, we shared our stories and set our intentions for the quest. Unsurprisingly, our group theme was *home*. Our concepts of home varied, but our stories reflected our common struggle as women to create a deep sense of home that provided safety and freedom, roots and wings. My personal version of this theme was to summon a home that would provide these things. Clearly, my work was cut out for me.

We set our intentions and made prayer ties. My intention was to call for a vision of my future home and bring it into being. Above all, I wanted a home with love at the center, a sacred place that would nourish all three of us. Every evening, for a whole month, I made my prayer ties—cutting out little squares of red, yellow, black, and white cotton, folding them into little pouches, filling them with dried tobacco, and tying them together in a long string and prayed for my home.

The day before the vision quest, one of my freelance clients called me.

"When you're sitting on that rock in the Karoo, would you contemplate coming to work for us as an employee?" she asked.

"I'll think about it," I said, smiling to myself.

It was working!

When I set off from Cape Town, it was pouring rain. It had already been raining in the Karoo for several days, and the usually dry riverbeds were overflowing. The last stretch of the journey was on a gravel road, treacherous at the best of times but now with a slippery gauntlet. The bridge over the first big river was closed with three large barrels bearing *no entry* signs. The water was already flowing over the bridge, and the road ahead was barely visible. I considered my options. The quest had begun!

Crossing a flooding bridge is not sensible, and I wouldn't recommend it, but missing my vision quest was not an option. Summoning my courage, I moved the barrels out of the way; it was the only direct route to Nauma. With my heart in my mouth, I drove through the floodwater and made it to the other side. Later that day, the bridge was washed away and would not be rebuilt for another two years.

Chapter 2 | Dragon Fire

With the first obstacle surmounted, I proceeded very cautiously along the slippery gravel road, through several flooded riverbeds, hoping that this tumultuous landscape did not augur what was to come. As I rounded the last bend, a large cobra was crossing the road. I slammed the brakes, skidding to a halt as it slithered into the Karoo scrub. My heart was pounding. I'd never seen such a big cobra. I took note; questing is all about reading the signs, and the snake was a powerful totem.

Soon after arriving at Nauma, I set off with my minimalist quester's backpack—a sleeping bag, a few clothes, a torch, matches, water, and my prayer ties—and walked through the scrubby Karoo veld toward the gorge at the far end of the farm. I followed the river south and scouted for a suitable spot to make camp. After the rains, the river was in full flow. I was in luck! In this arid environment, the abundance of water would be a welcome respite from the Karoo heat.

In a womb-like gorge, I chose a large flat rock alongside a rock pool, which I called Mint Pool because of the wild mint growing in the water-fed cracks and crevices. On one side of the gorge was a rocky overhang, which would provide shade in the mornings. On the other side was a shrub-covered kopje with plenty of brushwood to make a fire. These were important considerations. Scouring the riverbank, I collected small rocks and staked out my circle next to the rock pool. This was another rule of vision quest—don't move around; stay in your circle and go within.

For three days and three nights, I kept vigil in my circle. By day, the gurgling river kept me company, and at night the fire. Fire and Water. Earth and Sky. The smell of buchu and mint. In the watchful stillness of the gorge, I listened to nature, tuning into the subtle language of signs. There was a swallow's nest in the rocky overhang. Two busy parents circled around me all day long, feeding their young. The swallows reminded me of my quest for home. Unbidden, the dragon woke up from its slumber and entered the circle too.

During the day, I stared into the rock pool and saw the dragon. It had the face of sadness. At night I stared into the flames of my small fire and confronted the dragon. It had the face of grief. We had been warned about the shadow quest that emerges from the shadows, demanding center stage. It is like a supporting act to the main event and must come first to clear the way for the intentional theme of the vision quest.

It seemed like the shadow act was unfolding for me. Instead of a vision, I was blindsided by a torrent of emotion. Endings have always been difficult for me; letting go is not my strong point. With the settlement signed, the partnership was well and truly done. I thought I had let go, but the shadow quest told a different story. So often, we think we've let go, only to find that the hooks and attachments to the past are still there. They may be subtle, but they keep us tethered, nonetheless. The shadow quest brought every little ensnaring filament to the fore, inviting me to let go even more.

I cried more tears. How was it possible that I could produce so much water?

After the Separation, friends offered their advice, "Don't wallow. Keep busy and move on." How wise, and yet how misguided! I would have drowned had I wallowed. And yet, when pain cuts deep, there is no other way but to feel it, or you numb yourself forever. We heal by feeling, gradually integrating the shattered pieces into our heart, mind, and soul. This can't be done overnight. And it cannot be done by ignoring it either. The transformation that happens when you are willing to be still with your pain is revolutionary. This is not wallowing; it is an active process of transmutation from one state into another.

Alone in the wilderness, I confronted my soul-pain head-on. I screamed it to the rocks, the sky, the earth. At night, I howled to the moon. For the first two days, all the pent-up grief of the last few years poured out until I was empty. Hollowed out, I immersed myself in the rock pool and let the rain-fresh river wash me clean. I surrendered to its soothing embrace and let go a little more.

On the second night, I was ready to let my old life go. I let go of the notion that partnership, even with a soulmate, is forever. I let go of the perfect mother, who is a martyr to her children. I let go of the castle and the unbroken family who once inhabited it. I named all the hurts and

Chapter 2 | Dragon Fire

resentments, which still simmered and moaned like prisoners within the castle walls. Then I offered every last piece to the hungry flames and watched them burn. Fed by the flames, the dragon was quiet. In the liminal space between my old life and the vision still forming inside me, the old story and the new, I fell into an exhausted sleep.

The shadow quest was done. Unplanned and uninvited, it was a powerful rite of passage that signaled the real start of my new life.

Long fingers of light shook me gently awake. It was time to call for a vision. As the swallows circled around me, I dreamed of my new home. I let the picture paint itself rather than being the painter. I saw every detail: a house with good vibes and lots of light; French doors; flow; a patch of lawn; a big tree with a swing; sunny veranda; a view of Table Mountain. I saw the money arriving in my bank account and felt the sweet satisfaction of rooting somewhere, at last.

As the sun dipped behind the kopje, I prepared for the last night of solo time. With the vision formulated, it was time to ask for my home. The fire crackled as I waited for the waxing moon to rise above the kopje. A waxing moon, Jade once told me, is the best time to manifest. *How fortuitous.* As the generous moon shone over my stone circle, I fingered my prayer ties and asked for the home I had envisioned. With my heart as full as the moon, I kept a prayerful vigil all night and gave thanks for what was to come.

The next morning, I awoke to an unfamiliar sound, a soft swishing on the rocks. Just at the edge of the stone circle was a large puff adder, a venomous viper with a nasty temper if disturbed. Moving almost imperceptibly against one of the stones as it shed its skin, this puff adder was seemingly oblivious to my presence. I watched spellbound. If you have ever seen a snake shed its skin, you'll know that it is a slow process, the old skin coming off in bits and pieces. The puff adder at the edge of my circle was a big snake; this shedding was going to take a while. Watching it, old childhood memories surfaced.

When I was growing up, my family lived in Grahamstown (now Makhanda) on the edge of town or the edge of the forest, depending on your point of view. The forest was our back garden. My three brothers and I ran wild in that forest, catching snakes and bringing them home. My mother's only rule: no venom in the house. We never held snakes captive for long. The turnaround was quick. While in our care, my brothers fed them; my task was to tame them. I played my violin, which seemed to calm them. My mother called me a snake charmer. Secretly, I wanted to make my snakes dance, like the Indian snake charmers whose cobras spread their hoods and swayed to the pipe music.

The closest thing to snake-swaying was a rather funny incident when I was eight years old. On that occasion, I took two little house snakes—totally harmless, I might add—to school with me. At break time, I put them in my violin case. When I went to my violin lesson, the snakes had disappeared. While my violin teacher was tuning my violin, the snakes emerged from the sound holes, and they were swaying! I was transfixed, a mixture of wonderment and horror rendering me helpless in the face of impending disaster. Things unraveled quickly. At point blank range, the swaying serpents scared the living daylights out of my poor violin teacher, who fled from the music room screaming blue murder. She was from England, poor soul. Not surprisingly, she refused to teach me after that, which was nearly the end of my budding musical career.

Snapping out of my reverie, I watched the puff adder swaying against the rocks. Did I still have the touch of the snake charmer? There was no one around to witness my silliness, so I began to sing very softly until, at last, the shiny-skinned snake slithered away, leaving the old skin like an offering at the edge of my stone circle.

After the cobra sighting on the road, I should not have been surprised that the snake would show up on my quest and offer its medicine. Snake medicine is all about transmutation, the power of shedding the old skin and rebirthing into a new soul-skin. Like the snake, I had outgrown the skin of my old life. Remarkably intact, there was a wholeness about the puff adder's cast-off skin, and that is how I wanted to remember my old life—not as broken, but as something outgrown. It would be impossible now to fit back into my old identity or outworn relationships. Something fundamental had been transformed, and the shed snakeskin was my proof. This was snake medicine, indeed.

Back at base camp, we hung our prayer ties over the sweat lodge and entered its steamy belly. As the heat intensified, we surrendered to the steam and sang rounds of song. Later, we told our stories, and my vision took shape in words. It felt daring, audacious to ask for an actual house. Rule number one of manifesting is to be strong in your vision and intention and then let the Universe take care of the rest. This is all very well in theory, but could I really trust the Universe to deliver my heart's desire?

I needn't have worried. As it turned out, the Universe's organizing power was swift and precise. A few days after the vision quest, a friend insisted that we view a house that had just come on the market. Approaching the house, the first thing I saw was a big plane tree in the front garden. As we walked through the house, the rest of my vision unfolded, just as I had seen it. With a little TLC, the house would be perfect. Without hesitation, I put in an offer. I didn't have the money yet but trusted it was on its way. Over a nerve-racking three months, everything lined up in the surface-world. I signed a contract for a permanent job with a niche consulting and publishing company. I signed the papers for a mortgage bond. I signed a loan agreement with my parents to bridge the remaining gap. Finally, I signed the legal documents to transfer the new house into my name. Against all odds, and after a lot of signatures, our home was on its way.

Equally important, I had experienced first-hand the spiritual Law of Intention and Desire at work, which states that inherent in every sincere intention and heartfelt desire is the means for its fulfillment. When we become quiet and beam our intentions into the field of pure potentiality, we harness the Universe's infinite organizing power, which can manifest our desires with effortless ease. This was a lesson I was never to forget.

COMING UP FOR AIR

Three years after we had moved out of the old family home, my boys and I moved into our reconfigured family home. Finally, I came up for air. We had survived the transit. We could move on. The boys took the move in their stride, this being the third since the Separation. Luca's pinched, pale face slowly relaxed, and he looked happy again. He was doing well at school, and more importantly, he had friends and passions—cricket, soccer, fly-fishing. He kept us constantly outdoors. Liam's multi-layered school outfits were a thing of the past, and his creativity was blossoming with story-writing, drawing, and music. He kept us constantly entertained. I planted herbs in a sunny courtyard and flowers in the small back garden to ground myself. We hung a swing on the plane tree in the front garden, just as I had seen in my vision. Our new life was taking some sort of shape.

The reconfiguration of family included an animal contingent. Animals bring a special quality; their presence is healing, and I figured we could use a little help. First, the kittens arrived, one each for the boys. Samon was an unusual tricolor mix of grey, white, and salmon pink. Kabushka was a scruffy cinnamon kitten who morphed into a magnificent ginger cat. Liam's shy rabbit Riverfoot arrived next. He lived wild in the back garden and ate all my flowers. My blue-black Labrador puppy, Indigo, joined the pack with gusto. Tropical fish tanks and goldfish in an outdoor pond appeared almost organically. Everyone had their pet-care jobs.

Liam once quipped, "We're part zookeepers, part schoolchildren."

I asked him which part he liked best. "Duh," he replied. That single syllable floated like a feather and landed softly in my heart.

Just when I thought the menagerie was complete, my friend Thandi showed up at our house one day with a large wooden crate. Thandi worked for Cape Nature on a wild animal rehabilitation program, so it was anyone's guess what was inside that crate. "I thought of you guys," she said, opening the crate to reveal a beautiful leopard tortoise.

The boys peered inside the crate, then looked up at me with pleading eyes. Thandi said the leopard tortoise couldn't be released into the wild because it had been in captivity for too long and urgently needed rehoming. I was a soft touch. Delighted to have a new pet, the boys called him Jeep and settled him into the front garden, where he munched on grass and kept the lawn neatly trimmed.

With everyone happily settled, my focus shifted from survival to stability. Home was our sanctuary, our *querencia*. In Spanish, *querencia* is a metaphysical place where you feel at home, a place from which you draw strength, and where you are your most authentic self. It comes from the verb *querer*, which means *to desire*. That about summed it up; I had desired this home into being. Here we could become our truest selves. Here I could place love at the very center of our home and our lives. Here I could listen to my soul and lay the groundwork for my mission.

Every morning, Table Mountain greeted me through the kitchen window. The view was never the same. In summer, the mountain shimmered in the early morning sun. In winter, there were silvery waterfalls gushing down the ravines. Sometimes, a rainbow appeared in the waterfall's spray. I drank in this daily offering of beauty and vowed to source my new life from its presence. Wired to the Earth's sacred grid, I felt steady again.

Here, I could stand at the foot of my beloved mountain and shout to the silver waterfalls, *Yes!* Oriah would be proud of me.

I had faced the dragon. It was time to head for higher ground.

DRAGON'S GOLD
Wisdom teachings from Chapter Two

- The dragon has many faces, but however it appears, prepare for transformation. While you might be tempted to get rid of your dragon, the wise heroine knows that dragon-slaying is not the answer. Rather, she seeks to befriend the dragon and follow it into its lair. This is where the gold lies in plain sight.

- Initiations, of whatever kind, are an invitation to embrace soul growth and transformation toward the next level of consciousness. From this perspective, the external catalyst—whether an event or a relationship—is simply a reflection of what most needs alchemizing in your inner world.

- Aligning with your deepest intentions is the fastest way to walk your path. When you are out of alignment with your soul's truth, this will show up in visceral ways, such as boredom, restlessness, depression, physical pain, or even disease. The panacea is going within to surface your truth and find the courage to act from a place of authenticity rather than expectation.

- What other people think of you is none of your business. Their thoughts are an extension of their energy, and should unwanted energy attach to you; it's best to shake it off like water off a duck's back. This is a variation of the second agreement in Don Miguel Ruiz's bestseller, *The Four Agreements*, which simply states: "Don't take anything personally." Sound simple? It's one of the hardest lessons on the path to self-mastery.

- Manifestation is an act of creation made possible by the Law of Intention and Desire. This spiritual law states that inherent in every heartfelt intention are the seeds for its fulfillment. When you beam your sincere intention into the field of pure potentiality, you harness the Universe's infinite organizing power to transform your imaginal desires into material form with effortless ease. When working with the power of intention, it is important to ask for the highest good of all concerned.

3

ALCHEMY

2005 – 2008

The highest form of magic is Soul Alchemy. Through Soul Alchemy, we transmutate the grotesque particles of our souls into the highest forms of gold.

– C. JoyBell C., author of *The Conversation of Dragons*

It was time to transform lead into gold. Although I had come a long way in letting go of the old life, I was still riding waves of anger about the Separation and how things had played out in the aftermath. I knew this was my personal jetsam—the lead that was weighing down my ship—and I was on an alchemical quest to get rid of it, throw it overboard, transform it. It was time to do whatever was needed to move forward and follow my soul's calling to heal myself and others.

My alchemical quest led me to many spiritual teachers who helped me through the fires of transformation and deepened my understanding of the healing arts. They inspired me to be true to my healer's heart. Soon after we moved into our new home, I embarked on formal training again, picking up where I left off in London and figuring out what kind of healer I was going to be. As it turned out, my training path provided the alchemy I sought. My personal transformation and journey as a healer were inseparable; I had found my way again on the path of the Wounded Healer.

The fires of transformation raged for several years. The dragon was at work! My dragon was a light sleeper and woke up all too often, pumping anger through my veins; it was an uncomfortable place to be. Anger is not an easy emotion to hold, especially for women. From a young age, we are taught that anger is bad. Women shouldn't be angry in the first place; if we are, we shouldn't express it. The problem is that anger is not the real poison—pretending not to be angry, then swallowing it, is. The Separation had surfaced my anger to a place where I could no longer push it down; swallowing it just wasn't possible anymore. And thank goodness for that. In the end, rage was my biggest teacher despite all my efforts to evade it.

Most cultures are afraid of female anger, and for good reason, perhaps, because if women listen to their anger, they cannot agree to play by the rules anymore. By leaving the marital home, I had broken all the unwritten rules about what a woman with children should and shouldn't do, what she should reveal about her truth, how much she should tolerate, and how much she should sacrifice to keep the family together. God knows I had grappled with these rules until it almost killed me.

In the aftermath of the Separation, I focused all my energy on crafting a new life as an indie mom, a life that was beyond mere survival and included the abundant joy of settling into our new home, but my anger tripped me up. I was angry with Patrick for having the upper hand socially. I was angry with myself for being so naïve and with Spirit for making my path so tough. I had paid a very high price for listening to my soul. Knowing I had lessons to learn and karma to burn was small comfort in the face of sometimes unbearable pain. That's when the gift of the red spade from my children came in handy to dig into the earth, giving my anger a release, but I needed something more than digging to satisfy the dragon. My therapist said, "You need to harness anger in service to the self."

This sounded like a version of riding the dragon, but how to ride it was the question. Until this point, I had listened to the dragon, heard its voice, and let it loose. Now I had to befriend this unruly beast, become one with it, like a rider and her horse.

TRANSFORMATION BY FIRE

My quest for soul alchemy led me back to Frieda. Under her piercing gaze, I felt stripped bare, naked, yet utterly held in her warm-hearted embrace. Her teachings over the next few years have guided me ever since. The core of her teaching was radical clarity and integrity. Frieda was uncompromising in her quest to live her truth and lead by example.

"Integrity means wholeness of being," she explained. "This happens when all parts of you are welcomed, witnessed, and understood."

In becoming whole, you discover who you are and source your life from an authentic place, speaking your truth with radical clarity, without hiding, without compromise. True integrity exists when your deepest yearnings and instincts forge your path when the inner world and outer expression match. This is what it means to live a soulful life.

Frieda's teaching tools were ritual and ceremony. She had trained in Swaziland and Botswana as a *sangoma*, an African shaman, and had been blessed in the Native American tradition to conduct ceremonial sweat lodges. "Ritual and ceremony connect us to Great Spirit, to the ancestors and other spiritual allies," she explained.

We journey to the inner realms through ceremony and call for the soul, enabling spiritual opening and intervention. This is the shaman's vehicle for change from one state of being to another—soul alchemy.

Under Frieda's sage wings, I experienced first-hand the power of connecting with the spiritual realms through ritual and ceremony. She taught me a kind of transformational intelligence that only comes through experience. Over the next three years, my spiritual work with Frieda took me through an intense purification process. Together, we sifted through layers of silt, searching for nuggets of truth. Who was I beneath the outer shell I had inhabited for so long? Now that the castle had been destroyed, at my own hand, what did I want to create?

What needed purifying for the journey ahead? She was a rigorous yet compassionate teacher.

In a succession of rituals, we plowed through ancestral wounding to purify my paternal and maternal lineages. On my father's side, my lineage is Dutch. My paternal ancestors arrived in Cape Town in the late 1600s with the Dutch East India Company. At that time, the Cape was a Dutch colony, serving as a refreshment station on the lucrative spice route to the East. My ancestors were among those who stayed in the flourishing settlement. On my mother's side, my lineage is Celtic. On her paternal side, my Celtic ancestors arrived in Cape Town from Ireland in the early 1800s, by which time the Cape was in the hands of the British. On my mother's maternal side, my English ancestors arrived in Algoa Bay (now Nelson Mandela Bay) in 1820 as part of a wave of immigration from the British Isles known as the 1820 Settlers. On their arrival on South Africa's shores, the 1820 Settlers were given farms in the Eastern Cape to create a buffer zone between the expanding Cape Colony and the indigenous Xhosa people living in the area. In this arid environment, and with little experience in farming, this was a tough assignment. Eking out a living on parched land in hostile territory, my maternal ancestors were evidently a hardy bunch, but it came at a price. This was where it all went wrong in my maternal lineage. The extreme harshness they endured, not to mention the unjust politics of the day, was the seed point for abuse in my maternal lineage, and transmuting this dysfunctional pattern was one of my soul tasks.

Alongside my personal work with Frieda, I participated in her monthly sweat lodges for women as often as I could. A sweat lodge ceremony is a powerful purification process. In the ceremony, the lodge becomes the womb, the container for the spirit of fire—the great transformer, and a space for the alchemical process. Time and again, those present entered the sweat lodge with heavy hearts and left with a feeling of renewal and lightness.

The sweat lodge was a dome-like structure made of branches and covered by thick blankets. It was much like a small teepee with space for about ten people to participate in the ceremonial sweat. Outside the lodge, there was a fire pit for the sweat lodge fire. During ceremony,

Chapter 3 | Alchemy

the firetender kept a large fire burning and, at regular intervals, carried hot rocks into the lodge, where the water pourer ladled water over them to produce steam. The water pourer is the person who directs the ceremony, determining the intensity of the heat and leading rounds of song while the occupants sweat.

The water pourer is a sacred role and one that requires a blessing in the Native American tradition. Frieda had received this blessing and had unusual skill in holding a powerful ceremonial space for the women to share their stories and release their troubles into the fire. At the start of every ceremony, Frieda said, "I welcome all parts of you," and invited the shadow out.

There was no hiding inside the lodge. Another layer was peeled off and released into the fire with every round of sweating. Every ceremony revealed a nugget of gold. When the fires died down, we emerged from the steamy womb-space, glistening with sweat, clear-skinned and bright-eyed. It was a rebirthing every time, every sweat lodge a small initiation along the path.

For a while, I stepped into the role of firetender. As the heat intensifies and the group sweats and moans, the firetender harnesses the spirit of fire outside the lodge to serve the alchemical process within. Working with the spirit of fire was like riding the dragon. There are two kinds of fire—destructive and transformative. The firetender's role is to harness the energy of transformation, which requires the utmost presence and patience. Sometimes the rounds of sweating would go on for hours on end.

When the Cape southeaster was blowing, the fire was a wild beast; fire and air—the dragon's breath. Holding the elements of wildish fire and tempestuous air for the duration of the ceremony was a lesson in harnessing power while letting go of control. I walked this edge again and again until I found the balance. The balance came when I could sit in my heart center, whatever the elements were doing, and connect with the women inside the lodge, allowing love to rise, despite the external forces within and between us. Those were the times when the dragon quietened, and the transformative fire burned brightest. I discovered that love is the greatest alchemical force in the Universe if only we can let it flow.

During those long evenings in ceremony, I became a vessel for every woman's story as they merged with my own. Our old stories dissolved in the flames as fire transformed us, allowing new stories to rise in our hearts. We emerged from every ceremony anew, dripping with sweat, naked bodies muddy, bedraggled hair, and our eyes shining. The joy after moving and transmuting so much pain was breathtaking; This was the alchemy of joining human hearts.

Through my ongoing personal work with Frieda, I became more alert to the subtle guidance from the natural world and learned how to interpret what showed up in my outer reality. During this time, I also became more receptive to the spirit world and received regular guidance from my ancestors. Slowly, I became more attuned to the dynamic flow between the visible and invisible worlds. I was learning to walk between worlds again, but now with much greater awareness than my childhood wanderings.

Shortly after the Separation, my great-grandmother Isabella started showing up at night. As I became more receptive, her communications were more frequent. Though I had never known her, Isabella was my mother's favorite granny. In spirit, she was a gentle, loving presence. She announced her arrival with a warm rush of energy that filled my heart. Sometimes she gave me messages; at other times, she was a comforting presence.

She also popped up in unexpected ways to answer the questions in my heart. On one occasion, when I was grappling with a difficult decision, Isabella came to the rescue in a rather creative way. Liam had recently started formal school and was off on his first school camp at a nearby nature reserve. I was one of the parents transporting the school kids to the camp. The last part of the trip was on a dusty gravel road, and my car was caked in dust when we arrived at the campsite. After offloading the children and getting them settled in their tents, the volunteer parents gathered for coffee before driving back. When I got back to my car, the word *Isabella* was written in large letters across the dusty doors. I laughed out loud! One of the kids, no doubt, but a clear message to me—*when you have a problem, ask your guides!* I couldn't help smiling at the ways Spirit got my attention.

Isabella's spirit was around me for several years, offering comfort, advice, and sometimes warnings from the other side. It was as if my ancestors were applauding my every step through her.

While I was questing for inner alchemy, Frieda was creating a vision for a spiritual center where ritual would be at the heart of transformational healing work. This was a big vision. She had inherited a large tract of fynbos-covered land in Hout Bay, but it took years of hard work to raise enough funds for the construction of a building. Eventually, the plans were drawn, and the process of birthing Phakalane began. Named for the hawks that circled overhead, Phakalane means hawk in Tswana, the national language of Botswana. Like the hawk, which is the symbolic messenger between the spiritual and physical worlds, Phakalane became a spiritual gateway for everyone who stepped onto the land.

In creating her vision, Frieda was a shining example of walking her talk. The building process was held in ceremony every step of the way; she personally blessed all the building materials that came onto the land, down to every wheelbarrow of sand. She was unerring in her attention to detail and spiritual purity. As I neared the end of my own transformation process with Frieda, her vision took form, and Phakalane Centre for Living Ritual opened its doors in 2007.

One of my greatest joys was being part of the birthing of Frieda's vision. Sadly, Frieda passed away in 2018, but her magnificent legacy lives on. Phakalane remains a sacred sanctuary in the heart of Cape Town, where others continue her life's work. It was my spiritual home for many years and the place where I took my first steps as a full-fledged healer.

But I am getting ahead of my story . . .

BACK ON A TRAINING PATH

My quest for formal training led me first to Kate and her Polarity course. I had been seeing Kate for energy work for a few months to help me find balance in the wake of rebound relationship wobbles. She was an exceptional healer, using a bodywork modality called Polarity Therapy, developed by Dr. Randolph Stone.[7] Polarity Therapy is a healing system that includes bodywork, nutrition, and self-awareness. The energy work is quite physical, using acupressure points to activate the flow of energy and balance the body's five elements—earth, water, fire, air, and ether. With my background in shamanic practices, massage, and shiatsu, and my Libran need for balance, it sounded perfect. The course was only six months, and it wasn't a qualification, but Kate was a consummate alchemist, and I was eager to learn from her.

At Kate's prompting, I signed up for the introductory Polarity course and picked up where I had left off almost a decade ago in London. For six months, our group of eight met every month for an intensive training weekend during which we learned the basic Polarity principles and bodywork sequences. Between monthly meetings, we had various assignments for putting principles into practice. The Polarity course put flesh on the bones of my purpose to heal myself and others and provided some important markers on my path. As much as I was learning about energy, it was also a deeply personal healing journey.

At our first training weekend, Kate spoke about the nature of polarity—opposing poles, light, and shadow. In a world of duality, there will always be both. We might come from Oneness and even yearn for it, but while we exist in a third-dimensional reality, we hold the tension of opposites. The art is to balance both in a never-ending dance. Kate warned us that we were entering the energy of the dance. We were inviting change into our lives. "Are you up for it?" she asked, looking around the circle to gauge the group's response.

There was silence. The others looked as nervous as I felt, but one by one, every person in the group raised their hands in agreement—*we*

---

[7] Dr Randolph Stone D.C, D.O, *Polarity Therapy, The Complete Collected Works on this Revolutionary Healing Art by the Originator of the System*, Vol. 1 and 8 (Book Publishing Company (TN), 1999).

were ready. The group quickly became a safe space for deep sharing and learning. Still raw from the ending of my rebound relationship, Kate's teachings were a balm for my soul. One of Kate's first lessons was that need overrides intuition. I could have done with that bit of advice before I dived into said rebound relationship! Looking back, I could clearly see how need had gotten the upper hand, repeatedly leading me to ignore my intuition. I put that one down to experience, lesson learned. Despite varied life experiences, everyone in the group had fallen into a variation of this trap at some point in their lives, and Kate's first lesson resonated with all of us. *Need overrides intuition* quickly became our group mantra, a reminder to pay attention to our intuition above all else.

More than any psychotherapist, Kate helped me move through anger. First and foremost, she gave me permission to feel angry.

"There is nothing wrong with anger, as long as you let it flow," she reassured me. "Think of emotion as e-motion, energy in motion. It has to move."

It's that simple; energy must move. Einstein himself said energy must flow. Only when it stagnates does it cause problems. Anger is a powerful energy; more than any other energy, it needs a pathway out of the body.

This lesson made me think about an amazing dragon story I came across on my travels. In Hong Kong, the dragon is a cultural icon, believed to be the bearer of good fortune. So honored is the dragon that the flight paths from the mountains to the sea are kept clear of obstacles to ensure good feng shui. Years ago, a hotel in Repulse Bay on Hong Kong Island was built directly in front of a dragon's flight path, obstructing the fabled dragon's direct access to the sea. This was considered such an affront to the dragon—and bad luck to boot, that the building was hollowed out in the middle to clear the way for the dragon's path. Keeping dragon and citizens happy, the hotel still has a gaping hole in the middle. Locals call it a dragon gate. This story reminded me of the importance of keeping the pathways open for powerful energies and spiritual forces to move through.

Kate reminded me that powerful energies should always be honored like the Chinese dragons; in honoring such forces, their purpose is revealed. *What if my anger had an important purpose?*

Kate taught us that anger is the boundaries coming in.

"Listen to what anger is telling you," she said. "Embrace it and learn from it. Eventually, you'll learn to feel the boundary and hold it without anger. This is mastery. This is true power."

Kate spoke a lot about self-mastery. One of the most important principles of self-mastery was to harness energy. Kate taught us to harness energy with intention. Her maxim was *where intention goes, energy flows.*

This spiritual law became another group mantra. It gave me a handle on my restless dragon. By this time, I had done my fair share of listening to the dragon, but it still had a lot to say. Apparently, there was a lot to learn, so cautiously, I invited it in.

Having glimpsed my angry dragon, Kate encouraged me to use movement to let it move through me like a wave. That summer, I swam every chance I had—in the tidal pool at Kalk Bay, in the cold Atlantic Ocean, in the dam up at Silvermine Nature Reserve, any water body would do. Like a dolphin, I propelled myself underwater with a butterfly kick, sounding the anger, feeling the bubbles rising to the surface. I called it the Dolphin Thrash; I'm pretty sure I invented it. By the end of the summer, I was a mistress at soundless underwater screaming. Mercifully, the dragon seemed appeased.

Toward the end of summer, Kate announced that we were going to work with the fire element. The dragon in my belly did a little jig. I reminded it that I still had a job to hold down, two young children to look after, and there was a limit to how many more dragon antics I could accommodate.

To prepare for Fire weekend, the group went on a liver flush detox designed to bring up fire energy. We ate fruit, vegetables, and tons of ginger, garlic, and chili for ten days to activate the digestive fire—a powerful alchemical force in the body. After the first few days, my body was burning, and if that wasn't discomfort enough, I was consumed with rage. In despair, I phoned Kate, convinced my body couldn't hold the energy.

"I thought I was done with rage," I told her, pleading for relief.

"Hang in there," she said. "The calmness will come. Usually by day nine or ten."

Sure enough, on day nine, I woke up feeling calm and peaceful. I felt as if my being had been washed in the night and soaked in soothing waters.

At our next training weekend, we learned the fire bodywork process—a sequence of energy points to activate fire energy and release anger. We practiced the bodywork on each other. When it was my turn to receive the healing bodywork, I set my intention to release any remaining anger, secretly hoping that the Dolphin Thrash and liver flush detox had dealt with the dragon. While my partner was working on me, I felt intense energy in my belly and then a rush of hot energy that surged up through my throat and out the top of my head, which felt as if it had been blasted open; much like a dragon gate. Caught in the dragon's pathway, my bodywork partner sprang back and called Kate, who arrived just in time to feel the tailwind.

"What just happened?" she asked.

"It was the dragon," I said sheepishly. "I think it's gone now."

The dragon might have gone, but the aftershocks of its potent exit were still coursing through me. While the rest of the group continued with the fire bodywork practice, I sat outside in Kate's garden. I was shaking all over, and my hands and arms were tingling intensely. The only thing that helped to soothe the residual fire energy was water. I sprayed my arms down with the garden hose, directing the energy into the ground. It was a whole hour before the tingling in my hands finally abated. At the end of the day, Kate said my etheric body was still shaking.

By the time I got home, I was in agony; my chest hurt, my ribs ached. The dragon had left a trail of wreckage in its wake. The next day

I went to the doctor and was diagnosed with a dislocated rib. It had been pulled right out of the cartilage in the sternum. My doctor said, "Don't move. Don't laugh. Don't even breathe if you can help it. Six weeks. That's how long it will take to mend." Every movement was extremely painful. Laughing just wasn't an option—try telling that to two young boys. My doctor was right about that, but she was wrong about the recovery time. I was about to learn first-hand that working with energy can produce miracles.

Despite the excruciating pain and shock that the movement of energy could cause such physical wreckage, I was in awe at the power of the dragon. I was left with no doubt about the power of energy and the importance of my dragon lessons.

Later that week, I went to Kate for some energy work to repair my shaken etheric body. While she was working on my chest, I felt as if I were falling, being sucked backward out of my body and into nothingness. Then I heard wolves howling—not one or two, but a pack of wolves in unison. As this was suburban Cape Town, my rational mind assumed it was dogs barking, but there was no doubt that what I heard was *howling*. The wolves howled and howled and howled; immersed in the pervasive sound, I saw myself as a Native American medicine woman.

At the end of the session, the vision faded like a dream on waking. I asked Kate about the howling dogs.

"What dogs?" she asked.

She hadn't heard a thing! Not even one barking dog.

"Sounds like a portal has opened," she smiled mysteriously.

I wasn't entirely sure what Kate meant by that, but the pain in my ribcage was completely gone the next day. Six days, rather than six weeks, a miraculous recovery by any standards. Dragon-wrought destruction had paved the way for an important teaching about healing.

On the final weekend of the Polarity course, we had to dress up as our Higher Selves and pretend to be who we really are—just for a day. After

Chapter 3 | Alchemy

my experience with the wolves, my Higher Self choice was obvious; I would be a Native American medicine woman. To my surprise, another group member, Petra, arrived as a Native American woman.

We gathered in a circle, taking turns speaking about who we really are and why we are here on Earth at this time. By now, we were on intimate terms, and this deep sharing felt safe, though very revealing. When it was my turn, the words tumbled out of my mouth with little thought:

> I am Medicine Woman. This is my true-est identity across time. I am here to offer healing and pass on knowledge to the tribe. The medicines I use come from my soul's knowledge gained over many lifetimes. I am here to bring back sacred feminine knowing—the wisdom of the heart—and help heal the collective female psyche. This will restore balance to the world.

I sat down, somewhat shocked by my words. Petra stood up next and told us about her soul identity. While she was talking, I was filled with an intense longing. For a moment, the veils parted, and I saw teepees in a valley. I could smell wood fires. Tears sprang to my eyes. When I looked up from my reverie, Petra's face had changed; her features were rounder. I saw her as she had been in that long-ago time and recognized her as my sister. It was a complete knowing, with as much certainty as I've known anything in my life. In that moment of recognition, I knew that I had lost her in that life we shared as sisters. She had died giving birth to her first child, and I, as the medicine woman, had not been able to save her. All this came flooding through me without any thought on my part—an instantaneous download.

Afterward, we hugged each other for a long time. Something extraordinary had passed between us, and we'd both felt it. From then on, Petra and I were bound together as soul sisters. Our two oldest sons would also become the very best of friends.

I didn't know then that this was just the beginning of many years of spontaneous timeline jumping. Kate was right—a portal had opened the day I heard the wolves howling. Since then, I have moved between these two worlds and timelines many times, connecting with my soul roots to complete an outstanding spiritual task.

METAPHYSICAL HEALING TRAINING

After these powerful experiences with energy, there was no doubt that I had to start working with energy as soon as possible. Small hurdle: I needed formal training and qualification as a healer. There was a perplexing array of modalities to choose from, and, unlike in my twenties, I no longer had the luxury of time to explore them all—time to get cracking.

Soon after the Polarity course with Kate, I met Viviane, another exceptional healer in Cape Town. She casually mentioned that she was offering Metaphysical Healing training for a small group of healers. She looked at me pointedly and said, "You're coming."

It was a Friday afternoon when all major shifts in my life seemed to occur. Viviane's eighteen-month course was starting the next day. I had less than twenty-four hours to make a commitment. There was no time to interrogate the content or make practical arrangements, but it wasn't really a decision. It was a directive from Spirit, and with very little thought, I jumped right in. These have always been my best decisions: follow the energy, and I'm right on track.

The next day I was sitting in Viviane's classroom, ready to start my formal training. We were a handpicked group of six. For the next eighteen months, we met on alternate Saturdays, and Viviane taught us spiritual law and energy healing. We learned about the human energy field, from aura to chakras and meridians, and an array of techniques to restore balance and flow. In class, we practiced on each other, and between classes, we worked with family and friends to gain experience. As our skills developed, we worked with volunteers who provided case studies for our written assignments.

This intensive immersion in the world of energy took up every minute of my spare time. All my training and practice had to be condensed into alternate weekends when my boys were with their father. In the early mornings before work, I sat on my meditation cushion, and in the quiet evenings, after the boys had gone to bed, I plowed through the prescribed reading list before falling into an exhausted sleep. The sweet thrill of being back on my path gave me grit.

As the training progressed, I discovered there was a lot more to becoming a healer than technique. It was also about self-mastery and becoming a pure channel for healing. Viviane taught us spiritual discipline in the tradition of the old mystery schools. She was a hard taskmaster. She laid a strong spiritual foundation for our healing work, leaving us in no doubt that becoming a healer is a deeply spiritual path.

As anyone on a spiritual path will know, it is a journey of opening the heart, and cracking its hard shell can be a quest in itself. Opening the heart takes us beyond the mind and ego into a deeper center of being. Working from the heart, a healer is better able to help others with compassionate detachment without getting entangled in their suffering or becoming depleted. In the long run, the art of healing is to be able to sustain your own life force energy at a high frequency so that you can assist others in sustaining theirs. This is what it means to hold the light.

"As a lightworker, you are a beacon of the light and a channel for the light," Viviane explained. "My job is to give you a strong spiritual foundation so that you can be both. This is your true power as a healer."

And so, Viviane set about fashioning her students. She called it an upgrade—adding more RAM to our internal computers to expand our capacity to hold and calibrate energy. Like installing next-generation software, the outdated programs, beliefs, and patterns unconsciously running in the background of our lives would be overwritten. For me, this meant challenging my notion of self and changing a lot of things I'd taken for granted.

"You can't be a healer for one day a week and then go back to your normal life," Viviane told us. "Becoming a healer is a lifestyle change."

More than a lifestyle change, my metaphysical training with Viviane was a paradigm shift.

TUNING THE INSTRUMENT

In Buddhist teachings, the mind is often likened to a pond. When the water is muddy, our thinking is cloudy, and reality is obscured. When the pond water is clear, we see things as they are and struggle less. A clear pond reflects truth; a muddy pond distorts the reflection, concealing the truth. Most of life is a dance, a constant movement between looking at the world through muddy or clear waters—between truth and distortion.

The path of a healer is to become the clear pond, in mind and heart, where the reflection is as close to truth as possible. So along with learning the practical aspects of working with energy, we were also tasked with becoming clear ponds—the empty vessel, the hollow bone for holding a pure space for others and channeling higher vibration energy. This takes work. It takes dedicated effort to become a finely calibrated instrument that can serve others effectively.

Viviane said, "Remember, *you* are the instrument of healing."

Tuning myself as an instrument of healing meant raising my vibrational frequency and expanding my light. Tasked with this lofty goal, I threw myself into a daily round of meditation and chakra cleansing to coax my light body into better shape. Since those early days at the Buddhist Retreat Centre in Ixopo, I had a regular meditation practice, but under Viviane's tutelage, my practice had to be upleveled. It was part of the upgrade.

Viviane also taught us to harness the power of a still mind. Mind power is a combination of focus, attention, and intention. This combination directs the flow of energy.

"Focus is the number one skill of a good healer," Viviane said. "When you're working with a client, your full presence is necessary. You can't be thinking about what's for dinner or making a shopping list. That won't serve your client."

Group consciousness meditation was our mind power training ground. With each person at home, our group met ethereally for an hour-long meditation. This was dedicated time to connect with each other between classes and experience the group energy remotely. It was also an opportunity to practice sending and receiving information. Every session, one of us communicated an intention telepathically, like planting a seed in the group matrix to be picked up and cultivated. Afterward, we compared notes. In the beginning, it was a bit like broken telephones, causing much hilarity. But slowly, we improved, and after a few months, we had aligned with the group consciousness and effortlessly *got the memo*.

OPENING THE HEART

While a focused mind keeps you calmly present, the most important channel for healing is the heart center. The heart is the central conduit for channeling Source energy. It is the bridge between the physical and spiritual worlds and an important portal between dimensions. A healer sees with the heart, not the eyes; quite simply, an open heart sees much more. So, opening the heart to see more clearly was an essential part of our training.

Being the Wounded Healer, the doorway to my heart was rather reluctant to open. Then at one of our Saturday classes, I received help from an unexpected source—Viviane's dog Persephone. A black glossy-coated mixed breed with long spindly legs, Persephone usually slept on her cushion, an unobtrusive presence in the shadows of our classroom. While we were doing an exercise to open our heart chakras, Persephone strayed from her corner and wandered around the circle. Stopping in front of me, she stood up on her hind legs and put her front paws on my chest. In this most undog-like pose, she kept her paws on my heart center for several minutes. Suddenly, there was a burst of energy, a bubbling in my chest, and with that, Persephone went back to her corner, seemingly unaware that she had immensely accelerated the opening of my heart.

Viviane taught us how to channel Source energy through our heart chakras at a technical level. The pathway of Source energy traveled through the open Crown chakra, into the Heart chakra, down through the arms, and out through the hands. When the heart chakra is open, this flow of healing energy is unimpeded.

"You are glorified hosepipes," Viviane said. "Channels for divine light. Don't let your egos get in the way. If your heart is turbulent, you block the flow of energy. Your job is to be a pure channel in service of the Divine."

Over time, I learned to feel the two-way communication between my heart and hands. When the heart energy is open, it automatically connects with the chakras in the hands, which become receptors too. With practice, I could feel my client's energy with my hands and *understand* what I was feeling in my heart. With this information, I could direct the flow of Source energy through my heart and hands to where it was needed in my client's body. My hands and heart became a bio-feedback system that bypassed the mind—and ego!

Working from the heart in this way is like switching channels from the rational mind to the intuitive heart. The heart is the epicenter of intuitive understanding. I came to understand it as a psychic bridge, an information processing center, where intuitive messages are received and understood. In a very real sense, the heart center is the main intuitive channel; when the heart chakra is open, the other intuitive channels automatically open.

Intuition is our heritage. It is in our blood, but our conditioning is designed to stem the flow. Until recently, children were discouraged from using their intuition and learned to disregard it. So, like a forgotten language, we must re-learn it. Anyone who wishes to access intuition can remember this mother tongue and activate it. It's just a question of how deeply buried it is and one's willingness and dedication to uncovering it.

People who are considered shamans, psychics, or clairvoyants are those whose intuitive channels are more open than average, and access to multi-dimensional awareness comes easily. For a multitude of reasons, they have learned how to access multi-dimensional awareness. Shamans call this non-ordinary reality. Accessing non-ordinary reality, and traveling to other dimensions or timelines, has been a human capacity since the beginning of time. As Earth descended into third-dimensional consciousness, most of us lost this capacity. It's as if a circuit in the human brain got switched off. With a bit of practice, we can turn the switch on again, and as a species, we are waking up to these abilities more than ever before.

My psychic radar was switched on in my twenties, so this type of multi-sensing was still close to the surface. Since my Paranormal Gap Year, the volume had been turned down significantly, but it had never completely switched off. I often received images and messages in my dreams and had flashes of intuitive seeing and knowing during waking hours. At times, this had been extremely helpful, but I didn't actively seek it out. However, as soon as I started my Metaphysical Healing training, my intuitive senses opened again, quite naturally.

As with any newfound skill, intuitive sensing requires practice and fine-tuning. Like learning a language, you need to speak every day to gain fluency. During the training with Viviane, my intuitive senses developed in leaps and bounds.

MULTI-SENSORY PERCEPTION

Our sixth sense is, in fact, an extension of our five ordinary senses and has multiple channels for communicating what is perceived. When we start using multi-sensory perception, intuitive information comes through seven psychic sensory channels. Here is a brief description of each of these sensory channels, known as the *clairs*.

- Clairvoyance is intuitive seeing (seeing images, visions, moving scenes).
- Clairaudience is intuitive hearing (hearing words, sentences, sounds).
- Clairsentience is intuitive sensation (feeling physical sensations in the body).
- Clairempathy is intuitive feeling (emotions and empathic feeling).
- Claircognizance is intuitive knowing (knowing with certainty without rational reasons).

- Clairolfaction is intuitive smell (perceiving a smell that does not emanate from the physical environment).
- Clairgustance is intuitive taste (perceiving a strong taste that does not have a physical source).

Many psychics or healers work with one or two dominant psychic channels of information and may never use all seven of them. Experience with these different types of sensory channels depends on the level and type of healing or psychic work we are called to do. My experience followed a typical pattern of progression from clairvoyance, as my main channel of receiving multi-dimensional information, to the opening of other channels through my work with clients. Sometimes the opening of a dormant intuitive channel was dramatic. This was the case when my clairsentience came through.

SARAH'S STORY

My first case study volunteer was a middle-aged woman called Sarah. An accomplished academic, Sarah was witty and charming and seemingly confident in the world. Her energy body revealed a different story. When I started working with Sarah's energy field, it appeared as if she were floating somewhere outside her body. I immediately felt a bit sea-sick, as one does in a rocking boat. As I scanned her chakras with my hands, as I had in my massage days in London, and with my third eye for visual information, there was almost no pulse, which meant very little energy flow.

While my hand was hovering over Sarah's solar plexus, suddenly, I couldn't breathe. It felt as if there was a tight girdle around my diaphragm. Tuning in further, I could see an etheric strap around Sarah's diaphragm, which had the effect of cutting her in half, the lower part of her energy body severed from the upper part. *No wonder she felt so ungrounded!* Still struggling to breathe, I removed the etheric strap and felt an immediate release in my body and a rush of energy into Sarah's solar plexus. At this point, I didn't know what the strap was related to or why it was there; it took much more practice before I would be able to get the full story. But when I told Sarah what had happened, she burst into tears and told me her story.

When Sarah was six weeks old, her mother went back to work and left her with her father, who was studying at the time. While he was busy at his desk, he strapped baby Sarah onto her compactum so that she wouldn't fall off. Even as a baby, Sarah probably left her body to escape the stress of being trapped like that.

Over the course of a few sessions, I cleared this traumatic imprint from Sarah's diaphragm and integrated the two halves of her energy body. As the energy began to flow again, it was possible to bring Sarah's energy-consciousness more fully into her body and strengthen her shaky grounding.

Working with Sarah was the first time I received information so clearly in my own body. My next experience of clairsentience was even more dramatic.

KAREN'S STORY

Another case study was an illustrator called Karen. She was recovering from glandular fever, and although she felt much better, she was constantly tired. In the first session, Karen shared with me that she was having relationship difficulties with her domineering husband, but she didn't say much more than that.

As soon as I entered Karen's energy field, I was gripped by a hand around my throat. It was so intense that I started coughing. I grabbed some water to stop the coughing, but the constriction in my throat continued, almost throttling me. Focusing on Karen's throat chakra, I tried to ease the constriction. Immediately, I was guided to remove an invisible hand around her throat, and as I did so, her throat chakra opened with a rush of energy. As her throat constriction eased, so did mine until finally, it dissipated.

Working with the blockage in Karen's throat guided us toward a deeper understanding of her life situation and the root cause of her illness. I could sense that the communication between her and her husband contained a lot of anger, bordering on violence. When I asked Karen about this, she confessed that he was emotionally violent and that once or twice he had put his hands around her throat. *No wonder I had felt strangled!*

Karen's illness was, in fact, a defense. The only time her husband had shown her any care or concern was at the height of her illness. Chronic illness had allowed her vital time out from the continual onslaught of his abusive behavior. As she gained an understanding of how the glandular fever was protecting her, we looked at other ways that she could set boundaries in her relationship and protect herself. Karen knew she should leave the marriage but didn't feel strong enough to take that step.

One of the important aspects of Karen's healing journey was finding her voice and speaking her truth about what was happening in her marriage. This took time, but slowly she regained her strength, both physically and emotionally, and eventually was able to end the marriage and start a new life.

Karen's real malaise was an ether block. Ether is a subtle element closely related to spirit and is concentrated in the throat chakra. When the throat chakra is blocked, it stops the flow of ether, which results in all sorts of problems. The throat chakra is the energy center that governs communication, self-expression, and sound. An ether block prevents us from expressing feelings and speaking truth; even more importantly, it prevents us from living truth. In a very real sense, an ether block is a truth block. When truth cannot flow, when the voice is muzzled, there is a profound loss of power.

An ether block interrupts the flow of intuition too. The throat chakra is right in the middle of the brow and heart chakras, and when it is blocked, the natural connection between the head and heart is severed. There is no coherence between the rational mind and the heart-knowing. An ether block cuts us off from this natural wellspring of intuitive knowing. At an even deeper level, an ether block has the effect of cutting us off from our soul's truth and destiny path. An ether block is no small thing.

Women are especially prone to ether blocks. Like Karen, many women have experienced ether blocks at some point in their lives, me included. Thanks to Kate, my ether block was cleared during the Polarity course. This had undoubtedly helped to allow my intuition to flow more freely, clearing the path for realizing my destiny.

TRANSMUTING ENERGY

After working with Sarah and Karen, clairsentience quickly became my dominant way of sensing. Once an intuitive sense has been activated, it still takes practice to interpret and trust the information coming through the psychic airwaves. My body unfailingly showed me where the main blockage in someone's energy system was located, which invariably led to the deeper layer of healing needed to restore balance. My body was never wrong with its signals, and I learned to trust it implicitly.

Faith was one thing; method was another. I still had an important methodological lesson to learn. This came with my next case study. Late one night, I received an emergency call from a friend asking me to help her teenage daughter Tamara, who had been involved in a car accident and was in the hospital with serious injuries.

TAMARA'S STORY

Tamara was in pretty bad shape. Although she had regained consciousness, her body had taken a beating. She had a cracked pelvis, a broken leg, severe whiplash, and minor head injuries. Tamara's injuries were similar to those I had sustained when I was twenty-one, not much older than her. Perhaps because of this, working with Tamara was physically intense. I found myself taking her pain into my own body and transmuting it through my energy system.

I worked with Tamara three times, each time carrying her pain with me for days. Thanks to her quick-thinking mother, she recovered from her physical injuries much more rapidly than expected and was likely spared further suffering down the line.

For my part, I felt drained and exhausted. I had over-identified with Tamara's physical pain. Without thinking, I had resorted to the old shamanic way of healing, transmuting energy through my own body. This was my default setting, and the clairsentience had heightened this tendency.

The primary role of a healer is to transmute energy—to be a kind of alchemist for the person seeking healing. There are many ways to transmute energy, and every healer works in a slightly different way, depending on which intuitive senses are dominant. The pitfall with clairsentience is that the visceral sensation makes it all too easy to take on the client's energy.

Working with Tamara taught me an important lesson about transmuting energy. Since my clairsentience had come on stream, I had been taking energy through my body in the old shamanic way. It was my default methodology, a residual memory from my shamanic past as a Native American medicine woman. In those times, shamans had the support of ceremony, times of fasting, and long periods alone in nature to purify their energy. Clearing the *shamanic body* was, in fact, a communal process. In the modern context, this old methodology simply isn't viable without the support of these community-held processes. The pace of healing practice is faster now, and my physical body would not sustain this old way of transmuting energy for my clients. More than that, I would be taking on karma at a rate that I could not clear myself.

My spirit guides chipped in, "The task of a lightworker is to use light to effect change. Don't get emotionally involved. Don't wade into the mud with clients. That way, you take on karma and add to the sticky energy."

I had to change my default setting and become a healer for the modern age. Above all, this meant transmuting energy with light while maintaining strong, energetic boundaries so that I didn't take on the sticky energies I was working with.

Chapter 3 | Alchemy

SPIRIT COMMUNICATION

My training was a steep and exciting learning curve. There was so much to learn about the world of energy and navigating the invisible realms. My next case study initiated me into spirit communication and the associated sensory signals.

JAY'S STORY

I first saw Jay shortly after his brother's tragic death. A few months previously, his beloved younger brother Frank had gone on an overnight hiking trip with a group of friends and had a fatal asthma attack. He had died on the mountain without his medication and far from the nearest hospital. Some of the group had gone looking for help, but by the time the paramedics got to him, it was too late. Jay explained that Frank had suffered from severe asthma as a child, but as an adult, it had been more manageable, so long as he took the right precautions. On that fateful day, he had forgotten his asthma pump.

Jay was struggling to accept that Frank had died a preventable death at such a young age. They had a strong bond, and Jay had always felt protective of his younger brother. How he wished he had been with him on the hike! Still, so soon after his brother's unexpected passing, Jay's grief was overwhelming when he came to me. After listening to this heart-breaking story, my intention was to help Jay process his grief and find acceptance. When I went into his energy field, the grief was palpable. There was a dark shroud over his heart chakra, and the rest of his chakras were barely spinning.

Shortly into the session, Jay's glass of water exploded with a loud ping, shattering into tiny pieces for no apparent reason. Jay shot up in astonishment, then laid back down. Suddenly, I felt light-headed, and my third eye was throbbing. Tuning into these sensations, I became aware of an unseen presence in the room. A cold shiver ran through me as I realized it was Frank's spirit. I asked Frank if he wanted to communicate with his brother and listened intently for a reply. His telepathic message came to me in short sentences. This is what he said:

> It was my time. Nothing could have prevented my death. Put down the guilt you are feeling. I am at peace. I will always love you, Jay. Love never dies. Please open your heart again and feel it.

And then I felt a shift in the energy as Frank's spirit left. I quickly scribbled down his words and continued with the energy work, focusing on Jay's heart chakra. Not only would I need to lift the shroud of grief, but it seemed important that I work with opening his heart again.

After the energy work, I conveyed Frank's message to Jay, who promptly burst into tears. Once the tears abated, he told me that this was the first time he had cried properly since his brother's death. This was a huge release for him. Although Jay still needed to grieve, I hoped his brother's communication would help him find peace.

Through this experience with Jay and the spirit of his brother Frank, I learned that messages from the other side could be very comforting to those suffering the loss of a loved one. Just knowing that the soul lives on and that the connection between them remains is a huge revelation for many. In the years to come, I would channel hundreds of messages from departed loved ones, which, without exception, helped the person left behind on the Earth plane.

Thankfully, I have never again experienced a spirit announcing its arrival by shattering a glass. I can only surmise that Frank's spirit had to create a rather dramatic disturbance to get my attention because it was my first experience communicating with a spirit other than my own departed relatives. Thanks to Frank, I was primed to connect with spirit energy. Whenever I felt sudden light-headedness and throbbing in my third eye, there was bound to be a spirit in the room, and I could adjust my focus and vibration to receive their message.

VIBRATIONAL ALCHEMY

With all the practice and varied case studies, my intuitive sensitivity and confidence blossomed. However, this heightened sensitivity came at a price. Each wave of attunement with a new intuitive sense was accompanied by physical discomfort. At first, I experienced frequent headaches. This was partly because my third eye had become so sensitive.

It was also because the high-vibrational energy I was channeling and processing was hitting against the denser energy of my auric field as it came into my crown chakra. Evidently, more upgrading was required.

Throughout my training period with Viviane, I went to her for regular upgrades that involved targeted transmissions of light into my energy system. These repeated light transmissions slowly calibrated my energy to a higher vibrational frequency, which helped my physical body harmonize with the higher energies I was channeling during sessions. It was a kind of vibrational alchemy, transforming denser vibrations into a lighter state.

Continually raising my vibration was a professional imperative. The higher my own vibration, the more effectively I was able to channel healing energy for my clients, and the more clearly I received intuitive information or spirit communications. Each time my vibration went up a notch, it also became easier to access my spirit guides in the higher planes.

For trained healers, information quality—not the volume—is most important. But the dense energy of our material world can interrupt the flow of higher vibrational energy, fragmenting intuitive information. It takes practice to maintain a steady flow of accurate messages. In the beginning, most of the information I received was in the form of static pictures or disjointed words. With practice, the visual images became more like movies with subtitles explaining what I saw.

Unlike my experience during my Paranormal Gap Year in my twenties, I now had the tools to support this psychic opening. Even so, I could still get easily overloaded if I didn't manage my energy. Sensory overload was not a new experience; I'd been intuitively managing my sensory exposure since I was a child. But the more my intuitive senses switched on, the more I actively had to manage the sensory streaming from the ordinary world. Most *normal* situations became much more taxing for me. Going to shopping malls, for example, was exhausting. With so many people in a confined space, the energy was intense and hard to shut out completely.

Out of necessity, I learned to close my psychic channels to mute sensory exposure when navigating ordinary reality. But even with good energy management, my life as a healer still required some adjustments. There were many places I couldn't stay long and some I avoided completely. Social events were manageable in bite-size chunks, but not much more. Noisy restaurants were taxing, though I found that if I sat in a corner facing the room, I could screen the flow of energies. Traveling became more challenging, too, especially if I had to spend a night in a hotel room, which was like trying to sleep in an energetic railway station.

Despite these restrictions, I adapted to having super-sensitive radar and reminded myself that sensitivity is a strength; it allowed me to be the finely calibrated instrument through which healing energy flowed.

Do all you sensitive souls out there hear that? Sensitivity is a strength—embrace it and find the gift in your unique blend of sensitivity.

BECOMING A MEDIAL BEING

As the metaphysical healing course progressed, my life changed. I had outgrown my old life like old clothes that no longer fit. Viviane said this was part of the upgrade, gradually replacing outdated software programs with more advanced ones suited for the next level of growth. It was a process of becoming. Stepping into the world of energy was a type of crossing. Once again, I felt as if I were moving between worlds: the visible and invisible—the world of work and children and social functions on the one side and the world of energy and soul on the other.

"You are the bridge between worlds," Viviane said. "Your task, as a healer, is to help people cross that bridge."

First, I had to find my own way across the bridge, applying spiritual law, following signs, and calibrating my own compass. As I attuned to the Universe's guidance, I became more aware of spiritual allies helping me make the crossing between the visible and invisible realms. Back and forth, I was becoming more surefooted in bridging worlds.

Chapter 3 | Alchemy

My friend Jade from the now-defunct jazz band said I was becoming a medial being. For clarification, she pointed me in the direction of our go-to guidebook, *Women who Run with the Wolves*, by the illustrious Clarissa Pinkola Estés. In the book, she says:

> *The medial woman stands between the world of consensual reality and the mystical unconscious and mediates between them... She is able to live in all worlds, the topside world of matter and the far world, or underworld, which is her spiritual home.*[8]

By the end of the training, I was comfortable moving between worlds, prepared for the medial role of being the bridge for others. Still, I was keeping one resolute foot in the known world. I knew I would have to leave my job at some point. My training path was making a beeline for the cliff-face; leaping off the edge was just a matter of time.

At our last Saturday class, Viviane channeled guidance from an Ascended Master for each of the students. The message for me was that I had to step out of my comfort zone. I knew this meant I had to leave my job, but I wasn't ready yet. The prospect of losing my financial footing terrified me. I had sleepless nights thinking about that fast-approaching cliff-face. As a breadwinner with two children to look after, giving up a regular salary did not seem sensible or even possible. Comfort zone or not, there did not appear to be a way through this impasse.

Could I trust that a more reasonable path would be shown?

INITIATION AS A BONA FIDE HEALER

After completing our training, Viviane's class gathered one last time for an initiation ceremony at Phakalane. With Frieda holding ceremonial space, Viviane gave us her blessing to practice the healing arts.

The night of the ceremony was stormy; the rain and wind lashed the sweat lodge as we gathered around the fire. This time I would be inside the lodge with my classmates. Tonight, I would join the rounds of

---

[8] Clarissa Pinkola Estés, *Women Who Run With the Wolves: Myths and Stories of the Wild Woman Archetype* (USA: Ballantine Books, 1992).

sweating and song as we released everything that wouldn't accompany us on our journeys as practicing healers. While the storm raged outside, we offered our old lives to the fire and called for our new lives to take form. At midnight, the wind dropped; we emerged exhausted and silently made our way to the sleeping hut and entered the dreamtime.

In the morning, we sat in a circle and received our formal blessings before making a vow to work in the light and serve the Divine. Like a Hippocratic oath for healers, we promised to work in accordance with the highest good of every person, and in every situation, we were called to assist. It was a powerful rite of passage.

Finally, I was a qualified healer. My training with Frieda, Kate, and Viviane was done. I was ready to answer the call.

DRAGON'S GOLD
Wisdom teachings from Chapter Three

- Ask your spirit guides for help. Spiritual assistance is always at hand if you make a sincere request and take the time to listen for the answer. Help may come in the form of a clear auditory message, a chance meeting, an eye-catching visual image, the lyrics of a song, or it may be delivered through another person. Your task is to stay tuned to the workings of the invisible world.

- Anger is a powerful energy and needs to move. Movement is initiated when you listen to what anger is telling you and honor the message. This is an important first step in spiritual alchemy. By honoring anger, purpose is revealed. Often, anger indicates a boundary showing up. When you listen deeply and let the feeling-energy move through you, rather than projecting it onto someone else, you'll learn to hold the boundary without the anger, and then you can graciously release it.

- Need overrides intuition. This unconscious override is one of the most common traps, especially for the naïve or unmothered heroine. The lesson here is to pay attention to your intuition before diving in boots and all.

- Where intention goes, energy flows. Learn to harness energy with focus and intention. Focus on what you want, not what you don't want in your life. Directing thought and intention for the highest good of yourself and those around you is an advanced form of self-mastery.

- Like an alchemist, the task of a lightworker is to use light to effect changes in vibrational substance. Don't wade into the mud with your clients or transmute their energy through your body. That way, you take on karma and add to the sticky energy. That's old technology.

4

ANSWERING THE CALL

2008 – 2010

Your soul is eternally calling you in the direction of your highest path. Answering your soul's calling is not about a single revelation; rather, it is a lifelong dance.

– Rebecca Campbell, author of *Light is the New Black*

Qualified and initiated as a metaphysical healer, I was ready to answer the call.

I wondered what my life would have been like had I answered the first soul call when my clairvoyance opened during my Paranormal Gap Year. What if I hadn't pleaded in that little stone church in France for the visions to stop? What if I had said yes to what life was giving me instead of running in the opposite direction? Was it my destiny, or was it my resistance that took me on the scenic route to becoming a healer?

There is no definitive answer to this, and perhaps, over the course of a lifetime, timing doesn't matter that much. A soul path is not one fixed route; there are infinite possibilities. Fulfilling a soul mission may even take more than one lifetime, so can we really judge the time it takes, in the cosmic scheme of things, to reach our destination?

What matters is that we become trackers—keeping our ears to the ground, listening for the call, seeking out the best route, following faint tracks into the wilds. A skilled tracker follows animals through their spoor: the tracks, droppings, scratch marks, and scents. If we are paying attention, there is so much to show the way. And still, there will be many forks in the proverbial road, and we'll be required to make choices, big and small.

If we don't know where we are heading at such points, we must ask ourselves the single most important question: Is this a path of heart? If the answer is yes, it's likely to take you closer, step by step, in the direction of your highest path. And that's the best that any of us can do. Keep moving, however fast or slow, in the direction we chose without looking back—we can never know what may have been on the path not taken. Each path has its own gifts, pitfalls, and unique challenges. Even a wrong turn is a teacher. Our task is to gather the gold along the way and keep following the golden thread toward our soul's calling, even if it means weaving this way and that and feeling a bit lost at times.

It is a misconception to think that walking your soul path is a direct route from A to B. Or that you'll always know where you are going. A soul path is made of baby steps, with a lot of plodding, wandering, backtracking, and occasionally big leaps forward. All you need to do is keep tracking the signs and take the next step. This is how we follow the call of destiny and create it as we go.

Destiny is a mysterious mix of free will and choice, karma and fate, and there is no magic formula for the perfect path. Weaving your destiny is a co-creative process. The choices we make *create* our path and, ultimately, our destiny. Conversely, destiny itself will *guide* those choices if we seek its direction and allow it to unfold. It is like being in a giant feedback loop, or as Rebecca Campbell observed, a lifelong dance.

Chapter 4 | Answering the Call

Even when we know our purpose, the path is not always clearly laid out before us. It still requires close attention to the signals and signposts along the way. I had known from a young age what my purpose was and had many mystical experiences to make sure I would get with my soul's program. However, the question of timing for staying the course was a bit more complex. I've come to understand that on life's path, we have both karma and purpose giving directional signals. We can be advanced in one and not the other, and this affects the timing of choices.

One of the primary arenas for karma is relationships, in all its permutations—family, romantic partners, friends, work colleagues, and clients. It is like a cosmic play; anyone can enter onto the stage for short cameo appearances or major roles. We even carry ancestral karma, giving us the opportunity to resolve issues that persist in the family lineage. It is through the complex web of relationships that we learn the lessons of love and loss, joy and grief, trust and betrayal, and all the expressions of being human. Most of us are entangled in these karmic lessons, in one way or another, while trying to figure out our higher purpose. Those rare few who have it sussed when it comes to relationships may be adrift when it comes to purpose. Others may have a clear sense of purpose but are bogged down by karma.

I fell into the last category, with rounds of karma to sift through before I could fully step into my calling as a healer. I reminded myself that my purpose included healing myself, which had to come first. As it turned out, the circuitous route I traveled yielded many gifts—primarily, the benefit of life experience, which undoubtedly allowed me to approach my clients' issues with greater sensitivity and insight. The biggest gift of extra time was that I got to be a mother first, a life experience that opened my heart and taught me about the mysteries of love in a way that no training or monastic setting ever could. In my working life, I also acquired a veritable arsenal of practical skills: as a young journalist, I honed my writing skills; as a massage therapist in London, I learned the body with my hands; in my publishing job, I was a wordsmith and team manager. A long detour, perhaps, or a gathering of gold for my work as a healer.

THE CURRENT OF DESTINY

After being initiated as a qualified healer, I answered the call with a resounding, *Yes!* If I'm honest, it was tempting to stay in the comfort zone of a well-paid job and avoid rocking the boat of my children's reconstructed world. But perhaps precisely because I did not answer the call in my twenties, I was not going to hesitate this time. Now in my early forties, I was ready to plunge into the current of my destiny and trust the flow.

In one of my favorite books, *The Alchemist*, Paulo Coelho's central character Santiago says:

> *When someone makes a decision, he is diving into a strong current that will carry him to places he had never dreamed of when he first made the decision.*[9]

I recited these words gleefully to anyone who questioned my wisdom, and there were many, as I slipped deeper into the current of my journey. Of course, I knew this strong current would also move through my children's lives. But I had done my homework and was poised for not-yet-dreamed of places.

As we got ready for work and school every morning, I kept my eye on the mountain from the kitchen window. It was an ever-changing picture, no one day the same: tumbling clouds draped like a tablecloth over the mountain's flat table-top; shrouds of mist; sheets of rain; spectacular rainbows; in winter, cascading waterfalls gushing down its slopes. The mountain's capricious offering always made me feel connected to the elements; it was my barometer. As I contemplated my destiny path, I felt anchored at the base of this powerful energy center—rooted in the only place I had ever felt home.

What better time and place to take the next step on my healer's journey?

Not without trepidation, I started making changes in the outer world. The first step was to negotiate a part-time week at my publishing job—

---

9 Paulo Coelho, *The Alchemist* (Harper One, 1993).

asking meant revealing my soul's aspirations and coming out of the spiritual closet. I didn't hold out much hope, but I figured it was worth a try. To my surprise, one of the directors I spoke with immediately got it, as if she had seen this coming, and persuaded the other directors to accommodate my request. Spiritual allies appear in the most unlikely places. We quickly reached an agreement, and as soon as the next book went to print, I was free to pursue my healing work two days a week.

CROSSING THE THRESHOLD BETWEEN WORLDS

At the beginning of 2009, I opened my energy healing practice at Frieda's new center, Phakalane, and dipped my toes into the life of a healer. Moving between worlds, I recalled Viviane's words about being a bridge for clients, helping them cross from the known life to the life that is possible when you embark on a healing journey or a conscious spiritual path. As a healer, I would have to sustain the connection with the soul-world and bring back the knowing, the insights, and the soul food to others.

At the same time, I was at a threshold too. My life was grounded in spiritual principles and practice, but it took time to find my feet in this new role and forge my identity as a healer. I might have been a bridge for others, but I was also traversing from the known to the unknown. My time at Phakalane was the bridge between my old life and my new life, the bridge that spanned the time it took me to move from part-time to full-time healer.

My first year of practicing as a professional healer was a steep learning curve—practice being far more nuanced than my training. Every client taught me something valuable. Like gems on the path, I collected every insight to build my psychic muscle, strengthening myself as the instrument for healing, and deepening my understanding of the energetic body. I was learning how to move up and down the vibration ladder, find the high and the low notes, learn the resonant chords, listen for the vibrational harmonies, and change keys according to the client. As my hands read the energy body, I became more proficient in seeking out the dissonant tones and tuning the body to a more harmonic key.

Like a musician practicing scales, I went up and down this vibrational ladder until it was second nature.

In the process, I was creating a body map, correlating symptoms with spiritual-emotional issues, learning how to listen to the body-mind, and finding the keys to initiate change for my clients. This required deep listening: to the client, the body-mind, the soul, the universal field, my guides. Listening from the heart and dropping the ego-mind and its judgments is a different type of listening. When judgment arose, I had to push the ego-mind aside mindfully. The moment you judge someone, you lose their trust and the opportunity to make a difference in their lives.

I soon discovered that heart-based listening was a critical skill that required tuning into multiple sources of information. When clients shared their stories, I tracked the threads—the choices, the patterns, the themes. While doing the energy work, I listened to the energy body, which told another part of the story, sometimes conscious, often not. Finally, I tuned into the quantum field, which held information about the client's soul journey and revealed the bigger picture of life lessons and soul contracts at play.

As information washed up on the shore of my intuitive heart-mind, I was guided to adjust and attune the client's energy body. It was an intricate dance of souls and energy—mine pulling out old energy and channeling Source energy, the client's responding, shifting, and integrating change. Like a beautifully choreographed piece coming together, our dance continued until the crescendo moment when the client's mind, body, and spirit found harmony.

Of course, harmony didn't always converge in one session. Sometimes the dance continued over multiple sessions and in the living of life between sessions, but if the client was listening to the music too, the healing dance gathered pace.

I loved this work. In the dance, I felt relaxed and alive. Healing days at Phakalane were a stark contrast to my deadline-driven bread-and-butter job, which left me feeling rushed and stressed rather than in flow with my innate pace. I knew that feeling in flow was a sure sign of stepping into alignment with my soul path.

GETTING TO KNOW MY HEALING TEAM

In the beginning, the pace of my new healing business was slow. It took time for clients to find me, for referral networks to fire up, and for the Universe to respond to my "Yes" message. As the instrument, I needed time to find new rhythms and get to know the inside of a new life. I was also getting to know my healing team as old and new spirit guides showed up to offer their assistance.

At that time, my main spirit guide was a Native American medicine woman called Chenoa, which means *white dove*. She had a calming, peaceful energy, and I felt a strong bond, almost a kinship with her that made trusting her guidance come easily. My great-grandmother Isabella also popped into my healing room offering guidance of a more personal nature. She had helped me through some tough times during the transformation years while I was navigating a divorce and a career change, and her presence was always a reassuring support as I honed my skills.

As new guides turned up, it took time to get to know them and establish trust. One of the first was a rather short and slim elderly Chinese man wearing blue worker's overalls, who was always grinning slightly, as if somewhat amused. I noticed he usually showed up when I was working on physical conditions—ailments, illness, broken bones. Since his guidance included medical knowledge, I asked him if he'd been a doctor.

He started laughing, apparently amused at the question and my obvious puzzlement at his uncharacteristic worker's attire, then whispered just one word, "Mao."

Oh right, the penny dropped. I had to laugh at my own preconceptions about how a doctor should look. From then on, I called him Doctor. In this line of work, it's important to get rid of your preconceptions. They get in the way of what you need to see. I noticed that the more I kept my mind out of the way, the more I saw, and intuitive information flowed more consistently.

As new would-be guides arrived in the healing room, I was learning the importance of discernment—not everyone was hired for the job. I was quickly realizing that just because I heard a spirit guide, it didn't mean that what they had to say was valuable. Some brought high-level guidance, while others were lower energies that jumped into the psychic airspace like gatecrashers at a party. Those whose assistance I welcomed were the light beings, who offered valuable guidance and whose presence filled the space with high-vibrational energy, supporting the healing process. Among these light beings were angels, archangels, and ascended masters, as well as my personal teachers, such as Chenoa and Doctor, and benevolent ancestors, like Isabella. Those I kept out of the healing room were displaced beings who hadn't crossed over to the light planes and were needing rather than giving help, as well as negative entities attempting to hijack the airwaves and offer their two cents worth. My job was to discern between the astral rabble and the real guides and to send the low-vibrational lot packing.

In my training, I had learned to screen all the spirit beings that came forward with offers of assistance by applying the Law of Challenge. This spiritual law states that if you challenge a spirit entity three times in the name of God, or whatever is holy, it must reveal its identity or disappear. In practice, this meant asking every spirit being that entered the healing space the question, "Are you a being of light?" three times over and noticing the response.

Under scrutiny, a low-vibrational being would often waver, look away or simply disappear. Sorting out who was who kept me on my toes, especially when clients arrived with their own guides in tow. The room could get quite crowded!

On one occasion, my colleague Ginny came for a session, along with her extra-terrestrial guide. There were some funny moments.

GINNY'S STORY

Ginny was a practicing healer in my emerging network. After a series of challenging sessions with her clients, she asked me to clear and balance her energy. As a healer, Ginny understood the importance of taking responsibility for her energy and seeking help when needed. As soon as I stepped into her energy field, an unfamiliar being appeared and tried to take charge. He was an odd-looking extra-terrestrial entity with a large dome-shaped head and misshapen nose. After my initial surprise, I checked his credentials and was assured that he was a light being, working as a guide for Ginny.

Assured of his intentions, I followed his instructions to hold Ginny's head and place crystals in strategic places while he rewired her scrambled energy circuits. This was new to me, but I let him take charge while I simply observed the process. *If only every healing session was that simple!*

Ginny got up smiling and said, "Oh, I forgot to warn you about my guide. Peculiar looking chap. I hope you didn't get too much of a fright!"

We laughed, and I told her how her alien guide had taken charge. "I haven't found anyone who can work with my bossy ET guide," she said. Apparently, I had passed some sort of test.

After that, Ginny came for regular rebalancing. She was a Starseed soul, and normal healing techniques didn't work. Starseed souls are those that originate from other parts of the Cosmos and may have little prior experience of living on planet Earth. Many Starseeds struggle to connect with Earth energy and ground themselves, and the usual grounding techniques of connecting with the Earth and bringing Earth energy into the energy body, simply don't work. For example, grounding with Earth energy was positively destabilizing in Ginny's case. So, following the instructions of her bossy helper, I learned to work with a variety of quite alien techniques, excuse the pun, to reset her energy system and ground her with crystal energy instead.

KEEPING THE ENERGIES SPARKLING

Another light being who quickly became an indispensable member of my healing team was Mika, a spirit helper who arrived at the end of each session to help me clear the room of residual energies. During their sessions, my clients released a lot of old energy, and if this debris was not regularly cleared, it hung around the space like a dark cloud. Working in an energetically dirty space is just bad practice, and I was hugely grateful for Mika's assistance in keeping the energy sparkling, especially after a heavy session.

Similarly, managing my own energy in the healing room was no longer nice to have; it was an essential part of the job. After every session, I cleared and rebalanced my energy to release anything I might have taken on from the client. This was as much for my own well-being as it was to ensure that, as the instrument of healing, I was a clear channel for the next client who walked through the door.

The more I worked with clients, the more I realized that my vibration was a significant part of the healing experience. If I were a still pond, I could more easily pick up the energetic ripples in the client's field and smooth them over. When someone arrived in an agitated state, I could calm them down almost instantly by getting them to sync with my breathing. Nine times out of ten, my clients would enter a deep state of relaxation and often fell asleep during the healing session.

Keeping myself in a calm state was not just about my energy when I was with my clients. It required a dedicated effort in and out of the healing room to counter the stress of juggling a deadline-driven job, single-mothering, and my new role as a healer. If I was to be of the highest service to my clients, I had to meditate and clear my chakras every morning, drink plenty of water, and spend time in nature to recharge. That's a lot of self-care! But I couldn't help my clients with their energy bodies if my own was depleted.

Little by little, my lifestyle changed. On the weekends, I began to spend whole days on the mountain to release the week's stress and rebalance my energy. One of my favorite ways to detox my energy was to *listen to rivers*. As often as I could, I hiked up one of the river gorges in Newlands Forest to a secluded spot where I sat in meditation, listening to the sound of running water. As the river's song soothed me, I would imagine the pure mountain water washing me clean as all the week's stress and accumulated stale energy was released and carried downstream. In the winter months, when the mountain waterfalls were flowing, I'd also indulge in an icy waterfall shower any chance I got.

Running water is a powerful cleanser. Waterfalls are especially potent. One of the reasons for this is that pure water carries negative ions that balance the positive ions, which build up in the energy body due to electromagnetic pollution and stress. Water is also infused with cosmic energy, which helps to nourish and balance our energy bodies. In shamanic traditions, the water element is considered a powerful purifying force, particularly for the emotional body. For some people, living near a river or a large water body, like a lake or the ocean, is a prerequisite for their emotional well-being.

Since I didn't live near a water body, frequent pilgrimages to the mountain rivers and the ocean were an integral part of my new life, and the boys happily joined in. Beyond clearing my energy field, maintaining a high-vibrational frequency became a daily task. I extended my long-time daily meditation practice to include grounding work, chakra clearing, and pranayama breathing techniques. There were tweaks to my diet, too. I moved to a largely plant-based diet, stopped drinking tea and alcohol, and upped my water intake. Using the protocol from Kate's Polarity course, I did regular detox, gradually ridding my body of toxic residue. At first, the detoxes had a powerful effect on my physical body. Over time, the detox effects became more subtle, affecting the emotional and mental bodies more than the physical body and releasing old emotions, cell-bound memories, and beliefs.

After every detox, my intuitive senses were sharper, and I could hear my guides more clearly. It was a bit like tuning a radio station to the correct channel, removing any static or interference. To this day, regular detox is an important part of my spiritual toolkit to make sure that as the instrument for healing, my energy is like a clear, running stream.

OPENING NEW PSYCHIC CHANNELS

Seeing clients every week was also expanding my intuitive range. After all the river-listening, it's not surprising that the next psychic channel to come online was clairaudience. I had some experience with clairaudience when I heard my spirit guide instruct me to unfasten my seatbelt just before the car crash—undoubtedly saving my life. But since then, my main psychic channels had been clairvoyance, intuitive sight, and clairsentience, feeling physical sensations that alerted me to what was happening in a client's body. Now suddenly, my clairaudience opened up like a symphony, temporarily overshadowing my other intuitive senses. It was like switching from watching TV to listening to a podcast. For the next few years, clairaudience and clairsentience became my main psychic channels.

As my clairaudience developed, I experienced ringing in my ears for several uncomfortable months. At first, I thought I was suffering from tinnitus, but my guides assured me it was an energetic shift as my clairaudient ear attuned to a higher vibrational frequency. I just had to hang in until there was greater alignment with the incoming frequencies. The painful ringing did eventually go away, but multi-sensory perception comes at a price!

The first time I experienced clairolfaction—the psychic sense of smell—it took me by surprise. Fortunately, my client Nisha immediately validated the unusual sensory information; otherwise, I might have dismissed it as my imagination. Since then, clairolfaction has often come in useful as a visceral connection with a client's buried memory.

NISHA'S STORY

During one of my first sessions with Nisha, I became aware of a strong cooking smell. Taken by surprise, I thought that perhaps Nisha had been cooking that morning, and the smell was lingering on her clothes. A part of my mind shifted into logic mode trying to rationalize the smell, but when a stronger waft hit me, I recognized it as the unmistakable smell of samosas frying in oil. Getting my logical mind out the way, I tuned into the psychic smell more intently and saw Nisha as a young girl with an elderly woman. I asked Nisha what samosas meant to her, and she immediately burst into tears sharing memories about cooking samosas with her grandmother on Saturdays to sell at the local market. Those Saturdays with her grandmother were the happiest times of Nisha's childhood—her granny being the stable force in her otherwise turbulent world.

Nisha's grandmother had passed on many years before but communicated this olfactory message to remind her granddaughter of these happy memories. A happy memory can be an anchor for the traumatized inner child to start the healing process. After this experience, Nisha was able to forge a visceral connection with her inner child, which initiated a deep process of reclaiming the dissociated parts of herself. Nisha had a rough childhood, with an unpredictable father who was verbally abusive toward her mother. Now in her thirties, the prompt to see me was recurring laryngitis and general anxiety. In a hoarse whisper, she explained to me that with each bout of laryngitis, she lost her voice. She told me she'd lost her confidence too.

Establishing a connection with her inner child paved the way for a deeply transformative healing process. From an energetic perspective, inner child issues are often lodged in the sacral chakra, the emotional reservoir in the energy body. If the sacral energy is blocked or stagnant, it affects the flow of energy in the lower energy body, particularly the neighboring base and solar plexus chakras. Sacral blockages also affect the throat chakra, which is paired with the sacral chakra from an energy anatomy point of view.

In Nisha's case, restoring her life force energy resulted in a focus on the so-called troublemaker trilogy—the sacral chakra, the solar plexus, and the throat chakra. The root cause of Nisha's throat issues was in her sacral chakra, the energetic home of the wounded inner child. It was not surprising that our work to reclaim Nisha's energy strength would initially be concentrated in this area of her energy anatomy to clear the blockage and boost her energy. Through steady work to clear her sacral chakra and reboot her troublemaker trilogy, Nisha's energy started to flow again. Within a year, her threadbare voice mended, and her confidence blossomed. She had literally found her voice!

At our last session, Nisha excitedly told me that she had resigned from her dreary job in the retail industry to pursue her artistic endeavors, including making pottery and jewelry. Her inner child was ready to play. And with that, we were ready to end our journey together. As a thank-you gift, Nisha gave me the most exquisite porcelain bowl with delicately painted angel wings. I've treasured it ever since.

Years later, I bumped into Nisha at a pottery market where she was selling her beautifully crafted handmade wares. I hardly recognized her. Beaming, she told me she was going on an extended trip to Peru to pursue her shamanic training. Not only had she found her voice, but Nisha had also found her soul purpose.

INNER CHILD HEALING

Working with inner child energy was a recurring theme in the healing room. Like most of us, many of my clients had experienced some degree of wounding in their childhoods. If we haven't processed our childhood wounding, the painful emotions or trauma will be held in the energy body, resulting in a blockage or stagnation in the natural flow of energy. Energy blockages drain our life force energy. In a very real sense, inner child wounding keeps our energy locked in the past, resulting in less energy available for the present. Until the past experience is dealt with and released, the wounded inner child holds the adult hostage.

Inner child healing usually involves working with the sacral chakra. As the emotional reservoir, the sacral chakra is often turbulent, frozen, or otherwise choking up the works. Suppressed emotion sits in the energy body until it is surfaced and expressed in some way. If emotions aren't felt and stay underground, the lower energy body becomes stagnant. In terms of the elements, the sacral chakra relates to the element of water, which seems to be especially troublesome for women, whose inner well may be stagnant, contaminated, dried up, or otherwise malfunctioning. Energy healing clears the waterways and restores the well-point.

One of the most important aspects of inner child work is discerning whether a client is ready to face their childhood wounding and then adjusting the pace of the healing journey accordingly. Nisha's inner child was ready to heal, so her healing journey progressed relatively quickly. Sometimes an inner child connection is more elusive. This might be because the client is not ready to face an old trauma. In such cases, it's important to respect the client's inner boundaries and not push them faster than the most vulnerable parts of their psyche can go. Jasmine's story is a poignant example of needing to slow down due to the severity of the original issue. Hers was a long process of gradually engaging with her inner child through the help of a professional team to support her healing journey.

JASMINE'S STORY

Jasmine was an up-and-coming singer, a rising star in the local indie music scene. At twenty-two, she was the lead vocalist with a popular band and was writing original songs. When she came to see me, Jasmine was suffering from repeated bouts of laryngitis. Losing her voice on a regular basis was affecting her budding career, and she was worried about the long-term effects of straining her voice. Her doctor had warned her that if she didn't rest her voice, she might cause permanent damage to her vocal cords. This was the impetus for coming to see me. In a hoarse whisper, Jasmine told me that despite her success on stage, she was feeling drained and stuck, as if her creative juices were simply drying up.

Jasmine's recurring laryngitis and the impacts on her voice suggested that her throat chakra was blocked. I wondered why laryngitis had come to the fore now and what the root cause might be. My gut feeling was that her physical malaise had its roots in the emotional realm. When I asked Jasmine about her childhood, she shook her head and said she didn't have any memories before the age of ten. The only information she shared was that her mother had remarried when she was two, and her stepfather had raised her. She didn't know her biological father. It is unusual not to have memories from the age of about three or four, and this void in her memory suggested that she might have experienced some kind of trauma as a child. I made a note to tread carefully with my questions, trusting that Jasmine's energy body would reveal what type of healing was required to help her get through this impasse.

When I enter someone's energy field, I usually get an immediate sense of their vibration and overall state of being. Then, as I tune in further, I receive more detailed information, much like going through someone's house one room at a time. Going into Jasmine's energy, the lights in the house were switched off, and I couldn't see a thing in the murky darkness. I felt as if I were wading through a quagmire of thick mud—no wonder she was feeling stuck! With no light illuminating her metaphorical house, I had no idea where to start. I had experienced the presence of dark energy dimming a client's inner light, but this was different. It was as if Jasmine herself had switched off the lights.

All I could do was stay in the void and channel light into her energy field. As I did so, her energy slowly shifted, and I heard faintly repeating rounds of the opening lyrics of the famous UB40 song "Red Wine." By now, I trusted my clairaudience enough to know that this was significant information, although I didn't know what to make of this lyrical message. It seemed to be a communication from Jasmine's soul rather than my spirit guides. What was she trying to tell me? Was the message literal or figurative? Did she have a drinking problem, or was this related to her childhood? Whatever the truth of this message, it was a cry for help. While I continued to channel high-vibrational energy, I stilled my mind to receive more information.

At this point, my spirit guide Chenoa appeared and told me that as a young child, Jasmine had been sexually abused by her alcoholic stepfather, but that this repeated trauma was so deeply buried in her subconscious mind that she no longer had access to these early memories. Here was the meaning of the lyrics. Red wine was Jasmine's red flag, triggering unconscious memories of her stepfather's alcohol-fueled behavior. Chenoa warned me that surfacing this memory into consciousness now—or too quickly—would cause further damage. Jasmine wasn't yet ready to face this deeply buried childhood trauma. I had to respect her inner boundaries and not push her too quickly—not for a long time. Before she could integrate the underlying trauma, Jasmine would need the help of a psychotherapist to delve into the hidden recesses of her unconscious mind.

Following Chenoa's guidance, I understood that my task at this time was to focus on getting Jasmine's energy flowing. This would allow me to clear the ether block and open her throat chakra to provide relief from the persistent laryngitis—the immediate priority.

At the end of our first session, I suggested to Jasmine that she see a psychotherapist in addition to the energy work with me. In a complex case like this, a slow process of self-discovery in a safe space would support her in uncovering and processing the trauma of sexual abuse. Thankfully, Jasmine was committed to her healing journey and was open to this approach.

Within a few sessions, we were able to clear her throat chakra and start the process of healing the laryngitis. Now that she was addressing the root cause of laryngitis and speaking her truth in therapy, her body no longer needed to hold onto this blockage. Within a few months, the laryngitis cleared up completely. When she was ready, we embarked on a gradual process of clearing residual trauma imprints related to her childhood experience of sexual abuse that were evident in her sacral chakra.

We continued our work together for nearly two years, during which time Jasmine was able to remember and process the painful experiences from her childhood. The last leg of this healing journey was helping Jasmine open her heart, which she had long ago slammed shut to protect herself from further hurt. The way into her heart was sound; I literally had to sing her heart open. It was fascinating to me that song was how her soul had communicated with me right from the start.

Working with Jasmine and her traumatized inner child was a profoundly moving experience. As her healing journey progressed, her creative juices started flowing again. Not only was she singing without impediment, but her songwriting had taken off to such an extent that her band landed a big recording contract. This happy outcome was only possible because Jasmine had the courage to dive into her painful past and embrace her wounded inner child.

At her final session, Jasmine told me that she had started dating. Smiling shyly, she said she had never dated before and was both nervous and excited about this new adventure. I wished her well, knowing our work together had come to an end. When she walked out of the healing room, a confident young woman in full bloom, I couldn't help wondering what would have happened had I not respected Jasmine's inner boundaries when she first came to see me.

SPIRITUAL PERMISSION

Permission for healing is non-negotiable. It is one of the spiritual laws of the Universe and an important part of the Code of Conduct of a professional healer. In my practice, all new clients sign a form giving their written consent for healing for themselves, a minor, or an unborn child. In addition, I asked every client's higher self for permission before entering their energy field. Even if a client has consciously given permission for healing, I might still get a *no* from their higher self, in which case I would not proceed with the healing. This rarely happened, but when it did, we explored other avenues to give them the help they were seeking.

When it came to inner child work, I learned that respecting the inner child's boundaries was another more subtle aspect of spiritual permission to consider. Jasmine's story highlighted the importance of respecting the boundaries of the inner child. Even though Jasmine gave me permission for healing, it took time before her inner child gave the green light to access the traumatic memories from her childhood.

There are times when it is not possible to get permission from a client directly, for example, when someone is unconscious or in a prolonged coma. A family member asking for help is not permission but a request. In such cases, it's important to get permission from the client's higher self before proceeding with any type of energy work.

The first time I encountered this tricky issue was when I worked with Kamscilla, who was lying in a coma in a hospital.

KAMSCILLA'S STORY

In the winter of 2009, the swine flu epidemic hit South Africa, and the creeping death rate started to make headlines. While in the hospital with severe swine flu symptoms, Kamscilla contracted a drug-resistant secondary infection and lapsed into a coma. She was in the intensive care ward on a respirator, and the doctors had told the family that there was nothing more they could do for her. Even more poignant, Kamscilla was a new mother; her first child was a baby boy, just a few months old.

The request for healing had come from her distraught husband, Mukesh. I met him at the hospital, and on our way to the high-security ward housing the city's swine flu cases, I explained that I would need permission from Kamscilla's higher self before I could offer any healing. I made sure that he understood that I would not go against her soul's free will should she not want our help.

In the ICU ward, the nurse on duty instructed me on the infection protocols while fitting me with a surgical mask and gloves, then took me to Kamscilla's cubicle. Drawing a curtain around the small cubicle, she smiled at me kindly as if to say, *it won't make any difference, but we appreciate your efforts.*

The doctor arrived in the ward, and the nurse took her aside to explain my presence. The unfriendly look she shot my way was not as benevolent. I guessed she was unhappy with me infringing on her territory. But to her credit, she came over and wished me luck.

Alone with Kamscilla, I placed a bubble of white light around the two of us to create an energetically sealed space. I held her hand and introduced myself, explaining that Mukesh had asked me to help her. The only response was the very loud noise of the respirator. I tuned in more closely and quickly found that Kamscilla's consciousness, though still within her auric field, was entirely out of her body. I asked Kamscilla if she was aware of her surroundings and critical condition. I heard a clear yes—the lines of communication were open. So, I asked her higher self for permission to proceed.

While I waited for the response, my heart sank. Kamscilla's hesitation was palpable. After a long silence, she communicated that she wasn't sure whether she wanted to live or die. She was figuratively sitting on the fence about her life-or-death choice. I asked her if she would be willing to have a conversation with me, assuring her that I would not interfere with her free will—only she had the power to choose her course.

I was all too aware of the gravity of the ensuing conversation. It was critical that I keep my influence out of the mix. I asked Kamscilla why she was unsure about coming back and what followed was a flood of words and images about how unhappy she was; she'd been suffering from chronic depression for years, and the birth of her baby pushed her over the edge. She felt powerless to change any of it and just wanted out!

While she was talking, my spirit guide whispered the words *baby blues*. Careful not to persuade her, I told Kamscilla what I knew about postpartum depression, that this could be treated, and she didn't have to suffer in silence. I spoke to her the way I would to any young mother with the baby blues. We also spoke about her baby, the little boy who needed his mother.

While we were chatting telepathically, I realized that Kamscilla's ego-mind was speaking and not her soul. So, I adjusted the vibrational frequency of our exchange and tuned in to a higher level to connect with her soul. This time I got a different story. Her soul communicated that the act of choice itself was Kamscilla's lesson. She needed to learn that she had far more power than she realized. In this moment, she had the power to choose life or death. While relaying this message to Kamscilla, she went quiet.

I told Kamscilla that there was no rush to make a choice. She had all the time in the world. A coma will go on for as long as the soul requires to make this kind of choice. It is a kind of protective safe zone. Reassuring her that I would not attempt to bring her out of the coma, I asked her if I could ease her heartache.

By raising the vibration of Kamscilla's heart, I hoped she would be more able to make a choice in line with her highest good. Clairvoyantly, I saw her higher self nod in agreement, so I focused on her heart chakra and started clearing out the sticky energy of depression, replacing it with higher vibration love energy. Had Kamscilla been conscious, I would have done more extensive work on her sacral chakra, but I was bound to respect her spiritual boundaries.

When I felt a shift in her heart space—a faint lightening of spirit, it was time to stop. In closing, I reminded Kamscilla that she had free will, and the best thing she could do was to allow her soul, rather than her ego, to guide her in this important choice.

When I left the ward, I found Mukesh waiting for me, his face stricken with worry. Gently, I explained that Kamscilla was on the fence about her life choice and the best we could do was support her by holding her in a loving space. I was confident that the next twenty-four hours would be revealing but couldn't tell him, with any certainty, what Kamscilla would choose. We cannot know another soul's path. It was not for us to know what was in her—and her baby's—highest good or what their soul agreement might be. When I walked out of that hospital ward, I honestly had no idea where Kamscilla's soul would lead her and did my best to detach from the outcome.

Still, much to my relief, Mukesh called the next day to let me know that Kamscilla had regained consciousness. At that point, she was not yet out of the woods because her lungs were still riddled with infection, but a week later, she was discharged from the hospital and reunited with her family. Whatever she had been through on the other side, I had no doubt Kamscilla had learned a powerful lesson and that her life would not be the same going forward.

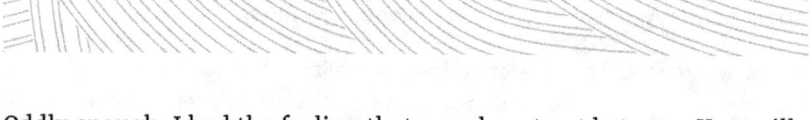

Oddly enough, I had the feeling that a soul contract between Kamscilla and myself to teach each other a valuable lesson about the power of choice had also been fulfilled. I had helped her make a powerful choice about her life, and she taught me the importance of respecting a soul's free will, however incomprehensible and however much, from a more limited perspective, I might wish for a particular outcome. A humbling experience, I learned how important it was never to go against spiritual law.

This experience also underscored the importance of not being attached to another person's healing—or one's own *success* as a healer. Being attached to a particular outcome, for whatever reason, is the ego's concern and stifles free will. In Kamscilla's case, I had to make a concerted effort to release my desire for the outcome that everyone wanted. After seeing her in hospital, I even cut energy cords between us to ensure that I wouldn't unconsciously influence her decision-making process.

Even though, as a healer, I might be asked to give assistance, it is not up to me, or any healer, to decide what is in another person's highest good. Healing is a powerful energy and using it in a way that interferes with someone's free will or karmic lessons has consequences. Undue influence may deprive the client of an opportunity to learn a significant life lesson and progress on their path.

While the issue of spiritual permission is often glossed over, it is important to understand the complexity of spiritual boundaries. There are several reasons for being so rigorous in this regard:

Privacy. Going into someone's energy is like accessing a database of information about their soul's journey. It is a violation of personal space and privacy to enter without permission, much like hacking their computer or personal data. Without permission, a person could be left feeling violated and vulnerable. This does not serve their healing.

Receiving. Healing is always more effective if it is actively received by the client. This can only happen with explicit permission from both an ego and soul perspective.

Karmic lessons. Permission on a spiritual level is equally as important as the client's verbal consent. Despite a client's conscious desire for healing, at a spiritual level they may need to experience discomfort, for example, through illness, to serve a soul lesson or purpose intended for themselves or others. Giving a healing without spiritual permission risks depriving the client of an important life lesson or opportunity for growth.

Right timing. Spiritual law states that everything happens in divine or right timing. If spiritual permission isn't forthcoming, it may not be the right time for that person to receive healing.

Right person. It is possible that a particular healer is not the right match for the client. This might be because that healer doesn't have the right skill set for the healing required, or in less frequent cases, there may be a spiritual contract where a specific person may be required to work with another soul.

GROUNDING IS OUR FOUNDATION

The experiential teachings were coming thick and fast. My task was to reflect, distill, and integrate what I was learning. The next field of learning was grounding—my Achilles heel.

Grounding is the very foundation of being in human form. I came to think of it as the anchor that tethers energy, as spirit and consciousness, and form, as the physical body, to the present moment.

After the car crash, it had taken me a long time to come back into my body, and quite frankly, it was easier to float off into the ether. This untethered state was not ideal for working with clients, which requires a solid presence to hold energy and remain centered. Firm grounding and mindful presence are the foundation of all energy work and an absolute must for creating a safe container for clients.

During my training, I worked on my grounding religiously, learning many tricks and tools along the way. Now that I was a practicing healer, I had to level up. The more grounded I felt, the more I noticed the lack of grounding in my clients. I was astonished to discover that, with few exceptions, my clients were poorly grounded and disconnected from their bodies to varying degrees. Most people were in their heads, cut off from their lower energy bodies and natural connection with the Earth. There were many reasons for this, the most pervasive culprit being a fast-paced city lifestyle with a multitude of associated stressors. Trauma was a culprit too.

Chapter 4 | Answering the Call

The deleterious effects of stress were evident among a range of clients: young professionals working their way up corporate ladders; working mothers juggling demanding jobs and children's schedules; people living in poor communities on the Cape Flats and struggling to make ends meet. There were countless variations of stress and the ways in which it manifested in people's energy systems.

In my first year of practice, Fazlin was one of those clients who presented with severe stress symptoms.

FAZLIN'S STORY

In her late twenties, Fazlin was a high-achieving young professional. She had grown up on the Cape Flats and overcame many obstacles to obtain and excel at her tertiary education. She was hard-working, focused, and ambitious.

Following a recent promotion in her corporate job, she had been suffering from severe migraine headaches. She described feeling heavy pressure on top of her head, accompanied by visual disturbances and dizziness, and generally *being in a fog*. In the mornings, she was aware of background zinging, which intensified during the day. The headaches were intensifying in severity and frequency. Between almost weekly migraines, she said her head felt fuzzy most of the time. She had consulted her doctor and a specialist who suspected a tumor, but a brain scan was clear. Having run out of medical explanations, Fazlin turned to energy healing for help.

In addition to the migraines, Fazlin was experiencing several stress-related symptoms, including performance anxiety, poor sleep, and feeling overwhelmed. Listening to her story, I noticed that she used the word *pressure* repeatedly. An increased workload and demanding boss were creating pressure at work. Her family situation was also challenging. She described the financial pressure of being responsible for other family members, including supporting her mother and putting her younger brother through university. Her older sister expected her share of handouts too, and there were frequent arguments about money, indicating underlying issues related to family dysfunction.

After getting her permission, I got to work and found that Fazlin's energy body told a revealing story. She was operating almost entirely from her head. Her mental energy was firing on all cylinders, while her lower energy body was an energetic void. Her base chakra was completely blocked, with no natural flow of energy from the Earth. Likewise, her crown chakra had collapsed, which meant there was no natural flow of Source energy into her energy system. With very little natural energy flowing in to replenish her system, Fazlin was operating essentially through sheer force of mind and will. Also, without an outlet, the built-up excessive mental energy had created a spinning vortex in her brow chakra that was like a pressure cooker in her head. No wonder she was experiencing migraine headaches.

At Fazlin's first session, I focused on balancing her chakras and restoring the natural flow of energy through her system. First, I repaired the collapsed crown chakra and activated the base chakra allowing me to draw Source and Earth energy through her system. Once there was a stronger vertical energy flow, I could release the spinning vortex of energy in her head.

There are many triggers for migraines, but in Fazlin's case, it was clear that the trigger was the pressure of stress overload. Although managing stress more effectively would help, the key to reversing her migraines was grounding and restoring the flow of energy throughout her system. Clearing blockages in her lower chakras would improve energy flow and upgrade her system's natural capacity to process stress.

While we had made a good start, Fazlin would need to connect with her physical body and learn how to ground herself for lasting change. I showed her a simple grounding exercise and impressed upon her the need to do this every morning. I suggested she see me weekly for a few months so we could work on the different aspects contributing to the migraines. Fazlin was committed to regaining her health and quickly agreed to my recommendations.

As we continued our work together, Fazlin's healing journey included three core components: grounding and stabilizing energy flows, stress management, and boundaries at work and with her family. To upgrade her energy system, we focused on strengthening her grounding and boosting natural energy flows to increase her body's capacity to process stress and improve her resilience. For stress management, I taught her breathing exercises and practical techniques for releasing excessive emotional and mental energy. We explored her stress triggers so that she could identify, and respond to, stressors before they overwhelmed her. We also discussed her role in the family system and her tendency to be over-responsible for the well-being of her siblings. Soon, she began to see the connection between her stress levels and the onset of migraine headaches.

After the first month of treatment, Fazlin felt much better and reported significant changes. She felt more grounded and centered in her body. This gave her more capacity to process stress. She was also far more conscious of stressors and was actively pre-empting the triggers and processing stress before the pressure built up. As a result, her anxiety was greatly reduced, and her sleep improved. In the first month of working together, Fazlin had had only one bad migraine, and the daily *fuzziness* in her head became a thing of the past.

Fazlin also made some important lifestyle changes. In addition to her daily grounding, she started an exercise routine to release stress. At work, she moved to a different department where she had an easier relationship with her boss, which considerably reduced her emotional stress. She was also more aware of her role in maintaining the family status quo and was ready to do the deeper work needed to change this pattern and establish better boundaries.

The ungrounded clients continued to arrive in droves. While the reasons for poor grounding varied, from high stress levels to underlying trauma, the energy patterning was similar. In most cases, like Fazlin, energy was concentrated in the mental body, while the lower energy body was cut off from the natural flow of energy from the Earth. Many of these ungrounded clients were partly out of the body, meaning their consciousness had become disconnected, to varying degrees, from their physical experience of embodiment.

Grounding work is a combination of plugging into Earth energy and ensuring a healthy upward flow of energy through the body, activating the base and Earth star chakras, and connecting consciousness with the physical body. Once the energy body is grounded and consciousness is embodied, addressing the root causes of energy imbalances from trauma and stress is far easier.

The need for grounding was so universal that my healing sessions now included a simple grounding exercise to empower clients to manage their own energy. I was amazed at the results. After just a few weeks of practicing the exercise, most clients reported feeling much calmer and more centered. However, in a few cases, the grounding tools didn't work, and I was curious to find out why. As if in answer to my ponderings about grounding, Catriona turned up in my healing room. She had been struck by lightning and survived to tell the tale.

CATRIONA'S STORY

When Catriona came to see me, she was desperate. A thirty-something redhead, Catriona was tall and willowy. With a big sigh, she told me she was exhausted and hadn't slept for five years. This sounded quite extreme, but I noticed how pale she was and asked about her health. She was allergic to just about everything. Despite a severely restricted diet—no gluten, dairy, eggs, sugar—she had leaky gut syndrome and didn't absorb nutrients. With the support of a nutritionist and a homeopath, her digestive issues were showing some improvement, but nothing seemed to help her sleep. She felt she had exhausted all avenues for healing.

While Catriona was telling me her story, I noticed that she was physically and energetically thin, as if she were hardly present. Listening closely, I wondered if there had been a significant change in her life five years ago, the point at which sleep had become elusive.

"What happened five years ago?" I asked.

"Oh," she said, almost casually, "I forgot to mention that I was struck by lightning."

There it was. I asked her to tell me her story.

On a camping weekend with friends, Catriona had been watching one of Mpumalanga's spectacular afternoon thunderstorms when a fork of lightning struck her, knocking her out cold. Later, her friends told her that she was "lit up like a Christmas tree" with her arms stretched out in a wide arc and her body vibrating for a few moments before she collapsed. Her friends thought she was dead, but Catriona regained consciousness shortly afterward, and they rushed her to hospital. Catriona's right arm was badly burnt and paralyzed, but, quite miraculously, she made a full recovery physically. However, the emotional and energetic wounds ran deeper and left lasting scars.

Working with Catriona's energy quickly revealed that her energy anatomy was completely scrambled. The electromagnetic field of her aura was in tatters, appearing like a burnt rag at the edges. Her primary energy circuit was also malfunctioning. The central channel of energy—the shushumna—which carries energy up and down the spine, from the base to the Third Eye, was barely pulsing. The two major meridians on either side of the central channel —the Ida and Pingala nadis—were also damaged. These two meridians carry energy in a clockwise loop—the Ida to the left of the spine, taking energy upwards, and the Pingala, to the right of the spine, taking energy downwards. This core energy circuit is pivotal in ensuring a healthy vertical flow of energy between the chakras.

Catriona's central energy flow was in total disarray. Instead of a vertical line, the shushumna zig-zagged from right to left and the currents in the Ida and Pingala nadis appeared to have been reversed. There was also energetic *scarring* in her right arm and even in her liver where the lightning had carved hidden grooves. Much like a physical scar, energetic scarring appears as a dark patch, or distortion, in the cellular tissue and can be seen clairvoyantly.

With so much energetic damage, it was not surprising that Catriona was struggling to be present in her body. Her energy felt more like that of a discarnate spirit than an embodied being. I suspected that Catriona's soul energy had left her body to survive the trauma of the lightning strike and hadn't come back. As a result, her grounding was non-existent.

In the first session, my aim was to rebuild the template of Catriona's shattered energy system. I set to work rewiring her circuits and repairing her aura. I cleared the electrical shock of the lightning strike and calmed her central nervous system. At the end, I tried to bring some of her soul energy into her body, but she point-blank refused. The best I could do in that first session was repair the extensive damage and lay the groundwork for further healing. My guides whispered that she needed *earthing*, not just grounding. I wasn't quite sure what this meant.

After such a life-threatening shock, bringing Catriona's soul energy into her body and grounding her would take time. Her physical symptoms would not resolve until she was fully in her body again. As our work together progressed, we discussed her resistance to being embodied. She explained that she was "terrified of being here, feeling separated from God," and "longing to go home" to the realm of spirit. Experiencing such fundamental terror meant it was far more comfortable for Catriona to center her awareness in the etheric realms where she felt light and free. Given this profound disconnection, I realized that Catriona's healing journey would require a much deeper level of grounding than I had ever done and include a spiritual dimension about choosing to stay embodied on the Earth plane.

Over the next few months, Catriona made steady progress. Little by little, her sleep improved, and she had more energy to get through her day. As her energy circuits settled, it became easier for her to connect with her body. At home, she practiced her grounding exercises, and during our sessions, I was able to start bringing her into her body and plugging her into Earth energy.

In our conversations, we explored the spiritual issues underlying her resistance to embodiment. Catriona was a spiritual seeker engaged in a range of spiritual practices. For all her seeking, she began to understand that she was sitting on the spiritual fence and had to make a choice. It came down to making a commitment to her current incarnation and all its associated lessons. Like Kamscilla, her first lesson was about the power of choice. I gave her homework questions to ponder. Can you embrace your original choice to incarnate? Why might your soul want to be embodied? What are you here to do? And what is getting in the way? Every week, the conversation about her life questions continued.

One day, Catriona arrived in my healing room with a big smile. She looked energized, almost radiant, as she told me she had signed up for a three-year film course. Until then, I had never seen her excited about anything. In an animated voice, she told me that she had wanted to make environmental documentaries and "tell stories about the Earth" for as long as she could remember, but the lightning strike had knocked her off course.

"Sounds like you've decided to stick around for a while," I teased her.

"For now," she smiled. "And I'm getting married," she added shyly. "Well, not just yet, but I've said yes to my boyfriend. He has been asking for ages, but I just couldn't think long term."

After working with Catriona for nearly a year, I came to believe that the lightning strike was, in fact, her attempt to exit. She hadn't been committed to seeing this lifetime through. It wasn't my job to persuade her either way, but in our work together, she had faced the root conundrum and was making her own choice to stay on the Earth plane. She was earthing.

MULTI-DIMENSIONAL GROUNDING

My work with Catriona expanded my understanding of grounding to include a spiritual dimension, leading me to the concept of multi-dimensional grounding.

Multi-dimensional grounding starts with the premise that we are spiritual beings engaged in a human experience. To fully experience being human, we first must embrace being in human form—in a particular body, in a specific life, at a particular time. This is what it takes to integrate the spiritual and human aspects of existence. Being fully grounded means that we need to be present in all aspects of being— mind, body, and spirit. It's easy to understand the physical and mental aspects of being. Spiritual energy is a little more elusive. One way of thinking about spiritual energy is relating it to our connection with an unseen spiritual force, for example, a higher power, God, or Source, and seeing ourselves as part of a greater spiritual reality underlying our very existence. This relates to our connection with the existence of the soul and its expression in our current lifetime. A felt connection with the soul will naturally give rise to stronger soul energy.

On the other hand, if we are disconnected from the soul, our soul energy may be weak or fragmented, resulting in diluted energy strength for our life purpose. Multi-dimensional grounding strengthens our connection with the soul, bringing all aspects of being together, so we can draw on our full energy strength to engage with life and walk our path. This is what it means to be fully, or radically, present.

Based on this understanding, there are three important dimensions to grounding:

> *Embodiment.* The body is the foundation of being in human form. It is the vehicle for your soul's experience on the Earth plane, the container for the life that you're living. It is the temple that houses your spirit, the instrument for your soul's evolution. To be well grounded is to be at home in your body temple.

Earthing. This is your energetic and spiritual bond with the Earth. When you are grounded, you are naturally connected to the stream of Earth energy available to you. Without this connection, you are cut off from this vital life force energy. Earthing is literally plugging into this energy source. To be well earthed is to be at home on the Earth plane.

Embracing. Fully embracing your incarnation on the Earth plane is the spiritual dimension of grounding. This means accepting the lifetime that you've chosen, warts and all, so that you can be fully present. It means uncovering your soul's mission and getting on with it. To embrace an incarnation is to be spiritually at home in the present and committed to being here, right now.

These three Es are the pillars of multi-dimensional grounding. As I was discovering, very few people are grounded in all three aspects. And yet multi-dimensional grounding is vitally important for our health and well-being as well as our spiritual growth. A disconnection in any one of these three dimensions creates an imbalance. Remember Fazlin's story. She was present mentally, excessively so, but she was disconnected from the energetic, physical, and emotional aspects of her being. This created such an imbalance that her head was literally crying out in pain. It was impossible for her to fulfill her potential when her energy was so distorted.

The spiritual dimension of grounding is especially tricky. As I gained experience, I started to look at grounding through this lens and listened more deeply to what clients were saying. Many with a strong spiritual connection were not at ease in the world because they felt they didn't belong. These clients were regularly disconnecting from the body, often through meditation, to experience a more enjoyable lighter, higher vibrational frequency. This is a form of resistance to embodiment, and I saw it in many variations. Some, like Catriona, verged on a kind of *soul exit*. For her, the separation from God—her experience of Source, was so painful that her connection with the Earth plane was tenuous, at best, until she was able to embrace her embodiment. Although Kamscilla had already started exiting by going into a coma, she was able to come back and pick up the threads of her life by making the choice to embrace her incarnation.

Many of my spiritually ungrounded clients were trying all sorts of practices to become more present: grounding tools, mindfulness, and various forms of meditation. Working with them was a revelation. I realized that you could ground yourself until the cows come home, but if you're sitting on the spiritual fence, it won't work. For people who are more comfortable in the lighter realms and find the density of being in a physical body challenging, being present is an upward struggle. At the end of the day, it is not possible to be fully present unless the spiritual dimension of grounding has been resolved.

What is the panacea to this widespread resistance to embodiment?

The way I saw it, the answer lay in making a clear choice; a choice to embrace the life that you have, the path that you have walked so far, including all the heartache, the losses, and the things you regret. This starts with making peace with all your life experiences, and choices, until this moment. Regret is an obstacle to multi-dimensional grounding and presence. Once you accept that where you are right at this moment is a result of past choices, you can fully participate in your destiny from a place of conscious choice rather than being a victim of circumstance or fate. This is what it means to embrace this incarnation. It is the ultimate commitment.

When you are fully committed to being here, the other dimensions of grounding fall into place. Multi-dimensional grounding happens naturally. This deeper level of grounding brings forth heightened presence, or what I've called radical presence, which makes it that much easier to pursue your soul purpose. Ultimately, everyone's soul purpose is to attend Earth School with whole-hearted abandon, to experience the joys, the suffering, and everything in between, to learn from these experiences, and to grow. Absenteeism doesn't serve your soul. Your progress will be much faster if you are fully engaged and open to everything life brings your way.

Within the collective crucible of soul growth, we have individual purpose, a soul mission to discover and pursue. Your chances of walking a conscious path in alignment with your unique purpose are that much greater if you have worked on the three Es of grounding and made Earth your home.

GOING SOLO

The procession of ungrounded clients at Phakalane reflected something about the state of my own multi-dimensional grounding and presence. It was easy to see that working two jobs and context-switching between the world of energy and the deadline-driven publishing world was stressful. With so much to-ing and fro-ing, it was hard to stay grounded, let alone maintain a clear, running energy stream. I might have developed empathy for the corporate ladder-climbers and stressed-out working mothers who sought my help, but my grounding was suffering too. Keeping a foot in both worlds was taking its toll.

This dawning realization forced me to face the bigger question of embracing my soul mission with full commitment. When I was twenty-one, I had made a clear choice to continue my current life rather than exit. Now I had answered the call to be a healer, but was I really giving it my all? Was I prepared to quit my salaried job and become a full-time healer? Did I have the courage to take the next big step along my path?

These questions nudged me forward. The truth is, at that point, my yes to the call was lukewarm, and the Universe was likely to respond in a similar fashion—lukewarm signal begets wishy-washy response. And yet there were very real constraints, including keeping a home going and children fed. But knowing how energy works, I would have to shout *Yes!* Oriah-style for the Universe to deliver the solution to my stressful juggling act. I had seen this happen when I called in my home and on countless other occasions for lesser things. Now I had to take a leap of faith and trust the Universe to catch me.

The first step was to respond to my heart's longing for my own healing room. Phakalane was a wonderful springboard, but it was time to create my own space with my own energetic signature. When my clients arrived at Phakalane, they encountered the center's powerful energy first and then, looking slightly bewildered, found me at the back of the building. There was an energetic filter between me and my clients, which took time to dissolve. Driving across town to Hout Bay also took time out of my crammed schedule. So as much as I loved Phakalane's peaceful setting on the mountainside, it was time to make a change and create my own space.

My mind made up, I took out a second mortgage, drew up plans to convert my garage into a cozy healing room, and contracted a fabulous two-women building team to make it happen. It was a scary leap of faith. By the end of 2009, global economic woes had reached South Africa's shores and plunged the country into recession. Admittedly, it was not the best time to be making plans to leave a secure job and start a new business. My family thought I was mad and didn't hold back in voicing their concerns with varying degrees of tact. My older son was worried about his mother's financial savvy and the implications for his lifestyle. He had a point.

"No one will actually pay for woo-woo," he lamented.

My father was concerned about the wisdom of starting a new business at the height of a recession.

"No one will have spare cash for non-essentials," he cautioned.

He was more polite than other commentators, but these were valid concerns, echoing my own fears, of course. Still, another flame burned more strongly—a deeper knowing that this was my destiny path, and the Universe would support me if I was committed. Commitment to my soul mission required the rather elusive ingredient of trust. In less trusting moments, a niggling voice reminded me that I had only been seeing clients two days a week. How would I suddenly fill five days and make enough money to survive?

However, my girlfriends cheered me on. Kath said, "Build it, and they will come. You'll see."

I hoped Kath was right! Here I was wading into debt to finance the building project. The plans had been passed by the local municipality. I had already thrown good money at my dreams. It was too late to change my mind. So, I silenced the niggles and soldiered on. Nine months later, my garage-turned-workspace was finished. Toward the end of 2010, after nearly two years as a part-time healer, the builders handed me the keys to my new healing room. Now all I had to do before I got cold feet was hand in my resignation at the publishing company.

As it turned out, the Universe already had this covered. Before the proverbial ink had dried on my resignation letter, the company announced a restructuring process in which the publishing wing was severely trimmed. I was one of the casualties. Although not completely unexpected given the economic times, it was a shock to be retrenched. My ego wobbled for a while until it caught up with the fact that being retrenched was a wonderful gift. Here I was, about to go solo and a generous retrenchment package arrived on a platter. This is the abundant Universe in action! And what a timely reminder that when we respond to our soul's calling, the Universe will conspire to support us in the most unexpected ways.

Once my ego got with the higher program, I sourced within me a deep sense of security about striking out on my own. Marianne Williamson once said, "you can lose a job, but you can't lose your calling." This was a different concept of security to hang my hat on and teach my children. I joked that we might be eating peanut butter sandwiches for a while, but there would always be food on the table. Although it was tough in the beginning, I never once doubted it.

A ROOM OF MY OWN

Everyone needs a room of their own. It is a source of solitude and solid grounding in the world—a sacred space. For the next seven years, my healing room was my sanctuary and a refuge for thousands of clients.

Setting out as a full-time healer in my own healing room was a watershed moment. I took a month off to transition between worlds and attune my new workspace for the task ahead. When all was cleared and calibrated,

Chapter 4 | Answering the Call

I invited my inner circle of girlfriends to a blessing ceremony, where we spent three hours grounding my healing room and calling in the spirit team that would accompany me on the next leg of my journey. These women were my spiritual allies, and I was deeply grateful for their unerring support.

Working from home base made it much easier for me to bridge worlds and keep my feet more firmly on the ground. With one job to focus on, it was almost effortless to hold my center. My boys loved having me around too. Even as my client load steadily increased, my time was more flexible. In the afternoons, I could pick them up from school and hang out in the kitchen while they ate lunch. These were precious moments.

There were other perks too. When the first client arrived, my younger son's ginger cat Kabushka joined us. From then on, he was a faithful attendant in the healing room, waiting at the door every morning to be let in and leaving long after the last client had left. On the odd occasion when he didn't show up, I knew it was because he, too, had to take a break and recharge. I felt privileged to have an animal helper. In return, I thanked him at the end of every day and regularly cleared his energy. It goes without saying that he was showered with love.

Working with Kabushka was an eye-opening and humbling experience. My clients loved his comforting presence in the room, especially the children. I noticed that I felt more grounded too. As our working partnership progressed, Kabushka became more active in the healing process. When a client arrived, he was usually fast asleep at the foot of the healing bed. As soon as the client lay down for the energy work, he woke up, often moving position to lie on the most troublesome chakra. Client willing, he would lie there for a while before settling down at the foot of the bed again to hold the energy. On occasion, Kabushka would sit bolt upright and fix me with a green-eyed stare before jumping off the bed. This was a signal that there was a heavy energy to release. He was both warning me and getting out of the way. Time and again, clients remarked that it felt as if there were someone standing at the foot of the bed. Kabushka was a big presence, and it is not surprising that people perceived his energy as another person in the room.

Kabushka worked alongside me in my healing room for just over seven years until he retired. During that time, he soothed many clients just by his presence and offered his gentle healing energy to those who could receive it. His biggest gift to me was that he kept my heart open. Just looking at him filled me with love.

Chapter 4 | Answering the Call

DRAGON'S GOLD
Wisdom teachings from Chapter Four

- Walking your soul path is seldom a direct route from A to B. At any given point, it's unlikely you'll be able to see your destination. A soul path is made of baby steps, with a lot of wandering, circling, backtracking, and occasionally big leaps forward. There is no magic formula for the perfect path. All you need to do is keep taking the next best step. This is how you follow the call of destiny and create your path as you go. Synchronicity and flow are sure signs that you're on your highest soul path.

- Destiny is a mysterious mix of free will, choice, and karma. Living is a lifelong dance between these creative forces. Karma is a constant companion, informing circumstance and range of choice. The choices you make, whether conscious or unconscious, dissolve and form karma and create new experiences. Over time, experience carves a pathway, which ultimately becomes your destiny. At the same time, destiny itself will call to you from the future and guide your choices.

- Grounding is the very foundation of being in human form. It is the anchor that ties energy (spirit and consciousness) to form (physical matter) in the present moment. To be fully grounded is to be radically present physically, mentally, emotionally, and spiritually. Multi-dimensional grounding brings all these aspects of your soul energy together, so you can draw on your full energy strength to engage with life and walk your highest path. To be fully present, you must first embrace being in human form, in a specific body, at a particular time, and in a unique set of circumstances.

- As a healer or teacher, you are a guide for others to embark on a healing journey or a conscious spiritual path. You are the bridge between the known life and the unknown. During the traverse, you sustain the connection with the soul-world and bring back the insights and soul food for others until they can cross the bridge themselves.

- The art of healing requires a deep respect for spiritual permission and inner boundaries. It is not up to healers to decide what is in another person's highest good. Healing is a powerful energy and using it in a way that interferes with someone's free will or karmic lessons has consequences. If a healer jumps to the rescue without first gaining spiritual permission or respecting inner boundaries, they might unwittingly deprive their client of the opportunity to learn a significant life lesson.

5

SOUL ROOTS

2006 – 2012

The doors to the world of the wild Self are few but precious. If you have a deep scar, that is a door, if you have an old, old story, that is a door . . . If you yearn for a deeper life, a full life, a sane life, that is a door.

– Clarissa Pinkola Estés, author of *Women Who Run With the Wolves*

Embarking on a training path in 2006 opened a portal through time to my soul's journey. During my energy work with Kate, the howling wolves sang the prelude to the multi-dimensional story of my journey as a healer. As I was to discover in the coming years, connecting with my soul's journey gave me extraordinary insight into who I am. It took me to the real ground of my being, my soul-skin. Knowing my soul roots gave me a far deeper sense of belonging than I had ever conceived. It was a kind of coming home.

Over a period of six or seven years, I relived important aspects of my soul's journey in a series of vivid memory fragments, which arose spontaneously when the time portal to past lives opened. Although highly inconvenient at times, revisiting my soul roots in this visceral way was an important part of my training and profoundly influenced my growth as a healer. It was a parallel learning process. In present time, I was learning the art of healing while simultaneously journeying to other lifetimes to retrieve my soul's knowledge about the ancient art of shamanism. In the beginning, jumping timelines, often without any warning, was strange and disorienting. But after a while, these forays into non-ordinary reality became more ordinary.

Once again, I was going between worlds. However, this time it wasn't a mythical topside world and underworld working with feminine archetypes to make sense of my story. Now I was going backward and forward in time, tracking my journey as a healer across many lifetimes, but like most multi-dimensional experiences, there was no linear sequence to these stories.

Fragment by fragment, I gathered the memories and strung them together like beads on a necklace, the thread weaving the beads together into some sort of coherent narrative. As it acquired form, my necklace became a visual reminder of multi-temporal experiences. This was soul lineage work—restoring the connection to who I had been over the course of many lifetimes and who I was becoming in my current incarnation.

While I revisited many lifetimes, there was one lifetime as a Native American medicine woman in the mid-1800s that I went back to repeatedly, each time gaining further insight into its significance on my journey as a healer. This extraordinary experience gave me a visceral connection with my soul roots as a shaman in the Navajo tradition. This was my bloodline as a healer, and I needed this deeper understanding of my shamanic roots to embrace the truth of my calling fully.

Beyond understanding, revisiting my soul roots was a process of clearing old wounds and karmic baggage. We all have an ancestral lineage with family ties and a soul lineage with karmic ties. Sometimes these bonds intersect, but sometimes not. Exploring my soul lineage was a profound sifting process: reviewing soul contracts, understanding enmeshments, cutting karmic ties, and resolving unfinished business. It was like tying up loose ends, as one does before the next cycle begins.

Chapter 5 | Soul Roots

NAVAJO MEDICINE WOMAN

The day I heard the wolves howling, the portal to my life as a Navajo medicine woman opened. After that, the memories kept coming, in small fragments at first, later gathering more flesh on the bone, until slowly, a comprehensive narrative emerged.

During the Polarity course with Kate, I learned I had been a Native American medicine woman in the American southwest in the mid-1800s. This was Navajo territory before the White settlers moved into this area, forcing the Navajo people into reservations further south. As the medicine woman in my community, I tended to the sick and spent long periods alone in the wilderness gathering plant medicines. I also assisted the shaman of the tribe in harvesting visions for our people. In his absence, it fell to me to play this visionary role. With the advance of the settlers across the American west, it was a tumultuous time of great change. The Navajo Nation was not spared. Perhaps because of what happened to my people then, or perhaps because of the weight of responsibility I felt for their fate, I was carrying unresolved sorrow about this lifetime.

In that life, my sister—Petra in this lifetime—died in childbirth, for which I felt personally responsible. In the flashbacks of that lifetime, I also caught glimpses of a man called Standing Bear. He appeared in nearly every memory fragment, so I came to view him as my Navajo husband or lover.

And then I met Brad.

Shortly after I had finished my training as a healer, I went on a hike in Orangekloof with Brad, a new friend from my hiking club. Accessible only by permit, Orangekloof is a conservation area at the back of Table Mountain with pristine indigenous forest and a rocky river gorge. The vibration there is pure and clear. After a long hike up the gorge, we stopped for a rest. I was sitting on a large boulder, and Brad was standing on the other side of the river, pointing downstream. Seeing him in profile, I felt a jolt of recognition and suddenly felt myself going into trance. By now, I was familiar with this feeling of spiraling backward out of my body and slipping into a dimension of heightened sound, texture, and feeling.

In Brad's profile, I saw Standing Bear. I was gobsmacked. And then I received a clear vision of him in my Native American life: he was on a horse, preparing his warriors for battle and giving commands for the foray ahead. In my vision, Standing Bear had a build similar to Brad's—wiry, compact, with a strong jawline. He was beautiful in an unusual way. Commanding his warriors with graceful ease, he was clearly a respected leader. He had a serenity about him, a quality also apparent in Brad.

The pull to go to Brad was so strong that I boulder-hopped across the river and hugged him—*no, held him*—in an embrace that spoke of the sorrows of that previous time. Genocide leaves a deep imprint. This was a man I hardly knew in this life yet holding him in the hushed forest seemed like the most natural thing in the world. The odder thing, come to think of it, was that Brad responded as if he knew who I was. Neither of us said a word and the memory slowly faded.

On the long walk back down the river gorge, I asked him tentatively, "what were you doing around 1850?"

I've never asked anyone that sort of question, let alone out of the blue with no conversational context! Without skipping a beat, Brad started talking about the American southwest and the sad fate of the Native Americans in one of the biggest genocides of the colonial era. It was as if he were *expecting* my question. I had goosebumps.

This is how Brad and I became friends and then gradually, predictably perhaps, lovers. He had spent much of his early life in the United States, mostly in Colorado. He'd grown up roaming the wide-open spaces of the American wilderness, and this had shaped him. He spoke passionately about the Rocky Mountains, the Sierra Nevada Mountains, and places like Yosemite National Park. As a student, he had walked the John Muir trail in sections and described the experience as "being one with God." Perhaps because of these early experiences, he was a free spirit, an out-of-the-box thinker. Being in his company was never dull. Our time together was bound to be extraordinary.

For the next four years, whenever I was with Brad, the portal to our past lifetime opened and the story of the life we shared unfolded in a series of visceral memories. These flashbacks were spontaneous, bursting through ordinary reality at unexpected moments, usually triggered by a feeling, a glimpse, or some other visceral connection with that timeline. Just the sound of the wind rustling through poplar trees could instantly take me back to my Navajo roots.

On one occasion, Brad and I met for lunch at a quirky café called KwaLapha, which in isiZulu means *place here or place over there*, depending on the emphasis. There was a magnificent wild fig tree in the middle of the room, and the roof around the tree was open to the sky. It was a cold, wintry day, and we were given blankets to keep warm. Seeing Brad with his blanket wrapped around his shoulders gave me a jolt of recognition. Once again, I saw him as Standing Bear. Without any of the usual warnings of timeline jumping, I was back in Navajo times, sitting around a fire with Standing Bear and others in our tribe. This time I was completely overwhelmed by love. The physical pressure in my heart was so intense that it felt as if my ribs were going to crack. I couldn't move, and I couldn't come back. Brad ordered our food while I stayed in a trance-like space, love spilling through me. I already knew that I had loved Brad in our previous life together, but this was the first time I had felt it so strongly in this one.

In present time, our relationship was not conventional in any sense of the word. It was casual yet intense. We never spoke of commitment, or future, or any of those grown-up things that usually creep into a relationship. Perhaps this was because our connection was so bound up in our shared past. There was also a shadow from that lifetime I couldn't shake—echoes of control by the men in the community, including Standing Bear. The culture of male dominance also meant that as a medicine woman, I was *lesser* than the male shaman in the community hierarchy. Inevitably, the discomfort of the memories from those old constructs of male-female relationships colored my feelings for Brad.

Or perhaps talk of future plans was thwarted by my insistence that no man was going to share my sanctuary with the boys. Our *querencia* was sacred. I had made a promise to myself; never again would I drag my children through the mud of my relationships. Or perhaps it was simply because we both knew that one day, Brad would return to America and the wilderness he so loved. Whatever the reason, and by unspoken agreement, we danced between the past and the present and left the future out of the equation.

For now, we enjoyed our time together, most of it spent exploring the lesser-known trails of Table Mountain—whole days walking and hanging out in wildish places where the veil was thinnest. In Brad's company, I was as likely to be in the present as I was to be dropping into the distant past. Each time I came out of trance, Brad helped me process what I had experienced, never asking for anything in return. When I asked what was in it for him, he said, "I owe you a debt of gratitude. You'll see." This was relationship of the rarest kind. We shared the depths but not the mundane, and in the four years of roaming the mountain together, we helped each other work through a lot of karma.

One morning, about two years after meeting Brad, I woke with a feeling of expansive openness. It was as if the veils had parted in the night and forgotten to close. I felt in touch with all the lives I had ever lived. There was nothing specific but a palpable connection with a thread of soul-level experience. I stayed in this otherworldly space as I went about my day, wondering what was coming. And then I got a call from Brad. He had fallen while rock-climbing over the weekend and broken two ribs. I didn't usually do healing work with friends, but this was an emergency, and I jumped right in.

Chapter 5 | Soul Roots

BRAD'S STORY

Brad was in severe pain. His doctor had strapped his ribs and told him not to move for six weeks. For a runner and rock climber, this was a grim prospect. I had experienced this type of pain and the impossibility of keeping still when I had dislocated a rib during the Polarity course a few years previously—or more precisely, when the dragon's rapid exit during the Fire bodywork exercise had wrenched my rib from the sternum, opening a dragon gate for its outbound flight. How ironic that Brad was now in the same boat as I had been when the portal to our past life together had first opened!

As soon as I entered Brad's energy field, I felt as if we were being sucked backward into a different dimension. When the energy settled, I found myself in a teepee with an injured man lying on some blankets on the ground. I was the medicine woman among several people crouching over the injured man, Standing Bear. This was very different from being in present time and *witnessing* a distant life. I was actually *there*. Strange as it was, I stayed with the visceral impression of being the medicine woman and tuned into Brad's chest area. As I did so, his body jolted violently; I felt it inside my own body, a jarring ripple like a series of doors slamming shut while gunshots rang in my ears. As the medicine woman, I saw the desperation in Standing Bear's eyes and felt my own panic rise as I realized that he was close to dying. All of this happened in a flash, reliving what had happened to him—to us.

Returning my focus to Brad in my healing room, I was shown two bullet wounds in his etheric body, an imprint from his past life injury. I could see one bullet hole very clearly, and another hole where the bullet was still lodged in the sternum. I set to work to remove the bullet and repair the damage. While I was extracting the etheric bullet, there was a sudden, strong gush of energy and, with it, a wave of heart-wrenching grief. By clearing the old gunshot wound, I had tapped into Brad's grief about the devastating advance of the White settlers and unlocked an ocean of pain. My task now was to release this dense pocket of grief that was like a black box in his heart.

While working, I was given a message from my guides to relay to Brad, "It is time to let go of this pain. The past does not exist in this dimension." I knew the message was for me too.

After dissolving the vibration of grief, I was guided to perform psychic surgery on his broken ribs. As I worked, I felt the bones knitting together again. When the healing was complete, Brad sat up wide-eyed and described in detail what he had just experienced—a Native American woman working on him while he was lying wounded, fighting for his life.

"You saved me then," he said.

I nodded in understanding.

"And this time, I felt the bones mending while you were working," he continued.

Again, I nodded but didn't want to count on a miraculous recovery. Time would tell.

That evening Brad reported that the excruciating pain was no worse than a nagging ache. He did not even need to take painkillers. A few days later, the remaining discomfort had completely dissipated, and he started running again, a full month before the doctor's prescribed recovery time. I was stunned. This was beyond what I thought possible. For the first time, I had embodied my past-life shamanic self to offer healing. Even though I would do many past life clearings in the future, I would never again feel so viscerally that I was present in the past timeline. On reflection, I believe this was only possible because Brad and I had shared the very same experience.

What I took from this profoundly moving experience was the knowledge that anything is possible in the world of energy. It was clear that psychic sensing is just as powerful across time—tastes, smells, sensations, and emotions from a distant past can be powerfully experienced in the present. One explanation for this is that time is not linear; everything exists simultaneously. Another explanation is that, regardless of time, the sum total of the information held in someone's energy field can be accessed intuitively. The way I experienced this phenomenon in the context of healing is that multi-dimensional information connected to a soul's journey, whether past, present, and possibly even future, exists in the quantum field and is directly accessible through the portal of a person's field. In other words, information—not time—is the connective tissue of the Universe.

Miracles can happen with the right mix of intention and belief and the right synergy between healer and recipient. With Brad, I experienced first-hand that the recipient is as important to the healing process as the healer. The transmission of healing energy is a dynamic process; it works best when the recipient is open to receiving healing and believes that change is possible. If there is a soul contract between a healer and recipient to clear some old karma, miracles are sure to happen.

There are many types of soul contracts, some of which involve resolving unfinished business from a past life. I have no doubt that Brad and I had a soul contract to help each other to clear the burden of grief we were both carrying from our shared Navajo lifetime. The experience of his people—our people—being wiped out in the 1850s had been so traumatic that it had left a deep imprint in his heart. My part in our soul contract was to help Brad release this grief. The broken ribs were the pointers to the original wounding. His miraculous rib-mending, in current time, signaled the completion of this unfinished business. This was the debt of gratitude to me Brad had spoken of earlier. His role in our contract was undoubtedly to connect me with my soul roots. He had come into my life so I could remember—and experience—who I was as a Navajo medicine woman and to help me develop unwavering faith in energy healing. If I had any lingering doubts about the *reckless path* I had embarked on, they evaporated right then and there.

SOUL WOUNDS AND UNFINISHED BUSINESS

As the Wounded Healer archetype, my personal journey ran in close parallel to my path as a healer. After working with Brad, a wave of new clients needing help with past life wounds showed up in my healing room. Once again, my own process was being reflected by the clients who sought my help. The most likely explanation for this trend is that our energy field acts like a magnet, drawing to it people whose energy is vibrating at the same frequency. It may also be because we need to learn certain lessons or face certain challenges in order to grow. Time and again, this mirroring process offered valuable insights for my personal growth while giving me a deeper understanding and empathy for my clients' travails.

With the help of my spirit guides, I quickly learned how to work with past lives. Developing my skills in this area required that I track the past life story to the point in time where someone is stuck. The unresolved issues associated with a past life sticking point—or blockage—show up in the energetic body as an etheric imprint. This can present either as an emotional soul wound, such as a painful betrayal, or a more physical soul trauma, such as a traumatic injury or painful death. There may also be soul contracts or vows keeping someone bound to the past. As a healer, you are the detective, finding the sticking point and then untangling the sticky threads.

My detective work began with the past life story. When working with a past life blockage, I would see a series of images, almost like a movie, showing me the highlights of the storyline and the key issue to be resolved. If the blockage involved relationships, I would see the main characters playing out a repetitive pattern between them. If there were soul contracts to be resolved, these were visible in the outermost spiritual layers of the aura. The last step in the detection phase was sensing the vibration that was keeping the old story or pattern in place. The next phase was clearing the soul wound or unresolved issue. After clearing past life residue, I found that changing the vibrational frequency was the most effective way to set someone free from the past. In this phase, I was the vibrational tuning fork, which involved attuning key energy pathways and chakras to a higher vibrational frequency.

You might wonder why we should bother with past lives when we are dealing with so much in our current lives. I agree. There is no need to go delving into past lives just for the sake of it, but if there is unfinished business from a past life, which is impeding progress in the current life, then why beat about the bush when we can go to root causes? All too often, the root cause of a recurring pattern or issue in the current life is buried in a past life.

Soul wounds and traumas from past lives can leave deep imprints. If the original trauma was severe, part of the soul might even have split off, resulting in a deficit of soul or energy strength for the current lifetime. In such cases, it's important to gather the lost soul energy and anchor it in the current energy body. When soul energy is fragmented, the hara—known as the tan tien in martial arts—will show signs of weakness. A pivotal energy node, the hara holds the vibrational keynote of our existence, holding us in an incarnated form, and it's crucial to work at the haric level to restore soul coherence and vitality.

There may also be contracts or vows keeping us bound to a situation or person. It is helpful to understand these deeper undercurrents in our lives so we can tend to our spiritual well-being. This is soul healing.

SOUL CONTRACTS AND SOULMATES

After healing Brad's ribs, the soul contract between us was partially completed. I wasn't yet sure of the full scope of our contract, but we were in the process of finding out. I had never had this kind of relationship with a man; we were extremely close, yet, for me at least, there was no pull to create a life together. At this stage, I was more committed to honoring my intention to remain single and maintain a stable home for my boys.

In western culture, we mistakenly believe that we have one soulmate and that meeting this one person will provide us with the experience of perfect love. This is based on a misconception about the life of souls. We belong to soul groups and have incarnated again and again with the same group of people in various relationship combinations. There will be a few souls among these with whom we have a particularly close bond and may even have had a romantic relationship within one or several previous lifetimes. The upshot is that there are probably several so-called soulmates out there. This explains the instant recognition or familiar feeling you might feel when you encounter one of these souls again. These soulmates will show up in our lives at pivotal moments, but it doesn't always mean that we should be in a romantic relationship or be with them for the rest of our lives. Compelling as it may be, it is so important to be discerning and seek a deeper understanding of why a soulmate has appeared on your path. It's all too easy to fall into the one-and-only soulmate trap.

Over time, I had come to understand that Brad was a trigger soul. A trigger connection is someone who comes into our life to resolve unfinished business, teach us an important lesson, or help us remember who we are. While our triggers were being revealed and resolved, I was content to enjoy our time together for what it was without further complicating my life.

It was not so simple for Zoey, a new client who arrived in my healing room in a tearful state. Her trigger connection showed up in her life soon after she got engaged to her fiancé, throwing her into turmoil.

ZOEY'S STORY

Zoey was in the midst of planning her wedding to a man she loved. A few months after she got engaged, a young man—let's call him Daniel—started working at her office. She described feeling an intense connection with him, almost a longing. She didn't understand this longing and hadn't acted on it, but there was a strong pull. "Almost an obsession," she told me sheepishly.

Zoey was perplexed that Daniel had shown up in her life just as she was about to get married. Was it a sign that she was making the wrong choice? Should she act on this longing? Was Daniel, in fact, her soulmate? These were the questions in her troubled heart. She told me that she was still committed to her fiancé but wanted to be able to go into marriage with a clear mind and open heart—a wise young woman.

Listening to Zoey, I suspected that there was some sort of soul contract between her and Daniel. Undoubtedly, it was significant that Daniel had shown up in her life at this precise point in time. The big question was the nature of the contract. Was it a call for Zoey to make a different choice? Or was there something that needed to be resolved before she could marry her fiancé? I hoped we'd be able to answer these questions for her.

When I entered Zoey's energy field, I immediately felt the familiar spiraling backward pull taking me into a past timeline. Then I received a series of images showing me Zoey's previous relationship with Daniel. First, I saw her in a nurse's uniform in a wartime situation, which appeared to be somewhere in France during the First World War. Zoey was tending to wounded soldiers in a Red Cross tent. One of these soldiers was the soul now called Daniel. In that lifetime, Daniel was an American, and during his long convalescence in Zoey's care, they fell in love with each other. It was a deep, intense love, such that they talked about getting married when the war was over. The future being so uncertain, Zoey wanted to get married in France as soon as he was fit enough. Daniel said he needed to go home first to sort out his affairs. He didn't tell Zoey that he had a girlfriend waiting for him in the United States.

When the war ended, Daniel went back to the States, promising to send for Zoey once he found his footing there. For a moment, the movie screen went blank. Then I saw Zoey on a train on her way back to England, her home country. Back in England, she received a letter from Daniel, telling her that he was getting married to his girlfriend in America, who had waited for him throughout his wartime absence. Zoey was devastated and felt deeply betrayed. In that life, she never got over the loss of her first love and closed her heart to men.

The storyline was clear. There was a karmic bond between the souls known as Zoey and Daniel, involving deep love, betrayal, and unresolved loss. This was the unfinished business between them. The vibration of longing was still palpable in Zoey's energy field. Little wonder that the longing had been reactivated when she met the same soul in her current life.

I told Zoey what I had seen. Hearing the story usually brings relief for a client and is an important starting point for resolution. I explained to her that the longing she was feeling belonged to a past life, not her current life, and this is what had to be resolved. With the resolution of her past life connection to Daniel, she would have greater clarity to answer the questions about her marriage plans. I reassured her that just because she had loved Daniel in a previous life didn't mean she had to be with him this time around. But it did mean that the unfinished business between them had to be cleared before she could make a heart commitment. Unfinished business can take hours, days, or years. At that point, I had no idea how long it would take to free Zoey from the past.

Over the course of a few sessions, I set about clearing the unfinished business between Zoey and Daniel. The first step was to look at the contract between their two souls. It is important to understand the nature of a spiritual contract before jumping to conclusions. The contract would offer insight into their current conundrum.

When I tuned into the spiritual layer of Zoey's aura, I saw two souls laughing together. It was clear that they were from the same soul group and had probably incarnated together many times over. This explained the deep connection and familiarity Zoey described. I asked about the contract and was told it had run over many lifetimes. In her First World War lifetime, Zoey had fulfilled her part by opening Daniel's heart again after his horrific experiences in the trenches of France. After so much hate, she had restored his faith in love. Now Daniel was to play his part in their current life to help Zoey open her heart to men again, so she could make a whole-hearted commitment and enjoy married life, which she had denied herself in her previous life. I asked their souls if they wanted to be together in this lifetime.

They both just laughed, shaking their heads, and said, almost in unison, "No, that's not the plan."

Did I imagine it, or did I see a wistful look on Zoey's face? At this point, I asked spiritual permission to clear the contract.

"Not yet," my spirit guides said. "Not until Zoey has learned the lesson."

With this understanding, the next best step was to cut the karmic cord between Daniel and Zoey, which would lessen the intensity of the connection between them. I was then able to clear the emotional imprints of longing, loss, and betrayal from Zoey's field. After a few sessions, Zoey reported that her feelings for Daniel were not as intense. In fact, she said, it wasn't even an issue anymore. She looked surprised, but pleased, with her statement.

Zoey was ready to revisit her questions. She was very clear about her choice. She wanted to open her heart to deep love with her fiancé and work on building trust. She realized that commitment itself was an obstacle. Bottom line, she didn't feel safe in a relationship, and marriage was a scary prospect. Zoey's main lesson was to open her heart again so that she could feel good about making a commitment.

Wisely, Zoey decided to delay the wedding until she felt ready. As she moved forward in her life, our sessions came to a natural end. About six months later, I bumped into Zoey in a coffee shop. She was showing her wedding dress to a friend. She bounded over to my table to show her dress to me, excitement lighting up her face. She was ready to move on! How funny that I should have been in that coffee shop at that moment. The Universe is a magical place.

As in Zoey's case, a soul contract may run over several lifetimes and cannot be cleared until a particular lesson, or set of lessons, is learned. Spiritual permission must always be sought before clearing a soul contract. Clearing a contract prematurely is an avoidance of the karmic lessons and will only cause more problems for the souls involved.

However, free will can also come into play. If a client insists on cutting a contract short, the healer's task is to ensure that the client understands the implications of avoiding the karmic lessons.

I have always counseled clients against cutting a contract short; however, this is rarely necessary. Invariably, people seek my help when they are nearing the end of a contract and need help with its completion. For the most part, my role is to help these clients release an old pattern, or emotional imprint, and uplevel their vibration to a higher frequency. When the vibration is raised, a soul agreement or contract may automatically fall away and not even need clearing.

One of the reasons that it is possible to clear soul contracts is that we are evolving and burning through karma and karmic lessons much faster now than in the past. In previous lifetimes, we may have been given one lesson to learn per lifetime, one partnership to master. Now we may have multiple sets of lessons and more than one significant partnership in a single lifetime. It is also possible to learn multiple lessons within one partnership, but this only works if both partners are committed to growth.

SACRED VOWS

A soul contract can also present in the form of a vow, which is like a contract with the self. Vows are by nature enduring and can last many lifetimes. They leave a binding imprint on consciousness and have a profound effect on the current life path, even if the context is completely different. As with any soul contract, it may not be appropriate to clear a vow, and spiritual permission should always be sought before interfering with a sacred promise. Working with sacredly held vows requires spiritual sensitivity.

I had encountered a few examples of old vows holding people back on their soul path, but none so deeply embedded as in the case of Gabby, who had repeated a similar vow over multiple lifetimes. In Gabby's case, the big question was whether the vow was still serving her highest good in her current lifetime.

GABBY'S STORY

Gabby was a psychotherapist with a successful practice. In her professional life, she felt strong and in flow; but when it came to relationships with men, nothing worked out. This was the reason she had sought my help.

"I'm brilliant at helping others with their relationships," Gabby told me, "But I can't seem to get it right in my own life."

I asked Gabby about her patterns with men.

"It always comes down to communication. I hold back from speaking my truth, and when I do, it causes conflict," she said.

Gabby was very conscious of her patterns and yet felt powerless to change them. I wondered what else might be going on. When I tuned into her energy, I was struck by her high vibration. She had a lot of light around her, a purity of heart, and yet there was an undertow of density in her field, which I perceived as a vibration of guilt. I then received a string of images about her soul lineage. I saw her as a nun in medieval Europe, a sun virgin in the Inca civilization of pre-colonial Peru, and flashes of many other spiritually oriented lifetimes going all the way back to Ancient Egypt.

As the movie of clairvoyant images was playing, my spirit guides explained that these were all lifetimes in which Gabby had lived her higher purpose to serve humanity and participate in raising consciousness. She was part of a group of souls who were setting up *grids of knowledge*, which, in times past, were held secret. One of her soul tasks was to preserve this sacred knowledge for a time when it could be more widely disseminated.

In these ancient lifetimes, Gabby had always taken vows to put her purpose of serving humanity first, which included upholding vows of secrecy and not compromising her soul mission with romantic relationships. In more recent lifetimes, this intention had taken the form of a vow of chastity.

I told Gabby what I had seen. She nodded fervently, saying she always felt so guilty about romantic partners and sexuality and had never understood why. Now it was apparent that, at a soul level, Gabby felt she was going against the sacred vows she had repeatedly made. Energetically, it was essentially one vow that had been reiterated throughout her soul journey.

Chapter 5 | Soul Roots

A sacred vow has a strong binding energy, and this energy was clearly still active in Gabby's consciousness. But was this vow still serving her highest good? Her heart's desire to have a romantic relationship was causing her to experience profound inner conflict that had been playing out in all her relationships.

My spirit guides suggested that this repeated vow was blocking Gabby's growth. They said:

> Times are different now; knowledge doesn't have to be held secret anymore. Gabby can serve humanity and achieve her soul mission with the support of a conscious partner. In this lifetime, she needs to work in partnership. There is new learning for her in this area.

According to my guides, it was permissible to release the vow and the beliefs that held it in place. With Gabby's permission, I started the process of clearing the vow. The first step was to address her guilt. This vibration would need to shift because the vow was being held in place, energetically speaking, at the level of the vibrational frequency of guilt. I was guided to use the Violet Flame of Transformation to dissolve the vibration of guilt.[10]

As Gabby's vibration shifted, I was able to clear the energy of the vow. The next step was for Gabby to transform her belief system that a relationship would compromise her spiritual purity and her soul mission. Now that she was aware of the vow, and the reasons for it, she would be able to consciously release this old promise as well as the outdated beliefs that held it in place. After just two sessions, I had every confidence that Gabby would be able to make fresh choices about being in a supportive partnership in line with the current times.

When working with a vow, it is important to look at the reasons why it was made in the first place, as well as the belief system and vibration holding it in place. So often, as in Gabby's case, vows were made at a time in history when consciousness was different, and they are no longer applicable to the current lifetime and paradigm. That said, it is

---

10 The Violet Flame is a unique spiritual energy used to transmute negative energy. Known as the Violet Flame of Transformation, it doesn't simply remove an energy; it dissolves it and transmutes it into light. By changing the vibration, the Violet Flame performs what can be thought of as energetic alchemy, transforming vibrational base metal into gold.

important to surface these long-ago promises to enable an informed choice as to whether they still serve the client's highest good.

Around this time, I had my own unfinished business to attend to, and coincidentally it involved a vow.

A BLESSING AND A VOW

There was one more piece of unfinished business from my Native American past, which presented itself one chilly Sunday morning on the top of Table Mountain. Setting off before sunrise, Brad and I hiked up one of the many gorges on the mountain's east face. As the sun came up, we stopped to catch our breath and take in the view of the mist-covered city below.

We could just make out familiar landmarks, the city lights tinting the early morning mist with a fuzzy orange glow. In the distance, a thin spiral of smoke curled up out of the mist, early morning stirrings in one of the many informal settlements on the Cape Flats.

Looking at the spiraling smoke, I became aware of an odd sensation in my hands. They felt thick, numb, and then started ballooning to what felt like five times their size. The bigger my hands got, the more intense the sensation got. As I had been trained to do, I moved my awareness into my hands, and then came the familiar spiraling backward in time.

> I saw myself with long black hair, dressed in an animal-skin skirt and buffalo-hide boots. I was standing on a hilltop, looking over a valley of smoldering earth, blackened trees, an odd teepee drooping from a pole, and a lonely spiral of smoke in the distance. There was no other movement, no sign of life. It was a scene of complete devastation. There was no one left. Every single person in the village below—men, women, and children—had been massacred. Even animals lay dead on the ground. Up on the hilltop, I was rooted to the spot, numb with grief and shock. I felt paralyzed, unable to move, the heaviness in my heart overwhelming. I was too late with my grim warning, the visions too ghastly to believe. I'd stayed out in the woods much longer than planned, checking and rechecking, refusing to believe what I was being

shown. Would anyone have believed my visions had I been back in time to share them? I cried out in pain. As the medicine woman, I should have warned my people and prevented this. As I looked over the battlefield, absorbing the gruesome consequence of my shortcomings, I vowed I would never be a shaman again.

The grief was palpable as these old memories surged through me—my heart was physically sore. At the same time, the energy in my hands was getting more intense, almost unbearable, alerting me to something unfinished.

"There is something you have to do," my spirit guide Chenoa whispered.

It hit me in a flash that Chenoa had been my living teacher, one of the wise elders in that lifetime. She smiled in acknowledgment and urged me to listen closely to what she had to tell me now.

As I listened to her soothing voice, I knew that I had to bless this killing field. In 1851, I was too devastated by the massacre to offer a blessing. But now, more than 160 years later, I was ready to complete this spiritual task. With that realization, I spread my arms out and sent a blessing back through time to every soul who had suffered on that fateful day. Finally, after what seemed like hours, the sensation in my hands abated. It was done.

And then the tears came. I sobbed and sobbed for everything I had gone through then, for what the Native American people went through as tribe after tribe was decimated in one of the biggest genocides of that century, and for the undefined sorrow I had been carrying in my heart for as long as I could remember.

The genocide of the Native American people signified a huge loss for humanity. With their Earth-based spirituality, there was the potential to seed a more harmonious energy-consciousness that might have taken humanity on a different trajectory. Anchoring this higher consciousness was part of my soul mission then, as it is now. The genocide was a clash of consciousness. In effect, the White settlers crushed the potential for a mass awakening that might have blossomed on Earth more than a century ago. This was the deeper sorrow afflicting my soul.

"Let it go now," Brad said. "It is done."

"There is one more thing I must do. Let's get to the top," I replied, feeling pulled to follow another intuitive impulse.

On the last part of the steep scramble to the top of the gorge, I told Brad about my vow never to be a shaman again. Revealing this to him laid bare for the first time a deeper understanding of why I had been resisting the call to be a healer in this life. A vow is a powerful thing, and mine had rooted in my soul. It was time to let it go.

At the top of Table Mountain, with Brad as my witness, I called out to the rocks, the sky, and the sea far below, shouting:

> I release the old vow never again to be a shaman or healer. Unwind, unbind, and set me free to be the healer I'm meant to be.

Over and over again, I shouted these words like a decree to the Universe until my voice was hoarse, and I felt the vow's energy flowing out of my hands, like a long string of treacle being pulled out of my being. As the energy of the vow was carried off in the wind, I felt a wave of forgiveness, not only for the White settlers for what they had done to my people but for myself, for not being able to bless the site of the massacre at the time. This was the spiritual task that had been calling me back through time. At long last, I had let go of a 160-year-old promise; it was done.

Slowly peace descended, shifting my entire energy body as if I had just put a huge weight down. My heart felt light and free, my soul untethered from some nameless shackle. But a surge of energy was still pulsing down my arms into my tingling hands—and then I got it! As a healer, the true power of working with healing energy is in allowing universal love to flow into the heart and travel out through the hands to others. Nothing should get in the way of the flow—not even a very old vow.

As we continued our early morning hike, I felt elated, buoyed by waves of gratitude for having been liberated from the vow's binding power and curiosity about who I would become without it. Such is the journey of the Wounded Healer.

SOUL RETRIEVAL

Unfinished business from a past life sends ripples through all future lifetimes, affecting relationships, work choices, and the ability to achieve your soul mission until it is resolved. Sometimes unfinished business manifests as a general feeling of being stuck. In my case, the unfinished business of an old vow to never again be a shaman was limiting progress on my path as a healer. In more severe cases, part of the soul may be stuck in the previous experience, resulting in soul loss, which can be debilitating at every level of being. In such cases, soul retrieval may be necessary for the person to progress. There may also be an important lesson to learn from the previous experience in order to move through the current impasse.

When a pattern or an illness keeps repeating, it is a sure sign that there is something to resolve. Times of crisis are a strong nudge from the soul—an indication that we have reached a still point in our spiritual growth and that the soul needs a breakthrough. It is crying out to be heard. There is always a message, but sometimes help is needed to decipher the soul's nudges, especially when the unfinished business is stuck in a past life.

Finn's wake-up call came in the form of a recurring illness. He knew there was something to learn but didn't know how to access the lesson.

FINN'S STORY

Finn was a likable young man in his early thirties. On a conscious spiritual path, he was eager to find his purpose. When he first came to see me, he was depressed and stuck. While traveling a few years previously, he had contracted a nearly fatal dose of malaria and since then had suffered recurring, though less severe, bouts of feverish illness. There was nothing doctors could do to help him. Medical science has been unable to completely eradicate this strain of malaria (Plasmodium vivax), which is responsible for persistent infections.

Apart from feeling below par most of the time, Finn was frustrated with his life path. Whenever he made progress, he would be laid low with another bout of malaria, or so it seemed to him.

Listening to Finn's story, I wondered what role malaria was playing in his life journey. When an illness, or any pattern recurs, it is usually because we need to integrate a lesson or let something go. What was keeping this parasitic energy alive in his mind-body system?

When I entered Finn's energy field, I immediately received a series of gruesome images related to a previous life in the American West. Dressed as a cowboy, Finn's body was hanging over a gully, a thick rope around his neck. My spirit team said that he had committed suicide and deeply regretted it. At a soul level, Finn felt ashamed because he had failed to complete his mission in that life. When I tuned in more closely, I could see that Finn's spirit was hovering over the dead body. In other words, an aspect of his soul had separated from the whole and was still stuck in that timeline. When this happens, usually when there has been severe trauma, the stuck aspect is referred to as a soul fragment and generally holds the energy and feelings of the original trauma. Retrieving a soul fragment—a process commonly known as soul retrieval—is a delicate process and can only be done with explicit consent and when the client is ready.

I told Finn what I had seen clairvoyantly, and he nodded fervently. He had always felt that part of his soul was missing, and he was game to try anything to get it back. My task was to retrieve this lost soul fragment and integrate it into Finn's current energy body. But first, some healing would be required to prime his unconscious mind for integration.

At this point, I had done many soul retrievals involving childhood trauma, but this was the first time I had located a split-off soul fragment in a past life. My gut feeling was that Finn would make faster progress if he could understand his choice to commit suicide in his previous life and forgive himself from the perspective of the circumstances in that lifetime. This approach would also help to dissolve the vibrations of shame and regret that permeated his energy field. Before embarking on the soul retrieval process, I guided Finn into a past life regression so that he could revisit this pivotal point on his soul's journey. It was a powerful experience, yielding many insights, and he was finally able to forgive himself for the choice he made to end his life.

It was still too soon in Finn's healing process to attempt a soul retrieval. The next step was to work with transmuting the vibrations of shame and regret which permeated his field and had most likely attracted the parasitical illness. Over the course of a few sessions, I focused on attuning Finn's vibrational terrain to a higher frequency and opening his heart energy. This would lay the groundwork for a successful soul retrieval.

When Finn was ready, we worked together to retrieve the soul fragment and reintegrate it into his current energy body. This required taking him back to the scene of the suicide once more and inviting the soul fragment to return to the whole. Having already gone through a forgiveness process, Finn could now view his suicide with compassion, without the twin charges of shame and regret. It was quick work to retrieve the *shamed aspect* and integrate it through his heart chakra.

After completing the soul retrieval, I saw Finn for one more session. In cases like this, it's important to check that the soul fragment has integrated properly and not split off again. When Finn arrived for his appointment, it was immediately evident that the soul retrieval had been successful. He greeted me with a big smile and reported feeling *alive* and much more hopeful about his future. For now, at least, our work together was done.

Although it would take time, it was likely that the malaria parasite would not survive in the new vibrational terrain of Finn's upgraded energy body. I know most doctors would not agree with this prognosis, but I had seen enough to know that the world of energy works in ways that medical science does not yet fully understand. Regardless of any medical explanation, the protracted illness had served Finn by bringing him to the point where he was able to surface a hidden trauma and retrieve a part of his soul that had been stuck in an abruptly ended past life. I hoped that having restored his soul energy to its full strength, Finn would be able to move onto a higher timeline for his current and future lifetimes.

SOUL TRAUMA

As my work evolved, I was doing more remote healing—similar to energy healing, except the healer and recipient are not in the same physical space. In the quantum field, distance is not an obstacle to the instant exchange of energy, information, and light due to a phenomenon called quantum entanglement. Once I connected with someone's unique vibrational identity, I was able to scan their energy field and transmit healing energy appropriate to their needs. Spatial distance doesn't make the healing process any less effective.

Through remote healing work, I was now reaching clients globally. One of the most poignant experiences I had with remote healing involved soul trauma that was surfacing in the life of a five-year-old boy called Charlie who lived in New Zealand. He had reincarnated there almost immediately after a traumatic death during the protracted armed conflict in Iraq that began in 2003. Clever soul for choosing such a peaceful country to lick his soul wounds from a war!

CHARLIE'S STORY

Charlie's mother was desperate when she contacted me. She described her young son as angry, easily upset, explosive, highly strung, and generally unhappy. It was painful to watch her little boy struggling so much. The family had tried everything from child psychologists, dietary changes, and even changing schools, but nothing had worked. Quantum energy healing was their last hope.

When I first tuned into Charlie's energy field, he didn't want me to come too close. To break the ice, as it were, I engaged him in telepathic conversation to establish a connection and make sure I had spiritual permission to work with him.

I asked Charlie, "what are you doing?"

"I'm busy. I have to hurry," he replied.

"Why are you in such a rush?"

"The train is coming. I have to be on the platform on time."

"Where are you going?"

"I'm going to fight a war."

At this point, my spirit guides informed me that Charlie had been a young American soldier, age eighteen or so, on his way to Vietnam. He was killed during his first tour of duty in the early seventies. I was then shown a series of images of a dusty, desert-like place with ruined buildings. It was very noisy, with gunfire, smoke, and chaos. I was puzzled. This didn't look like Vietnam.

"We are showing you Iraq," my guides whispered. "This is where Charlie is stuck."

How could this be? The Iraq War was too recent. Normally there are about thirty years between incarnations, but in rare cases, it may be much less. I silenced my rational mind to continue gathering information from Charlie's energy field. After the session, I did some quick math and determined that if Charlie had died early on in the Iraq conflict—perhaps in 2003 or 2004—it was possible that he could have reincarnated five years ago after a few years in the spirit world. Likewise, he would have reincarnated relatively quickly after his death in Vietnam. Evidently, Charlie's soul had reincarnated at rapid speed after both these short lifetimes.

It was clear that Charlie's soul was carrying two wartime experiences and probably a lot of trauma. While he was communicating with me telepathically, I could see that there were several discarnate beings around him. Charlie told me that these spirits were his friends who had died with him.

When I asked him why they were hanging around him, he said, "Because they understand. We all died together."

Charlie was stuck in his experience in Iraq. It would not be easy to persuade him to let go of his spirit buddies. The only way to release them from Charlie's field would be to change his vibration to a point where there was no longer a vibrational match between him and his wartime friends.

Over the next few months, in a series of remote healing sessions, I set about the multi-layered task of clearing Charlie's traumatic past life experiences.

The starting point was to clear the soul trauma. The distressing experiences in Vietnam and Iraq had left multiple imprints. Charlie's energy body was literally shaking with trauma. Jagged streams of energy were visible in his aura, especially around his head. Despite being in a new body, he was still carrying post-traumatic stress. The behavior he was currently displaying as a five-year-old child was, in fact, post-traumatic stress disorder from his previous lives.

The energetic imprints from Charlie's soul trauma were evident in all layers of his being. No wonder he was struggling in his child's body. There was a strong emotional charge, too, most notably intense anger, anxiety, and sadness. Charlie's heart chakra was burning, and it felt as if it might burst. There was no way for a young child to discharge this intensity of emotional energy without some help.

There were also physical imprints, including a large abdominal wound, which appeared as a gaping hole in Charlie's etheric layer. This wound was the cause of his death in Iraq. The etheric wound held a vibration of extreme anxiety, and my guess was that Charlie probably had frequent stomach aches for no apparent reason. His mother later verified this as true.

I cleared the energetic imprint of anxiety and repaired the gaping hole in his etheric layer. Once this was done, I was able to cut energy ties with his past life in Iraq. In a series of telepathic conversations, I explained to Charlie that he was no longer in Iraq. He appeared to be somewhat disoriented, which was part of the reason he was clinging to his spirit buddies. He seemed to understand, and I was able to reassure him that he was safe in his current life, in his child's body, and that it was time to let go of his past experiences.

After clearing the trauma of Charlie's experiences in Vietnam and Iraq, I focused on raising his vibration until it was no longer a match with his spirit buddies. By this time in our work together, Charlie was very chatty. I explained that his spirit buddies were keeping him locked in the past. He was in a new life now and needed to connect with living people who would understand and love him. Charlie nodded, and I suggested that he say goodbye to his friends in the spirit world while I set about releasing them one by one. Charlie was sad to see his spirit buddies go, but surprisingly, the process went quickly.

During our final session, my guides told me that Charlie had a big mission to bring peace to the world. As a soul, he had an advanced understanding that our species is governed by the laws of co-operation and connection—not competition and conflict, as has been the dominant thinking for so long. Charlie would be part of changing this outmoded paradigm. I relayed this information to Charlie's higher self. As a child, he would not be able to absorb this level of information. Still, it felt important that the message was integrated at some level of his consciousness so that it was more readily available to his future self.

My hunch paid off. At the end of this session, Charlie stood up tall and waved to me with a big smile on his face. I knew our work was done.

A few weeks later, Charlie's mother reported that he was a different child. He was happy and calm, and the explosive outbursts had stopped. Even the stomach aches had disappeared.

"It's totally changed our lives!" she exclaimed.

Chapter 5 | Soul Roots

In Charlie's case, the results of releasing soul trauma and post-traumatic stress symptoms were dramatic. Children are very receptive to healing and quick to change. Adults usually take longer because the patterns are more deeply embedded in their current life experiences. However, paying attention to obstacles on our path can serve to unearth these patterns and draw attention to soul trauma. If we are listening, the crisis or setback can initiate the process of addressing unfinished business and releasing old trauma.

Over the years, I have frequently come across souls who had experienced traumatic deaths due to war or persecution. A surprising number of my female clients had experienced being burnt at the stake in a past life. Witch-burning was especially common during the Middle Ages when Christianity swept across Europe, and many innocent men and women died at the hands of the Inquisition. Some of these souls were healers, herbalists, midwives, and teachers who were labeled as witches or heretics.

For many healers, religious persecution is part and parcel of their soul lineage. Many souls, especially women, carry this *witch wound* to this day. The soul scars of being burned at the stake are deeply etched into their energy bodies. In a few cases, I've seen branded stigmata in the etheric layer where the original branding has left an energetic imprint. In the past, many healers gave away their power as a direct result of torture and witch-burning. As a collective, healers suffered a severe setback at the hands of the Church in the Middle Ages.

Fortunately, the tide is turning. After centuries of patriarchy, women are rising up, finding their voices, reclaiming their power, and releasing the collective pain of the witch wound. Men are also shaking off the limiting shackles of patriarchal control and persecution. Expressions of the divine feminine and masculine are emerging and expanding. Everyone who does their inner work, and finds their authentic voice, their soul song, is strengthening our collective awakening.

One example of this was a Dutch man called Johan who contacted me because he had an irrational hatred of the Church, which was blocking his spiritual connection.

JOHAN'S STORY

During his past life clearing session, Johan had a vivid memory of being a teacher in medieval France. He saw himself in a monastery giving clandestine classes on esoteric knowledge. At a certain point during this lifetime, he was arrested for *spreading false heresies* and brutally tortured by the Inquisition. The energetic imprints of this traumatic experience were still evident in Johan's energy body.

Clearing Johan's soul trauma involved removing dense imprints in the spiritual layer of his aura and releasing the vibration of trauma from his high heart. The next step was to cut energy ties with his medieval lifetime. There were several rope-like cords at the back of his heart chakra connecting Johan to his torturer and with the Catholic Church. These old energetic attachments were blocking the flow of his heart energy. After cutting the cords and releasing the painful charge, we were able to discuss Johan's hatred of the Church and reframe his relationship with spirituality in line with current times. The final step in our work together was opening Johan's blocked crown chakra to enable a renewed spiritual connection.

Johan's experience was a deeply moving example of the lasting effects of religious persecution and the extent to which severe trauma can persist across lifetimes. Indeed, it's not uncommon for healer and teacher archetypes to have suffered religious persecution in a past life. As a result, the soul's call to be a healer or spiritual teacher in their current lifetime may be drowned out by the imprint of persecution, making them feel fearful of again facing harm for their beliefs and practices. Unfortunately, the belief that it is dangerous to be a healer, or engage in other lightworker practices, is deeply embedded in the unconscious mind resulting in a loss of power when it comes to expressing truth and spiritual gifts.

Chapter 5 | Soul Roots

For those who suffered at the hands of the Inquisition—me included—there are many aspects to the healing process and reclaiming power. First and foremost is clearing the soul wound and releasing deep-seated trauma that might be imprinted in the energy body. There are many ways to do this, but I've found that taking clients through a past-life death and connecting them with a higher perspective about the traumatic event is very effective. This approach yields an understanding of the lessons from that lifetime, bringing a sense of peace or completion. Once the trauma has been released, it's important to clear the belief that speaking their truth will draw punishment or death.

Thankfully, we live in a different era now. In most of the Western world and many parts of the Eastern world, it is acceptable to practice as a healer and speak freely about it. However, the subconscious mind hasn't always caught up and might still be clinging to outdated beliefs and fears. As in Johan's case, the healing journey required his willingness to unearth his unconscious fear of persecution and transcend it.

RELIVING MY DEATH

One of the last times I saw Brad was on a three-day trail with the hiking group in the Cederberg Wilderness area. It was early spring, the secret season in the Cederberg when the temperatures are already warming up, long before Cape Town shrugs off winter. With their dramatic rock formations, the Cederberg mountains are breathtakingly beautiful, especially when the wildflowers bloom.

Originally home to the indigenous Khoisan people, the Cederberg region is known for its sandstone caves and rock art. The hiking trail planned for our trip would take us to some of the little-known rock art sites. As we set out on the trail heading for our first stopover in a mountain hut, a storm blew in—a common occurrence in these capricious mountains. Lashed by wind and rain, we took shelter in a cave and made ourselves as comfortable as possible to endure the stormy night ahead. The temperature plummeted, and even with the fire we'd made at the cave's entrance, it was still freezing cold.

Wrapped up in our sleeping bags, we tried to get some sleep. As the wind whistled through the cave, I felt that familiar tug backward into a past timeline, and I was soon immersed in another past life experience.

> The world was white. There was snow on the ground, and the trees were bare. I was wandering through this landscape, dressed in ragged buffalo hide and worn-through boots. Frozen to the bone, I was foraging for food. Finding shelter in a cave, I lay down, slipping in and out of a delirious state. Barely conscious, I realized there was someone holding me. I knew it was Standing Bear. He had survived! He had been calling my name, trying to revive me, but I couldn't open my eyes. While I lay in his arms, Standing Bear told me that a few of his warriors had survived the battle and scattered in the aftermath. He'd gone back to the valley many times to look for me and others, but there was no one except his small band of warriors. They had been on the move for months, fighting back, trying to hold onto the land. As he told me his story, I could hear everything he was saying but couldn't speak. I was too weak, my lips frozen. I couldn't tell him how sorry I was that I didn't warn our people, that I saw the battle coming but hadn't wanted to believe the scale of it. I couldn't tell him that I had been there after the massacre, that I had stood above the valley paralyzed, unable to give the blessing I knew I should have given for the many souls who had lost their lives that terrible day. I couldn't tell him that during these same months, while he had been fighting, I had been licking my heart wound in this cave, barely managing to keep warm or feed myself in the dead of winter. Standing Bear held me for days, keeping me warm, squeezing water through my frozen lips, but he had found me too late. I died in his arms.

During that stormy night in the Cederberg cave, I relived my death in the 1850s and finally understood why the karmic cord between Brad and myself was so strong. As the dawn light entered the cave, it illuminated several faded rock art paintings of hunters and antelope on the cave walls. How incredible that these depictions of ordinary Khoisan life had withstood the harsh weather conditions for thousands of years. I lay in my sleeping bag thinking about time and timelessness, washed over by a feeling of deep peace.

Walking through the fragrant fynbos that day, I reflected on my journey with Brad over the past few years. We had helped each other in countless ways—clearing soul wounds, learning soul lessons, and supporting each other to heal. So much had happened in the non-ordinary world. In the ordinary world, the vibration of sorrow I had been carrying was gone. The weight of unfinished business had been lifted. By going back in time to bless the devastated valley where my people had been massacred, I had completed a spiritual task. Most importantly, I had released the vow I had made in that lifetime never to be a healer again. Now I could continue unencumbered on my journey as a healer in this and future lifetimes.

After reliving my death, I felt a sense of completion with my Native American life, the peace signaling some sort of conclusion. Did this mean my contract with Brad was done? Was I ready to cut our karmic ties? Ready or not, it happened far sooner than I expected.

CUTTING KARMIC TIES

After the Cederberg hike, Brad announced that he was going back to America. It had been a long time coming, but perhaps the extended time in the wilderness had awakened what was just beneath the surface. Brad wanted to *go walkabout*, not for days but months. In the American wilderness, he felt untethered in a way that wasn't possible in South Africa with its increasing limitations on personal freedom. He explained that the American southwest was the only place where he could be close to the wild heart of life that he so desired. I didn't need an explanation. Brad's soul was calling him home, simple as that.

A few months later, Brad and I said goodbye to each other. I always knew this day was coming, and yet saying goodbye to a lover is never easy. Endings are painful, whatever the reason. I may have had a spiritual understanding of how things were playing out and a finely tuned respect for a soul's call when it comes, but still, it felt like an abandonment. This wasn't rational or fair. After all, I couldn't offer Brad a vision of a shared future, but emotions, rational understanding, and spiritual knowing are three different things.

Just before Brad left South Africa, we did a ritual in Newlands Forest to cut karmic ties and dissolve our contract. I white-knuckled it through our gratitude-laden goodbye and then fell apart. I wasn't having much luck with men. Sometimes my journey as a healer seemed so much more sure-footed than my journey as an ordinary woman with a wounded heart and evidently a lot of relationship karma to burn.

A CROSSROADS ON MY PATH

Revisiting my soul roots and severing karmic ties with Brad was an important waystation on my journey as a healer. During the seven-year cycle since the Polarity course and the calling of the wolves, I had cleared a major obstacle on my soul path and reclaimed my power as a healer. In the surface-world, my healing business was growing, and there was a steady flow of clients. Much to my children's relief, we were long past the point of peanut butter sandwiches.

After Brad left, I felt an unexpected lightness, as if resolving that old unfinished business had set me free in some indefinable way. I emerged from this experience with a clear knowledge of who I am. Wearing my soul journey necklace was like donning the robes of the high priestess. It gave me a newfound confidence in my healing work and soul-level knowledge that surpassed my training.

Spiritual authority, Viviane had said, comes with absolute faith in the power of healing. With spiritual authority, you can command energy masterfully and rise above the doubts and fears that inevitably arise on the path. And yet, I found myself at a crossroads. Did I source my healing from my shamanic roots or my training as a metaphysical healer? What kind of healer was I going to be? The shamanic way was so familiar, but my spirit guides were telling me to leave the past behind. This was old technology, they said. It belongs to a different age. There is no time for lengthy ceremonies anymore. We are moving to a new age where everything is speeding up; humanity is evolving rapidly, and consciousness is expanding. There was also a danger that the shamanic way would take me into the old vibration of sorrow and loss. My healing team assured me that there was another way, with a different vibration. I was to become a forward-looking quantum healer with no ties to the past, but this would require a different vibrational compass.

The vibration my spirit guides spoke of was the hidden pathway I had yet to find. The art of the pathfinder is to read the signs, track the subtle spoor, and listen to the soul's whispers. This is how to forge a soul path and learn how to walk it, baby step by baby step. But first, there was another obstacle on my path. This time it appeared as the dragon of fear.

DRAGON'S GOLD
Wisdom teachings from Chapter Five

- Intuitive sensing is multi-temporal. Emotions, physical sensations, even tastes and smells, from a distant past life can be viscerally experienced in the present. One explanation for this phenomenon is that all information connected to a soul's journey, whether past, present, and possibly even future exists in the quantum field and is directly accessible through someone's current energy body. In other words, information—not time—is the connective tissue of the Universe.

- With the right mix of intention and belief and the right synergy between healer and recipient, miracles can happen. The transmission of healing energy is a dynamic process. It is most powerful when the recipient is open to receiving healing and believes that change is possible. If there is a soul contract between healer and recipient, profound healing is inevitable.

- Past life regression is an extremely helpful tool to understand your soul's journey, heal soul wounds and trauma, clear outdated contracts, and vows, and resolve unfinished soul business. Unfinished business from a past life sends ripples through all future lifetimes until it is resolved, affecting relationships, work choices, and the ability to achieve your soul mission. Engaging with your soul's experience across time allows you to connect with your soul essence and retrieve accumulated knowledge and gifts.

- Spiritual permission must always be sought before clearing a soul contract. A soul contract, which may run over several lifetimes, should not be cleared until a particular lesson, or set of lessons, is learned. Clearing a contract prematurely is an avoidance of the karmic lessons that will only cause more problems for the souls involved. Sometimes, a soul contract automatically falls away when a past life issue is cleared.

- Everyone has many so-called soulmates. This explains the instant recognition, or familiar feeling, you might feel when you encounter one of these souls again. Soulmates will show up in your life at pivotal moments. Compelling as it may be, this doesn't always mean that you should be romantically involved with a soulmate. It's all too easy to fall into the one soulmate trap! It's important to be discerning and seek a deeper understanding of why a soulmate has appeared on your path at a particular time of your life. A trigger soul, for example, is a person who comes into your life, for a limited period, to resolve unfinished business, to teach you an important lesson, or to help you remember who you are. And sometimes, a soulmate is the perfect romantic partner.

6

INITIATION

June 2011 – June 2013

Slaying [the dragon] isn't the Heroine's way. She would rather engage with the dragon than kill him, entice him into her purposely diverse team, harness his unique skills.

– Sharon Blackie, author of *If Women Rose Rooted*

Shortly after I set out as a full-time healer, I did a series of specialized courses to supplement my training. Having left my publishing job, I had more headspace to immerse myself in the world of energy. My children spent every second weekend with their father, and I used these mother-breaks to acquire more knowledge.

For the best part of a year, I spent all my free time studying soul retrieval, ancestral healing, medical intuition, spirit release, and space clearing. It was like doing one of those language immersion courses when you learn a foreign language and culture at high speed—only the language was quantum energy, and the foreign country was multi-dimensional time-space. In a relatively short time, I went from being able to get by in a foreign land to becoming fluent in a new language and well-versed in the quirky cultures of other dimensions. Although intense, I was exhilarated by the accelerated pace of learning and being able to apply new knowledge almost immediately.

Toward the end of 2011, I embarked on a two-year healing program with the London-based School of Intuition and Healing, which was setting up a branch in Cape Town. Conveniently, I was able to assist with the school's administration in exchange for my tuition. Combining the excellent technical training I was getting at the school with the more esoteric training I had undergone with Viviane put me on an even more solid footing as a healer.

The school's director Sue was one of the teachers for the healing program and an expert in releasing spirits and clearing assorted dark energies. In addition to taking classes with her at the school, I also took several of her short courses in spirit release. Eventually, Sue took me under her wing, and for a while, I shadowed her client sessions.

Initially, I grabbed the opportunity to receive this high-level mentoring and learn everything I could about working with dark energies. When I got *whacked* with dark energy and was not able to clear on my own, Sue and her team helped to restore my equilibrium. I felt safe and protected, and, at the same time, I had to keep my wits about me in this unfamiliar terrain while I rapidly acquired new skills. Although it was terrifying at times, I was seduced by the challenge of doing this more advanced, and at times dangerous, light work. We were light warriors clearing the darkness and helping people return to the light. There was both glamour and significance in this dark energy work.

All too soon, I was on my own. Sue had a new batch of students, and I was taking on my first dark energy clients without her protective guidance. My workday was quickly filled with a parade of earthbound spirits, low-vibrational entities, psychic attack cases, and even a few possessions. This work was not for the faint-hearted. By nature, I am a gentle soul—a colleague once called me a "princess of the higher realms"—and evidently, my inner warrior needed some voomah.

For the next two years, my journey as a healer morphed into the archetypal journey of the warrior. Not only was I doing the dirty work

Chapter 6 | Initiation

in the trenches by day, but there was a lot of after-hours work too. After every client, I had to clear my healing room of energetic residue. At the end of the working day, I had to ensure that my home and my children were strongly protected. On occasion, when a disgruntled spirit showed up in my bedroom, I had to work a night shift too.

Looking back, this period of intensive dark energy work was by far the biggest challenge on my journey as a healer. The dragon of anger I had worked so hard to temper morphed into a dragon of fear and was breathing down my neck. The Dark Energy Intensive was nothing short of an initiation. I was no stranger to initiation, but this was undoubtedly the toughest so far. Like it or not, I had to rise to the challenge.

THE DRAGON OF FEAR APPEARS

On the Heroine's Journey, initiations are an opportunity to test one's biggest fears, often through a time of darkness, which seeds the next level of growth and transformation. Such an initiatory process is never comfortable, but the time of darkness is a necessary waystation on the path to the light. It is the place that awakens us to a new way of being.

My personal challenge for this initiation was to overcome my fear of dark energy and, in the recesses of my soul history, a deeply ingrained fear of the occult. The fear, when it arose, was visceral. I felt it as a coldness coiling around my heart, tightening into a threatening grip that was somehow familiar. I couldn't locate this déjà vu feeling, but soon I began to have dreams about the occult, flickering memories of a distant life breaking through the surface too elusive to grasp. I just had to keep working with the fear as it arose during the Dark Energy Intensive and find my own compass through the darkness.

In rational westernized society, we are disconnected from the world of dark energy and black magic, dismissing its power as superstition. Although I'd had fleeting brushes with darker forces in the spirit world, I had been sensitive to spirit energy for most of my life, like most westerner initiates, I was naïve about the power of dark energy and had no inkling about the depths of the dark world I was entering.

Wading in where even angels were cautious, I was about to see things that would shake me to the core.

Through all the years of mothering and working as a healer, my feminine side had developed in leaps and bounds. Although I was my father's daughter, which meant that as a girl and young woman I had identified more closely with the masculine, the car accident when I was twenty-one forced the masculine to take a backseat. It was a kind of developmental U-turn, which catapulted me into a lifelong process of returning to the feminine within. After that, I did a thorough job of reclaiming the feminine and became far stronger in my feminine aspect. Navigating through life's twists and turns, intuition had become my trusty compass, and I never doubted it. Now I was being called to strengthen my masculine energy. My inner warrior had to show up and stand strong in the face of the demons I would face in the darkness.

In energetic terms, choosing to take on this work was the equivalent of putting up a huge sign at my gate that said *Dark Beings Welcome*, attracting them like moths to a flame as they emerged from the shadows. It was as if I were suddenly visible in this murky world, and my every weakness was about to be exposed and challenged. Even though I had committed to being an instrument of the light, in the face of darkness, my fear made me vulnerable to subversion and attack by dark energies. My experiences at the hands of the occult many lifetimes ago had left a deep scar. I knew I had to unearth and heal this old soul wound by facing the dragon of fear.

For the next two years, I flexed my psychic muscle with all the tricks of the trade I had learned from Sue. During client sessions, whenever my fear came up, I took up my sword and summoned my inner warrior. Despite my best attempts at warrior-courage, when that cold hand encircled my heart, I felt my vibration drop. The dragon of fear was lurking just behind every shadow in my healing room.

MENTORS AND HELPERS

Taking on my first solo dark energy cases, without the reassuring shelter of Sue's experienced wings, had me nursing my energetic wounds all

Chapter 6 | Initiation

too frequently. It didn't take long to realize that I needed support to keep my light burning bright while I went through this initiation. And when I stumbled, as I often did, I would need a more detailed map to find my way through unknown territory.

With little prompting, my old classmate Faye, who had gone through Viviane's metaphysical training with me and had since become a trustworthy colleague, offered to clear my energy every time I received an *energy whack*. Small and elfin, Faye was the most unlikely ally against the dark forces. In the beginning, being debilitated by the dark energy work was a rather frequent occurrence, and Faye became an expert in clearing unwanted energetic residues and restoring me to full strength. I joked that she was my secret weapon. She quipped that it was her karmic payback. To my mind, there is little doubt that I owe Faye a huge debt of gratitude.

During this initiatory period, Faye was also a mentor. Her invincible calm in the face of the most obnoxious spirits, and her humility despite extraordinary behind-the-scenes work, were an inspiration. She was, in fact, the real thing, doing the unseen hard work in the back room, while I was the anchorwoman delivering the message to the dark forces. I had seen many others involved in this type of work getting high on the cloak-and-dagger glamour of it all. Faye taught me to keep my feet on the ground and understand that it was a privilege to serve the light in this way. She seemed to know, long before I did, that it was a temporary transit on my journey. In hindsight, I realized that Faye handed me the map to navigate this road of trials.

Throughout the Dark Energy Intensive, I was also held by my inner circle, who were there for me at a moment's notice bearing their varied gifts of light—color healing for my bombarded aura, restorative massage, and remote protection on rough days. This group of generous-hearted women was a powerful presence in my life. Without these angels in the wings, I would not have been able to stand strong and develop my psychic muscle on the frontline of dark energy work.

THE ABCs OF DISEMBODIED BEINGS

On the frontline, the forces of dark energy showed up in many different guises. In the beginning, I had to quickly come to grips with who was who and what was what in the invisible realms.

There are many types of spirits, or disembodied beings, in the invisible world that may appear in a healing space. From the higher realms, there are angels, archangels, and various levels of spirit guides. These light beings offer guidance and comfort and are never attached to the denser vibrations of people or places. Also, from the light realms—or *spirit world*—are the spirits of deceased relatives who pop in to give messages to their living relatives. These spirits are simply using the open channels to communicate with their loved ones and normally move away as soon as the message has been received.

A more troublesome type of disembodied being is an earthbound spirit, usually a deceased person, who is stuck on the Earth plane for any number of reasons. An earthbound spirit is often attached to the energy field of a person or a place and may need help to cross over to the higher vibrational planes.

Yet another type of discarnate being is a low-vibrational entity emanating from the astral planes. Trapped in lower vibrational consciousness, a dark entity, sometimes known as a dark force entity (DFE), invariably has a destructive agenda and can cause a lot of damage on the Earth plane.

Knowing your ABCs in the invisible realms and recognizing the different types of disembodied beings is of the utmost importance for anyone working with spirits and energies. Failing to distinguish between entities could place both the healer and the client at risk.

Discernment during the healing session is the very basis of holding a safe space for clients. When opening energetic portals, many beings can jump into the space. Deceased relatives often use the healing room as a channel to communicate with their loved ones. Other beings may jump onto the bandwidth, too, some masquerading as either a relative or guide. When new guides show up in this arena, knowing which to work with and which to send away is a crucial act of discernment.

Chapter 6 | Initiation

The starting point for discerning what kind of spirit energy is present is to screen every disembodied being that enters the healing space. In most instances, an experienced energy healer will quickly sense whether the being has a positive or negative charge. If there is any doubt, using the Law of Challenge can resolve the question simply by asking the being present "Are you a being of light?" three times and observing the response. In my experience, a being of darkness will quickly shimmy away under scrutiny, while a being of light will answer *Yes* unwaveringly. Engaging with a disembodied being in this way also provides pause for assessing its energy. If there is any uncertainty about the beneficial nature of its presence, it's best to send it away.

One of the obvious differences between a being of the light and a being of darkness is that the former is usually forthcoming and willing to engage in a conversation. An earthbound spirit, for example, while it might be stuck in a dense vibration, might be actively seeking help to cross over. Low-vibrational entities, on the other hand, often hide from view.

Energetically, earthbound spirits and dark entities feel different to me. While an earthbound spirit makes me feel suddenly light-headed, a dark entity causes my vibrational frequency to drop sharply. Clairolfaction also comes in handy; when a dark entity is present, I often get a whiff of a bad smell, a bit like rotting eggs.

As a healer, it is essential to discern between what is yours, energetically speaking, what energy belongs to a client and what might be emanating from an external source. This fine-tuned awareness is especially important when working with dark energy, and the quicker it's fully developed to discern what's what, the better. The power of discernment in this new territory is a vital survival skill. Each healer learns their own signals for discerning the type of energy present and where it is coming from, much like compiling a personal dictionary in a new language.

During the Dark Energy Intensive, my discernment went up a few notches. The moment a client walked through the door, I could tell whether there was a low-vibe entity or earthbound spirit in their field. Sometimes I would be forewarned. Depending on which of my guides turned up in the healing room while I was preparing for my clients, I would be given a heads-up as to what was coming my way.

SPIRIT RELEASE

My initiation started gently enough with a procession of earthbound spirits, which were lodged in one way or another in my clients' energy fields. My task was to release these spirit attachments and help them to cross over to the light realms. In shamanic language, the process of assisting a spirit to cross over is called *soul escorting* or *psychopomp*. I preferred the term spirit release.

Following Sue's spirit release protocol, I found that earthbound spirits were relatively easy to release and assist in crossing over to the spirit world. However, in a few cases, the attached spirit was angry or vengeful, and this made for a more challenging task.

One of the most challenging spirit attachment cases was that of a young child who was being disturbed by the spirit of an elderly man. The little girl's mother was at her wit's end when she brought her daughter to see me.

LUCY'S STORY

When I met Lucy, she was four years old. Her family had relocated to England when she was two, and since then, her behavior had changed. She was sullen and rude and prone to explosive tantrums. Initially, her mother chalked this up to the family's relocation, but as time went by and Lucy didn't settle, her concerns grew. Lucy's behavior had become impossible to handle. She couldn't sleep on her own, claiming there was someone in her room, and she had begun making strange, nonsensical comments. Her mother was convinced that something sinister was going on.

My first impression of Lucy's energy was that she seemed angry. While we were talking, she was restless and interrupted us constantly, demanding her mother's attention. I hoped I would be able to get her to sit still for long enough to access her energy field.

Chapter 6 | Initiation

With Lucy sitting on her mother's lap, I quickly scanned her energy field to assess what might be going on. As I did so, an angry voice said, "She's mine." Tuning into this energy, I saw an elderly man in a double-story house with blue shutters. I described the house to Lucy's mother. She nodded, affirming the description of the house. The old man's spirit energy was concentrated around Lucy's head. This meant that he had attached to her mental energy body and was most likely influencing her thoughts. I would need to understand why before I could release him from Lucy's field.

Communicating telepathically, I asked the spirit to tell me his story. The old man told me that Lucy's family had moved into "his house," and he wanted them out. He admitted quite freely that he was using Lucy, as the most vulnerable member of the family, to create chaos so that they would leave. I wondered why he was so attached to the house. On further questioning, he told me that he was angry that he had died before his sickly wife because he needed to look after her. After his death, she moved into a nursing home, but he stayed firmly attached to their house, believing she would return. His wife hadn't returned to the house, and he was blaming Lucy's family for preventing her return. The old man's spirit seemed very disoriented, and I realized that he hadn't accepted either his wife's choice to move into a nursing home or his own death.

Acceptance was the starting point to releasing the old man's spirit from Lucy's energy field. Gently, I explained to him that the house had been sold and his wife wasn't coming back. I told him that she had chosen to move into the nursing home and that he wasn't responsible for her anymore. I urged him to let go of his attachment to the physical world, including his need to look after his wife, and to cross over to the spirit world. While communicating, I worked with his heart energy to raise his vibration and release his anger. Finally, as the old man's vibration shifted, I was able to assist him in detaching from Lucy's energy field and the Earth plane and crossing over to higher realms.

It was a rather challenging spirit release due to my young client's restlessness. Lucy refused to stay in the healing room, so we moved into the garden. I hoped being outdoors would settle her. While conversing with the old man's spirit, Lucy was feeding the goldfish in the little pond outside the healing room. Luckily, the fish had kept her entertained just long enough for me to complete the task. After releasing the spirit, I quickly restored balance to Lucy's disturbed energy field before she ran off to the swing on the other side of the garden.

By then, I was pretty sure that the old man's spirit was gone and hoped that the change would be immediately apparent in Lucy's behavior. The family was on holiday in Cape Town, so it wasn't until a few weeks later that I received an email from Lucy's mother. "I've got my daughter back!" she wrote.

Since their return to England, the rudeness, tantrums, and strange comments had stopped. Lucy was altogether a different, much happier child.

When working with an earthbound spirit, it's important to remember that the spirit most likely needs help and deserves to be treated with respect and compassion no matter what disturbance it might be causing. One way I have found to keep this at the forefront of my communication with a spirit being, especially one that is creating disturbances, is to use the following questions to help guide my approach: If this spirit was still in physical form, what would I say to the person in front of me? How would I reassure them? What does this distressed soul need to move on?

In terms of method, spirit release work is a combination of energy work—raising the vibration—and consciousness work—changing perception. It is important to establish why the spirit is stuck in the Earth plane. There is always a reason. Just listening to the story is helpful for the spirit who may have been trying to get someone's attention for a long time.

In some cases, an earthbound spirit is attached to a person or a place because there is an unresolved issue. In Lucy's case, for example, the old man's spirit had attached to her energy field because he couldn't accept his death or detach from his husbandly duty. In other cases, a spirit may be earthbound because its vibration is too low to cross over to higher realms. This happens when a spirit is extremely angry or sad and is stuck in this dense energy. I have also come across spirits that don't realize they have left their physical body, usually as a result of a sudden death, which left their recently disembodied spirit disoriented.

Before trying to release an earthbound spirit from a person or a place, it is important first to establish why it is there. The only effective way to perform spirit release is to help the spirit find resolution so that they can let go of the worldly issue that is keeping them stuck—force does not work. While every situation is different, there is usually a process of explaining to the spirit that staying in a denser vibration does not serve them. In order to progress, an earthbound spirit must detach from its old life and cross over to the world of spirit. There they can find healing and progress as a soul. Once an earthbound spirit grasps this higher perspective, it is usually short work to raise their vibration sufficiently to complete their transition to the light.

Even if an earthbound spirit seems innocuous, a spirit attachment is never a good thing. Spirit energy invariably has a negative impact on the host's energy, emotions, and, in more extreme cases, their behavior and even health. Ultimately, it is a form of co-dependency which does not serve the living host or the spirit.

In Lucy's case, the old man's spirit was affecting her emotional and mental well-being. Sometimes, the effect of a spirit attachment is more physical. This was the case for a cardiologist who came to see me because he was experiencing inexplicable chest pain. I found it curious that a medical specialist would come to an energy healer for assistance but soon understood why.

SANJIV'S STORY

Sanjiv was a young cardiologist at a local hospital. For the past few months, he had been experiencing strange sensations in his chest area, accompanied by twinges of anger and impatience. I asked Sanjiv why he had chosen to come to a healer rather than a doctor for an assessment. He explained that he felt intuitively that these unusual symptoms did not have a physical cause. Sanjiv was refreshingly open to what complementary healing modalities had to offer and commented that there was much that western medicine couldn't solve. This was going to be an interesting exchange!

When I tuned into Sanjiv's energy field, I was immediately aware of a spirit energy on top of his chest. On closer inspection, I gathered that the spirit was that of a male patient who had died on the operating table when Sanjiv was performing heart surgery. The deceased patient was angry with Sanjiv for failing to save him. His intense anger and inability to accept his death kept the patient's spirit attached to Sanjiv's energy field and mired on the Earth plane. He would need help to let go of his anger and stop blaming Sanjiv for "robbing him of the rest of his life," as the deceased patient's spirit put it.

Going through the spirit release process, I released the man's spirit and helped him to cross over to higher realms. For the rest of the session, I focused on rebalancing Sanjiv's disturbed heart energy. While clearing the residue of anger, which belonged to the departed spirit, I became aware of an underlying vibration of guilt that was keeping the anger vibration in place, like two interlocking molecules. For some reason, Sanjiv felt guilty about this patient.

When I told Sanjiv what I had found in his field, he wasn't at all surprised. He clearly remembered this disgruntled patient, who he described as angry and impatient. When I asked about the guilt, Sanjiv confessed that he felt that he had made a mistake during the surgery and hadn't yet come to terms with his perceived error. I suggested we do some further work to release this guilt.

After the spirit release work, Sanjiv reported that he didn't feel angry anymore, and the burden of guilt had lifted somewhat. From then on, he was more mindful of the energetic component of his surgical work and protected his energy before going into the operating theater. Over time, Sanjiv found that he was becoming far more intuitive in the way he worked with his patients, which he found to be extremely helpful when faced with split-second life and death decisions. Looking back, he understood that, in the case of the angry patient who had died on the operating table, he had overridden his intuition and followed protocol instead. With this understanding, Sanjiv could finally forgive himself and release his guilt.

One of the most unusual cases of spirit attachment I worked with was that of Sally. When she first came to see me, she had recently had a kidney transplant, and the deceased donor was still attached to her new kidney.

Chapter 6 | Initiation

SALLY'S STORY

When Sally arrived in my healing room, she was visibly unwell. She'd had a kidney transplant six months earlier, and her body hadn't accepted the donated organ. After several surgical procedures, Sally was still in pain and felt generally unwell. Since the transplant operation, she had been on immune suppressants, which were causing mood swings, and she didn't feel at all like herself. Sally's biggest concern was that if her body continued to reject the kidney, she might have to go through another transplantation, which was no small thing even if she were lucky enough to find another donor. She hoped I might be able to persuade her body to accept the new kidney.

When I went into Sally's energy field, I was surprised to find a spirit attachment in her aura. Tuning in further, it became apparent that this was the donor's spirit, that of a young woman who had died after being in a prolonged coma. I noticed two energetic ties binding her to Sally: one was a rope-like cord wrapped around her kidney, and another was attached to Sally's solar plexus. There appeared to be a power struggle between the donor and the recipient. No wonder Sally's body hadn't accepted the donor's kidney! To complicate matters, Sally's energy-consciousness was way out of her body, which meant that her energy strength was weak, making it easier for the spirit attachment to lodge in her field in an attempt to lay claim to the contested kidney.

When I communicated with the deceased donor, she seemed rather confused. She said she wanted her kidney back. When I explained that she was no longer in a physical body and would have no use for her kidney in spirit form, she said she wasn't ready to die. I explained that she was already dead, and it wouldn't serve her to stay where she was. I pointed out that hanging onto her old kidney, which she had agreed to donate, wasn't going to bring her back to life. In fact, holding on to her kidney and cording to Sally would keep her stuck in limbo indefinitely. She was also blocking Sally's chances of recovering and moving forward with her life. After a lengthy communication, the deceased donor finally agreed to let go of her *claim*, and I was able to cut the cords and release her earthbound spirit from Sally's energy field.

Once the spirit energy had been released, I could bring Sally's energy back into her physical body. My guide, Doctor, butted in at this point, saying I needed to *imprint* Sally's energy onto the new kidney. He said this would enable her body to accept it. Following Doctor's instructions, I cleared the donor's energy from the new kidney and then attuned it to Sally's vibration.

At the end of the session, Sally verified that the donor was a young woman. Nevertheless, she looked skeptical about my findings and whether this energetic intervention would make any difference. I suggested she come back and see me in a few weeks for a check-up.

When Sally arrived for her check-up, she announced that her body was no longer rejecting the kidney. She felt more like her old self and physically stronger too. Her medical team was lowering her dose of immunosuppressants, and for the first time, there was a positive prognosis for a life without dialysis.

In my work with spirits, I felt like a mediator, deploying all my communication skills to persuade stuck and disoriented spirits to let go of their issues and detach from the living person's field. It was quite an art. The only difference between mediation with living parties and mediating with spirits was that the conversation was conducted telepathically, and the final agreement was spiritually, rather than legally, binding.

This kind of spiritual mediation worked well with earthbound spirits. It was less effective and far more challenging, with low-vibrational entities with a more insidious agenda, as I was soon to discover.

As the Dark Energy Intensive progressed, more and more clients with dark entities in tow started showing up in the healing room. My initiation was about to go up a level. I quickly realized that I needed more assistance from my etheric healing team. Another tool of the trade was assigning a light being as a gatekeeper to protect the space, like a bouncer at a party door to keep gate crashers out. It took a while to find a suitable candidate, but eventually, Melchior showed up. He was perfect—a powerful masculine energy with a bright light that lit up my healing room whenever he was present. With this new member of my etheric healing team, I received an early warning when there were low-vibrational entities about.

LOW-VIBRATIONAL ENTITIES

Low-vibrational entities—or dark entities for short—emanate from a denser dimension, such as the astral plane, and vibrate at a low frequency. There are many different types of dark entities, varying in levels of consciousness and intent. Dark entities can be attached to a person's aura or more deeply embedded within the energy body, or they might simply be coming in and out of someone's energy field using some sort of portal to access the host's energy-consciousness. A dark entity has consciousness; it is not the same as a thought-form, which might appear as an entity but doesn't have its own consciousness. A thought-form is a projection from someone's mind, either that of the client or a third party, who may be projecting a particular thought-form into someone's energy field.

These dark entities are among us, floating like particles in the vibrational soup of the quantum field. Most of the time, we're not even aware of their presence, and they don't disturb us. But should we encounter a dark entity, it is advisable to get out of harm's way. As the saying goes, it is in a scorpion's nature to sting—and so it's best to avoid the scorpion and not tempt fate. In all likelihood, it is only if the scorpion gets entangled in our clothes, or hides in our shoes, that we are likely to get stung. The moral of the analogy? Low-vibe entities are unlikely to affect us unless they become entangled in our field, but they are best avoided.

Among the clients I worked with, I encountered various reasons for entity entanglements. A low-vibe entity might have attached to a client's energy because they are energetically porous. This vulnerability may arise because of a self-destructive lifestyle, such as alcohol or substance abuse. Illicit drug use, for example, provides a portal to the astral planes where lower, two-dimensional entities exist. Over the years, I had seen many drug users with weak and torn auras who were the unwitting carriers of dark entities. Cocaine and heroin were among the worst culprits. But during the Dark Energy Intensive, I became increasingly aware of the impacts of crystal meth—known on the streets as tik—which had become the drug of choice in Cape Town with some alarming hidden side effects.

One of my young clients was struggling to free herself from her addition to tik. I admired her immensely for her determination to kick the habit and wanted to help her. But her energy field was so damaged that it was unlikely that energy work would have any lasting effect unless she went through rehab and stopped using. The best I could offer was a temporary fix—clearing the dark entities from her aura and sealing her field—but it was highly likely that the entities would flock back as soon as she started using and opened the portals again.

After this and a few other heart-rending experiences with young drug users, I made it a policy that I wouldn't work with anyone using hard drugs until they had been clean for at least six weeks. This might sound harsh, but in the long run, I wasn't serving a client's highest good by giving them false hope of a quick fix before they had dealt with the root of the problem. It was not in my power to wave a magic wand unless they came to the party too.

Another reason someone might become an unwitting host to dark entities is if they dabble with spirits. I witnessed this firsthand when I worked with a teenage boy called Josh who was suffering from depression. During our conversations, he confessed that he and a group of friends were using a Ouija board to do seances. This was a dangerous game. By calling up spirits in this way, Josh and his friends were unwittingly opening portals to the astral planes that allowed dark entities to come through and attach to their energy fields. After months of doing these seances, Josh had accumulated an entourage of dark entities, and being host to them was draining his life force energy. No wonder he was depressed. With Josh's cooperation, it was quick work to remove the dark entities from his aura and repair it. Now it was up to him to stop inviting them in again. Fortunately, Josh understood the serious consequences of his innocent dabbling and assured me that he would stop attending the seances. Without the energy-sapping attachments, Josh would have a much better chance of overcoming his depression.

During the Dark Energy Intensive, I saw many clients with low-vibrational entities in their auric fields. Most were totally unaware of their presence and only too glad to be rid of their unwelcome energies. There were others who didn't heed my advice, despite the dangers. Time and again, I saw clients who wanted a quick fix but then left my healing room and continued with the same behavior, activity, or relationship that was causing the problem.

As healers, we cannot interfere in free will. Hard as it is to see someone taking a dangerous path, we must respect their choice. It might be that a client needs to learn something from a particular experience, and we cannot interfere with soul lessons, even if we think we know better. It was a steep learning curve for me. My lesson was to detach from the outcome while doing my best to help and remain compassionate. In choosing the path of compassion, I was constantly reminded of the pitfalls of any kind of misguided attempt to rescue rather than heal. Going into rescue mode would have been like pouring energy into a bottomless pit and would not have served anyone.

It was humbling to observe the imperative of respecting free will. Even if clients ignored the higher guidance that they received in the healing room and continued with destructive patterns, I had to respect their choices and do so without judgment. While there might be high roads and low roads, everyone has a right to choose their path and its attendant challenges. Through many of these clients, I witnessed the effects of free will, as well as extraordinary acts of courage, in shaping experience, life path, and destiny.

However, there are times when even free will is interfered with by psychic means, such as by psychic attack.

PSYCHIC ATTACK

The term psychic attack is used to describe the intentional use of energetic or psychic means to willfully manipulate or harm a person or their property. Even though it is a distressing experience, victims of a psychic attack have choice in deciding how to respond to this type of interference.

Psychic attack has many faces and is usually related to revenge, envy, or personal gain of some sort. In the worst cases, a psychic attack is carried out by a professional who has been paid to target the victim. More commonly, an intentional attack is carried out by an amateur with malicious intent to hurt or destabilize another person. A psychic attack can also be unconsciously carried out. This usually occurs when intense emotions such as anger or jealousy are repeatedly directed at another person.

The degree of harm caused depends on the attacker's level of skill as well as the nature of their intention. The cases I worked with varied accordingly. The intention behind a psychic attack might be to cause general bad luck, inflict pain or cause illness. It might also be used to prevent or damage a romantic relationship or undermine business success and market share. I've also witnessed cases where an attacker aimed to control someone's thoughts and actions, though this is rare. In extreme cases, an attacker might attempt to end someone's life through energetic means. Again, this is very rare, though I have witnessed interference of this malevolent kind.

The caveat here is that intentions are powerful. As a responsible, conscious person, you should always be aware of how you wield your mental power and never intentionally use it to harm another. If you work with energy, this principle is even more important. Working with energy carries enormous responsibility. According to spiritual law, using energy to create change carries exponentially more karmic effect than any other action.

Over the next two years of the Dark Energy Intensive, I would see many variations of psychic attack and learn to discern between professional, amateur, and unconscious attacks. In this arena, I encountered the collective heart of darkness, the ugliest shadow forms, and clients whose lives had been gravely affected. The flip side of the coin was that psychic attack also initiated profound healing journeys for those who were able to step out of the victim role.

In my training, I had been taught to block the attack, remove the harmful energy from a client's field and then help them to look at the dynamic at play. With psychic attack, there is always a dynamic between the perpetrator and the victim. Sometimes the dynamic is part of a soul contract to learn a life lesson or resolve old karma playing out from a past life interaction. Other times, an emotional wound needs to be surfaced and resolved. None of this interplay justifies a psychic attack, but it does mean that disarming a psychic attack often requires resolution at a deeper level.

In assuming the victim role, it is especially important that the person under attack looks at the part they might be playing in the exchange. With awareness, and changes in behavior, the dynamics between perpetrator and victim will shift, and the situation will automatically resolve itself. Fleur's case was a textbook example.

FLEUR'S STORY

Fleur was a light, bubbly soul. She came to see me because she had been experiencing debilitating neck pain for several months. It had started one day out of the blue, and despite countless visits to doctors and physiotherapists, she had found no relief. With so much light around her, I wondered what might be going on.

When I entered Fleur's energy field, I received a clear image of a blonde woman sitting with a voodoo doll sticking pins into Fleur's neck, much as you'd expect to see in a movie. The energy coming from the blonde woman was envy. I described the attacker as best I could, and Fleur immediately recognized her as one of her friends—let's call her Veronica. I asked her why Veronica might be jealous of her. I had an inkling of what was going on, but it was important for Fleur to understand the dynamic for herself.

I left Fleur with this question while I removed the etheric pins from her neck and blocked the attack. A voodoo doll is the simplest form of psychic attack, and it was easy to disable it. However, removing the pins was one thing; preventing Veronica from repeating the attack was another. There are many ways to stop an attacker from doing their dirty work. I chose the path of communication, giving Veronica's soul a choice. Communicating with her higher self, I explained that she was generating bad karma and that everything she sent to Fleur would be returned to her. I didn't return the harmful energy to her—that would be interfering in her field—I simply made her aware of spiritual law.

Fleur had no idea why Veronica would be so envious and was shocked that her friend had such strong feelings. I had to tread with great sensitivity. While clearing the attack, I had seen an energetic cord between Veronica and Fleur's husband, with whom my guides told me she had a fleeting affair. Veronica wanted him back and was jealous of his continued loyalty to Fleur.

After clearing Fleur's energy field, I told her very gently what I had seen. Hard as this was, it was not my role to protect her from an uncomfortable truth. Fleur was disbelieving and told me that her husband would never have cheated on her, though she conceded that Veronica had always held a torch for him.

"As far as I can see, the affair is over, and you have nothing to worry about," I said gently. "But it's best you get it out into the open and clear this energy between the three of you."

A few weeks later, a tearful Fleur arrived back in my healing room. Between sobs, she told me that her husband had confessed to a brief fling with Veronica a few months back. She was deeply shocked by the revelation. I asked about her neck pain. "Oh, that," she said. "It's gone."

She seemed to have forgotten all about the original reason for seeking my help.

The neck pain had disappeared the day after our first session. Now I needed to clear the shock and help Fleur work through the emotional distress of discovering her husband's infidelity. Fortunately, their relationship was strong enough that they were able to work through this challenge and find each other again.

Not every psychic attack was as simple to resolve. As I waded further into this murky terrain, the cases I was presented with became more complex. By far, the most common type of psychic attack case I worked with related to the business world, where competition for company ownership or market share was being played out in the shadows. In many of these cases, the conflicts I witnessed were in-house power struggles between business partners, where one of the business partners was using psychic means—often with paid assistance—to gain the upper hand. Invariably, my clients were the victims in these unfortunate situations and suffered from varying effects such as ongoing bad luck or ill health. Assisting these clients was a lengthy process of untangling sticky threads before there was a lasting resolution between the warring parties.

While dealing with the complexity of surface-world issues, I also became aware of underlying reasons for an attack, which were often rooted in a past life entanglement or karmic contract. I worked with many of these more complex psychic attack cases. One that stands out is Riana's experience of full-blown family warfare.

RIANA'S STORY

Riana was an elegantly dressed attorney from a well-to-do Afrikaans family. After a divorce a few years earlier, she had thrown herself into personal transformation work and was on a conscious spiritual path. I immediately warmed to Riana. She was quirky and lively, with an irreverent sense of humor. Our sessions were in English, peppered with the more poetic Afrikaans explanations and expletives when required. Despite the seriousness of our work together, we had a lot of fun.

Initially, Riana sought my help for physical reasons: constant fatigue, unexplained rashes, and a swollen stomach that no amount of exercise or dieting would shrink. She told me a bit about her history: a divorce, which seemed to be resolved, her distant relationship with a harsh father who had recently passed on, her close relationship with her elderly mother, and tricky dynamics with her older sister, Lizette.

When I asked permission to enter Riana's energy field, my guides warned me that there was *dark muti* afoot.[11] I was taken aback and proceeded with caution. What I found was shocking, to say the least. The outer layer of Riana's aura was cluttered with all manner of debris. Going further in, I found an etheric chicken's claw in her belly. This was classic African witchcraft, and I suspected that a dark *sangoma* was involved.[12] I asked to be shown who had projected the

---

11 *Muti* is a term for herbal medicine, common to most indigenous African languages in southern Africa and used in both South African English and Afrikaans as a slang word for medicine in general. *Dark muti* suggests that the medicine is being used for malicious purpose.

12 A *sangoma* is a traditional African healer and diviner. Well trained in the art of healing, *sangomas* are highly respected in their communities and part of the fabric of healthcare in South Africa. The vast majority of *sangomas* work in the light. However, there are also dark *sangomas*, or sorcerers, referred to locally as *witch doctors* who use their skills to perform dark magic.

thought-form of the chicken's claw and was shown two figures sitting around a fire, with all manner of pots and jars around them. One looked like a *sangoma*; the other was a more shadowy figure. My guides told me that the shadowy figure was Riana's older sister Lizette. What could possibly be her motive?

In our first session, I focused on removing the intrusions in Riana's energy field and blocking the attack. As I sealed her rather porous aura, I knew this was just the beginning. Until I could communicate with her sister and understand the underlying dynamic between the siblings, it was likely that Lizette would just renew the attack.

At the end of our first session, I told Riana what I had seen in her energy field. It is always difficult to give feedback like this to a client but much to my surprise, Riana didn't seem unduly taken aback.

"Lizette has been working with a sangoma for months. She is like an apprentice. I just didn't think she'd go this far," she said quietly. "But she has always been envious of me."

"Do you know why she is envious?" I asked.

"She always wanted my father's attention," she replied. "He didn't pay either of us much attention, but she competed with me in everything, trying to get it. It didn't help that I was very academic and more successful in my career."

Lizette was the classic Queen archetype, used to being in a position of power and looked up to by those around her. From a young age, she'd been intensely envious of Riana and bullied her. When a Queen misuses her power in this way, the shadow Queen takes over. As an archetype, the shadow Queen is a common theme in many cautionary tales about the misguided use of power.

It took months of sustained work clearing attacks and unraveling a complex family drama, which pivoted around this long-standing sibling rivalry and a contested inheritance. To make it more complicated, there were karmic cords, which looked like thick ropes, between the two sisters.

After the first few sessions, Riana's physical symptoms cleared up, but the energetic attacks continued sporadically. As our work together progressed, I was able to help her to set boundaries—spiritually and emotionally—so that she wasn't so porous. I also taught her how to protect herself and recognize the shifting energy during an attack. It is much easier to clear the effects of an attack immediately or soon after an attack.

At the consciousness level, we looked at Riana's role as the victim in this family saga and how she could move out of this position. The key was improving her sense of self-worth and stepping into her power. Riana had spent her life trying to please her father and older sister. As the victim of childhood bullying, she had a classic abuse mindset with low self-esteem and an expectation that she would be treated badly. As an adult, the bullying she had experienced as a child continued in a different, more insidious form. Slowly, we worked through the layers of abuse as well as the soul aspects of the situation. Her soul lineage was that of a healer and teacher. Not surprisingly, her current work as a family lawyer was also focused on helping people.

As our work progressed, the dynamics in her family were shifting. While she avoided seeing Lizette, her own healing was changing the constellation. One of the breakthrough moments was when Riana recognized her light and was able to step into the power of her spiritual authority. Ultimately, the big shift came when Riana was ready to cut karmic ties and clear the soul contract with Lizette. This was only possible once she had understood her role in the triangle with her father and could engage with her sister at a soul level.

When the time was right, we did a soul mediation process. By this time, Lizette was willing to engage with me telepathically. Together, we reviewed their soul history, which revealed a series of past lives involving intense rivalry, sometimes with fatal consequences. Lizette had been a sorcerer in one, using dark magic to disarm her rival, Riana. According to the soul contract in their current lifetime, Riana's lesson was to step out of the victim role and take back her power; Lizette's lesson was to step out of the shadow Queen role and use her spiritual power ethically.

It is not possible to clear a contract until the lessons are learned, but over the past year, both siblings had confronted their respective lessons. Their soul contract had been fulfilled. Spiritual permission was given to clear the contract, and with that, I cut the rope-like karmic cords that had bound Riana and Lizette in an unhealthy entanglement.

With the cutting of karmic ties, the psychic attacks stopped completely, though Riana kept her distance from her sister. One day, Riana called me to share that her mother had passed away and that together, she and Lizette had helped her to cross over in peace. She hoped this experience would pave the way for a newfound peace with her sister.

Over the course of Riana's healing journey, I had several encounters with the *sangoma* who was training Lizette in the dark arts. No doubt he did good work as well, but his dubious ethics threw up a slew of questions for me.

During my training, ethical conduct was the number one principle for a healer. It had been drummed into every student to work in the light and only ever in the client's highest good. At my Initiation ceremony with Viviane and Frieda, we had even made a vow to that effect. I could not imagine using energy willfully to harm someone. This is the equivalent of a doctor going against their Hippocratic oath. It sickened me to the core.

Although witch doctors in South Africa had a reputation for using dark *muti*, a trained *sangoma* was regarded more highly. Most *sangomas* worked in the light, offering their clients profound healing and spiritual guidance. I myself had directly benefited from Frieda's powerful transformational work. But sadly, there were others using their power to cause harm, which gave *sangomas* a bad name among lightworkers.

The whole experience with Riana gave me pause for thought. What did I need to learn? Working with psychic attack was undoubtedly part of my training in becoming more finely attuned to the psychic airwaves and adept at clearing complex entanglements. I also learned the tricks of the trade when it came to African *muti*. In hindsight, however, this experience alerted me to the shadow side of a spiritually conscious profession. It was disillusioning to witness the misuse of power by a respected shaman, but it taught me that spiritual purity doesn't come with the job title. The heart of darkness is part of the human condition and can show up anywhere. Perhaps most importantly, I was learning to bring compassion rather than judgment to bear on every situation and being I encountered, including the dark entities. There is a spark of divinity in even the darkest of hearts.

As Clarissa Pinkola Estés reminds us:

> *In mythos and fairy tales, deities and other great spirits test the hearts of humans by showing up in various forms that disguise their*

> divinity... *The great powers are testing to see if humans have yet learned to recognize the greatness of soul in all its varying forms.*[13]

The Dark Energy Intensive was an ongoing dismantling of my spiritual naivete. Not long after my encounter with the unethical *sangoma*, I was faced with yet another disturbing case. This time a spiritual guru was involved in a debilitating psychic attack on one of my regular clients. Seeking more power, he'd taken what is known as the left-hand path, with devastating effects on his followers. Even in spiritual circles, there are power struggles at play, but I hadn't been prepared for such darkness masquerading as light. The spiritual guru may have been an extreme case, but during this period, I came across other spiritual figures with dark agendas wreaking behind-the-scenes havoc in people's lives. It was eye-opening, to say the least.

Still, it is not all doom and gloom. If the victim of a psychic attack is willing to look at their part in allowing the intrusion, there are always lessons to be learned. Riana, for example, was among those who were willing to look at their role in the victim-perpetrator-rescuer triangle. As a result, she learned important soul-level lessons, and the psychic attack served her spiritual growth. There were others, however, who were not able to engage with the lessons or transcend the negative experience. This made the work of clearing a psychic attack or other forms of invasive energy far more difficult, if not impossible.

CURSES

Another type of interference with free will is a curse, which can distort perception and manipulate choices. Fortunately, curses are rare, but they do exist. Many clients arrived in my healing room fearing that they had been cursed, but in all the years of practice, I saw very few real curses. In these rare cases, a curse may be current, related to a past life, or ancestral. An ancestral curse might be in effect when an ancestor was cursed in the past with a specific instruction that the curse be passed down the generations, usually by the eldest child or by one gender in the family line.

---

[13] Clarissa Pinkola Estés, *Women Who Run with the Wolves: Myths and Stories of the Wild Woman Archetype* (USA: Ballantine Books, 1992).

One of my curse-carrying clients was the oldest child in an English-speaking South African family. His grandfather had grown up in an Afrikaans-speaking family at a time when the wounds of the Anglo-Boer war were still raw. When his grandfather married an English-speaking woman, he was disowned by his family, and a generational curse was set in motion to the effect that his oldest child, and the oldest child of each successive generation, would meet an untimely end. This was a grisly curse, but fortunately, it had little remaining power and was easy to clear from my client's field.

Another disturbing example of an ancestral curse at work was the case of Khanita, a beautiful young Muslim woman in her late twenties.

KHANITA'S STORY

Khanita came to see me because her eyesight was failing, with no identifiable physical cause. When I entered her energy field, it soon became apparent that the cause was energetic and that the source was an old curse laid onto her great-grandmother, who had been seduced by a beautiful foreigner and defied the laws of her culture by eloping with him. Perceived as a grave error of judgment in her time, the curse of dim sight was programmed to work through the daughters of successive generations to prevent them from looking at men and bringing disgrace upon the family.

Khanita's whole energy field was shrouded in mist, which was concentrated around her Third Eye and physical eyes, impairing both her intuitive sight and her eyesight. As she had approached marriageable age, it appeared that the mist effect had become more debilitating.

This was a powerful curse indeed, but fortunately, once a curse is identified, it is usually fairly straightforward to deactivate. In Khanita's case, it took no more than two sessions to free her from this past programming.

Far more challenging was curse-weaving, which is part and parcel of a professional and currently active psychic attack. A seasoned pro would know immediately when the dark energy matrix they have put in place has been dismantled. In one tricky case, when I'd successfully removed a curse from my client's field, the sorcerer responsible for weaving the curse threw a dark net over my aura and all manner of psychic weapons to boot. Suffice to say, it took several days and Faye's emergency assistance to clear the fallout. My initiation was getting tougher by the day!

In the event of a retaliation like this, I had been trained to do battle and defend myself, but Faye had a different view.

"Don't engage in psychic warfare," she said. "You only add fuel to the fire. If there is no energy to feed off, the attacker will get bored and go elsewhere. Besides, by engaging in psychic warfare, even in defense, you only generate more karma. Remember spiritual law?"

She raised a questioning eyebrow at me as if I should know better. I asked, "So, even if I am under attack, I must just sit it out and wait for the storm to blow over?"

Faye nodded wisely. "Eventually, you'll see it coming, and they won't be able to find you. If they do, then you send the highest vibration of love and compassion to these misguided souls and detach from the power struggle."

Clearly, I still had more to learn. My initiation was not yet over.

POSSESSION

In nearly fifteen years of practicing, I have only seen two genuine cases of possession, although many more clients claimed to be possessed. Possession is treacherous territory and takes enormous skill to deal with effectively. The reason for this is that the invading soul, or disembodied entity, has a strongly vested interest in remaining *in situ*; the other is that the host soul is either too weak to reclaim its energetic body and soul space, or is complicit in the status quo, deriving power or some other benefit from the invading entity. Until this Faustian pact is broken, an exorcism is near impossible.

Whatever the unconscious reasons for the entanglement, it is a place of torment for the client, and, in my eagerness to help, I waded in where angels fear to tread. Toward the end of the Dark Energy Intensive, a young woman called Xanthia came to see me. This extremely challenging case involved conscious collusion between my new client and a dark entity with subversive aims. As I was to discover, Xanthia was a conduit for a sinister agenda.

XANTHIA'S STORY

Xanthia was a waif-like woman with long black hair, very pale skin, and sad blue eyes. She was a Celtic beauty; only the sadness in her eyes dimmed her light. Xanthia was from Ireland and was visiting relatives in South Africa. In her lilting accent, she told me she had been to see a Catholic priest in Ireland who had deemed her possessed but was unable to help her release the possessing entity. Xanthia looked so fragile; I hoped I could assist her in some way.

Xanthia described her connection with an entity she called Red, which appeared as a bright neon red light and told her what to do. She explained that Red was almost constantly with her. Some of Red's instructions were inspired, but sometimes the guidance was destructive. Xanthia feared that she was possessed and wanted to be free of Red. She seemed sincere in wanting to release this destabilizing association.

At first, I suspected that Xanthia might be suffering from schizophrenia or some other mental illness. But when I went into her energy field, I immediately felt Red's presence. Several of my spirit guides formed a protective circle around me, warning me to be careful, and Melchior hovered overhead, poised for swift interception. I realized that Red was no mere entity but a powerful being from the astral planes, what some might call a demon with a distinct consciousness. In that moment of realization, Xanthia gripped my arm, sat up, and screamed right into my face. Her eyes were glowing bright red. Cold fear flooded my heart, and my vibration plummeted. What happened next was like a scene out of a horror movie.

Chapter 6 | Initiation

Xanthia jumped off the bed and started flailing about on the floor, yelling in a deep-throated voice that was not her own. Red was showing himself. Doing my best to remain calm, I knew that I would not be able to exorcise Red with my vibration having dropped so low. His energy was way too powerful.

Backed into a corner, I called on my healing team to assist. Almost instantly, a powerful energy surged into my solar plexus. At the same time, I felt myself growing taller, and my energy expanded into the room. Impulsively, I held my arms out like wings, and light streamed out of my hands, which felt as if they had become double the size exactly as they had when I was called to do the blessing over the decimated Navajo village, only this time the foe was right in front of me. In that moment, I realized that the dragon of fear had become my ally and was working through me to dissolve the demon's power. As this potent energy surged through me and blasted the demon, I was totally attuned with the dragon. Never have I experienced such potency, and, in that moment, I was utterly fearless in the face of the demon. Channeling dragon energy for what felt like several minutes but was probably only seconds, I harnessed the power of the dragon to banish the demon.

With spiritual authority that flowed from my entire healing team, I commanded Red to leave. With this, a neon red light shot out of Xanthia like a flame, and she crumpled to the floor. When I helped her up, she had a glazed look, and it was apparent that she had little recollection of what had transpired. I filled her in and, after stabilizing her energy, brought the session to a merciful close.

When Xanthia left my healing room, I was in a state of shock. Despite the dragon's assistance, it was a harrowing experience. Like a foolhardy initiate, I had ventured into dangerous territory. There are indeed demons among us. My energy field—and my confidence—was in tatters after my close-up encounter with one. I was extremely fortunate to have the dragon-as-ally. As Diana Cooper noted: "There are things that dragons can do, that angels cannot, for they can delve into deep, dense matter and dissolve it."[14]

---

14 Diana Cooper, *Dragons: Your Celestial Guardians* (United Kingdom: Hay House UK, 2018).

As luck would have it—or perhaps it was divine timing—the day after the session with Xanthia, I went on a four-day silent retreat at a spiritual center in the mountains. The retreat was a safe haven where I could lick my wounds and find my equilibrium. By the time I got home, I felt centered and calm again, but it was a long road to restore my confidence.

The encounter with the demon was a pivotal turning point. It also marked the beginning of my exit from the world of dark energy. From that moment forth, I screened every single prospective client before booking an appointment. By tuning into the energy of an email or phone call, I assessed the client's energy and turned away the heavyweights.

Every time a dark energy client walked into my healing room, the dragon of fear simmered. Over the next six months, I slowly regained confidence and realized that the cold hand of fear, which had so often gripped my heart, no longer had a hold on me. Instead, I smiled at the simmering dragon. Within a few months, I had the confidence to deal with anything that came my way—the weird and the wonderful—and to trust my instincts when the going got tough. I like to think that, along the way, I also helped many of my clients escape the quagmire of darkness.

TEACHINGS FROM THE DARKNESS

Everything comes into our field for a reason, but it took time to understand the teachings and integrate the lessons of the Dark Energy Intensive. The final initiation with the demon was undoubtedly an experience of dragon-as-ally rather than dragon-as-adversary. Through that terrifying experience, I had befriended the dragon. Having a demon elicit this next-level initiation only goes to show how, at times, the darkness serves the light.

Tough as it had been, the Dark Energy Intensive was a Teacher with a capital T. It was undoubtedly an initiation to overcome my fear, but I learned so much more along the way. At every level, I had to up my game considerably. The gifts from the darkness were manifold.

Chapter 6 | Initiation

The journey of a healer is all about stepping out of the comfort zone, not once, not twice, but continually. It requires inner work and a willingness to look in the mirror at every turn. In my healing room, I had a glittering silver-white mosaic mirror to remind myself that the lessons, and the gifts, are embedded in the reflection.

The spiritual Law of Reflection states that every single person or situation in life is a mirror of an aspect of ourselves. This is how we learn. This spiritual law reminds us to look in the mirror and discover what's hidden in the deepest recesses. As within, so without; the outside world reflects the inner world, ceaselessly presenting the lessons if we care to look within.

Demanding as it was, the Dark Energy Intensive taught me that everything comes into our field because we need to experience, learn, or resolve something. Like magnets with many facets, we magnetize both like-vibration and that which vibrates at the frequency of this deeper need. This is the Law of Attraction at its most subtle. If we are willing to peer into the shadows, there are always revelations. Spiritual law begged the question, what was the Dark Energy Intensive reflecting for me? What was the attractor point within me calling in this experience? The common thread with all my dark energy clients was fear. Overcoming fear was what I had to master.

The journey of a healer is a path of mastery, guided by spiritual law. This is the true quest. Peering into the looking glass of self-reflection cannot be avoided. Uncomfortable as it was, I had to look at the role of my own shadow in attracting the Dark Energy Intensive. This meant delving into every nook and cranny of my being and surfacing the shadows. The years of working with dark energy revealed so much of myself and was an opportunity, once again, to lighten my load.

While the years of transformational work with Frieda and Kate had been deeply healing, this initiation thrust me into the next level of purification. Where the dragon of anger had dogged me in my earlier work, now it was deep-seated fear—specifically, a terrible fear of the occult. With the help of a colleague who regressed me to the original horrifying ordeal at the heart of this deeply buried fear, I was finally able to clear its long-lasting hold over me.

There were other gifts too. With so much at stake, my intuitive senses had become finely tuned through the crucible of dark energy work, and I had developed a wolfish instinct for the traps and pitfalls in the invisible world. I also crafted a dictionary of signs and symbols that helped me navigate this territory and understand its inhabitants. I became much more proficient in transmuting energy and holding a solid space for my clients in the healing room.

My psychic antenna outside the healing room was also more finely tuned. I learned to tell instantly when there was active interference in my energy field. Sometimes I could feel an outside energy coming toward my field before it even entered my aura. This heightened awareness was ultimately the best protection. The more quickly I could pick up interference, the easier it was to clear or avoid altogether.

Over the years, I had learned many ways to protect my energy field, most of which involved putting layers of high-frequency light in various configurations around the aura to create an energetic buffer zone. Going through the initiation, I gained a far more nuanced understanding of protection. Put simply, I learned that creating a protection field from a place of fear simply does not work. It is like having a bucket full of holes. You keep filling it, but the water will just run out, leaving the bucket empty. One of the principles of energy work is *never leave a void*. Energy will always move to fill a void, so it's best to fix the leaky bucket!

The aura is an electromagnetic field and attracts like frequencies. If your aura is weak, thin, or full of holes, then external energies, including other people's negative thoughts and emotions, dark energies, and even viruses, are more likely to affect you. On the other hand, if your aura is strong and full of light, it acts as a shield in repelling lower vibrational energy. The light of a healthy aura will automatically dissolve lower vibrational energy of whatever kind and may even transmute denser energy in a space just by its presence.

Chapter 6 | Initiation

The best protection is a high vibration and strong inner light. It's one thing to put layers of light around your aura to keep it strong and healthy. This does help. However, the power of the light around your aura emanates from within. You can protect yourself with energetic buffers until the cows come home, but if your inner light is weak and your energetic boundaries are porous, the protection will be partial, at best, and will likely not last.

My quest throughout the Dark Energy Intensive was to transmute that hole-inducing fear and strengthen my inner light. Every morning I imagined myself holding the lantern of Source light high before entering the darkness. I visualized my healing room as a beacon of light, knowing that the dark energies would be drawn by the light, but if my lantern were burning brightly enough, the light would always win out.

In a dualistic dimension, there is both shadow and light in constant flux. Every situation has the potential for polarity. Sometimes, energy will be polarized toward the dark, and shadows lengthen. However, we are not always aware of the shadows we have encountered in this life and others that remain buried deep in our unconscious mind and energy field. Dark energy work is the great ouster for bringing shadows and secrets to the surface. With few exceptions, facing these shadowy places initiated a transformative healing journey for my clients.

Beyond learning new skills in working with dark energy, there were deeper questions to unravel. One of the recurring questions during the Dark Energy Intensive was why some people are vulnerable to spirit attachment or psychic attack and others are not. This was the subject of much discussion within my healing circles. One colleague remarked that psychic attack is just a projection of the client's shadow. I thought long and hard about this and concluded that she was both right and wrong. I didn't agree that psychic attacks are merely a projection. I had witnessed firsthand many a dark-art dabbler sending negative energy missiles into their victim's energy fields. However, my colleague was right in the sense that there was always a hook, a corresponding shadow in the victim's psyche that allowed an attack. By way of analogy, it's a bit like having an energetic docking station for an external device.

In more complex cases, there might be a deeper entanglement between the two souls involved. As we approach an era of higher consciousness, we are gathering all the karmic cords, all the entanglements, to untangle and free ourselves from the old stories so that we can evolve. And herein lies the crux of the issue. We cannot judge appearances. Light and dark often work together to bring balance. This is the spiritual Law of Balance and Polarity in action.

For this reason, it is so important to remain non-judgmental and compassionate when confronting the shadow. Compassion, however, is a frequently misunderstood concept. Tibetan Buddhist teacher Chögyam Trungpa Rinpoche coined the term *idiot compassion*, which has since been popularized by Pema Chodron in her acclaimed writings. Idiot compassion is a sentimental variety of compassion, which is often more about diving in to rescue someone from their suffering rather than offering genuine compassion. Idiot compassion seeks to avoid the discomfort of witnessing suffering and isn't really compassion at all.

Genuine compassion does not judge the human condition or the suffering. It offers kindness and care without seeking to rescue. This is possibly one of the most difficult lessons for the healer archetype. The Buddhist notion of *wise compassion* offers guidance on this point. Wise compassion extends loving-kindness to all beings without judgment about their situation or choices. There is an implicit understanding that there are invariably multiple—and multi-temporal—forces at play in every situation.

Working with dark energies deepened my grasp of wise compassion. Remaining non-judgmental in the face of the forces of darkness was an ultimate challenge but also invaluable to facilitating a lasting resolution. Dealing with psychic attacks had stretched me to the limits of my capacity for wise compassion. To wield malicious power from the shadows seemed to me like the height of cowardice. My inner judge was particularly disgruntled by the psychic attacks that emanated from within spiritual or shamanic circles. Time and again, I had to sit with the discomfort of these judgments and find a higher perspective. Who was I to judge someone's path or the pace of their growth?

In the end, it was humbling to realize that the only thing for me to do for my clients was to offer a higher perspective, a vision for someone's highest potential, and then hold a compassionate space for their healing process. This was a more masterful type of ethics than I had previously known.

With power comes responsibility, and even more so in the world of energy. Working with dark energy, in particular, refined my understanding of integrity and ethics. My time in the trenches highlighted the necessity of accredited training, where ethical codes of conduct are drummed into every aspirant healer. The salient points from a healer's code of conduct are:

- Always work from the heart—not the ego. This means that non-judgment and compassion are important no matter the context of healing.
- Always hold the intention to work in the light for the highest good of all parties.
- Never work on another person's energy field without their permission.
- Never send negative energy to another being—this goes against spiritual law.

This code of conduct for healers is the equivalent of the Hippocratic Oath for doctors, and qualified lightworkers take it just as seriously. However, I had seen how in the *good fight* against the dark forces, it was easy for the lines to get blurred.

In the cauldron of the Dark Energy Intensive, I came to understand that there can be no compromise when it comes to bargaining with the dark forces. Though I had been trained to engage in psychic warfare, in the end, I subscribed to Faye's view that we should never be tempted to trade like for like—tit for tat. This was Machiavellian thinking, and the end does not justify the means.

No matter how noble the aims, dark energy work operates in a third-dimensional matrix. For two years, I observed the dynamics of psychic warfare closely and felt that these power struggles belonged to an outmoded way of working for the light. I wanted to find another way. I knew my real work was fifth-dimensional. It was time for me to seek a higher path in every aspect of my healing work.

THE DEEPEST TREASURE

After two grueling years, The Dark Energy Intensive finally came to an end. All in all, it was a time of accelerated learning and overcoming inner obstacles on my journey as a healer. I was profoundly grateful to my inner warrior for rising to the challenge, but it was time to put the sword down.

My fear dragon had been guarding a deeply buried treasure. Like all true initiations, this period honed my instincts and initiated a higher level of consciousness. It was also an incredibly humbling experience, one in which I felt my frailties, faced my fears, witnessed my ego, and, through it all, had been guided and protected in miraculous ways. I came through it with a far more nuanced grasp of the world of energy. I also gained a close-knit group of like-minded colleagues, who became important spiritual allies and loyal friends for my journey onward.

Facing the dragon of fear had forged a new path. In the furnace of its fire-breath, the dragon of fear, so terrifying at first, had helped me dissolve a deeply buried soul wound. Despite my wariness, I had a newfound respect for the dragon and an unexpected ally in holding the lantern aloft in the dark.

With the benefit of hindsight, I understood that my soul had signed up for the dark energy work so that I could face my latent fear of the occult and step into my power as a lightworker. From this perspective, Xanthia was an unlikely spiritual ally. She presented me with the most extreme challenge I would ever face in my healing work, but she was undoubtedly the catalyst for the next step on my soul path.

Chapter 6 | Initiation

DRAGON'S GOLD
Wisdom teachings from Chapter Six

- What is happening at the soul level and in the invisible world is often more real than what appears in the visible world. What we see in the energy body, beyond the veil of ego and persona, is often closer to the truth than what is presented in the surface-world.

- The spiritual Law of Reflection states that every single person or situation in life is a mirror of an aspect of ourselves. If you are a healer, it is especially important to look in the mirror with unwavering honesty and confront the reflections. This is the true quest on the path of self-mastery and soul evolution.

- Among spiritual seekers, the need for a guru is compelling. While a guru may offer high-level knowledge or guidance, it's important to be discerning about the teacher and the teachings. Excessive attachment to a guru creates unhealthy entanglements and blinds you to hidden agendas. This invariably results in a loss of power.

- Always be aware of how you wield your mental power and never intentionally do harm to another. If you work with energy, this principle is especially important. Working with energy carries enormous responsibility. According to spiritual law, using energy to initiate change carries exponentially more karmic effect than any other action.

- Never interfere with free will. As a healer, or seer, you might give warning when a client insists on a dangerous path, but it is important to respect their choice. Genuine respect doesn't judge the path. Your client, or friend, might need to learn from an experience, and we shouldn't disrupt soul lessons, even if we think we know better.

- Energetic protection is multi-faceted. Most methods involve putting layers of high-frequency light in various configurations around the aura to create a protective buffer zone. While useful, this method has limited effect. For example, protection from a place of fear is not very effective. If you are emitting a vibration of fear, you'll be attracting like-frequencies. Ultimately, the best protection is to raise your frequency and strengthen your inner light. A strong inner light will automatically repel lower vibrational energy of whatever kind and may even transmute denser energy in a space just by your presence.

7

LIGHT

2012 – 2017

> When I teach, I am only trying to bring those who are willing to the River of Light, where we can drink and look at each other through awakened eyes.
>
> – Mark Nepo, author of *Drinking from the River of Light*

The end of 2012 was a turning point in my story. It was also a pivotal shift point for the planet. The Cosmic Moment on December 21, 2012, heralded the start of a rapid transition toward higher consciousness. The Cosmic Moment was the culmination of a ten-day window from December 12 (12/12/12) to December 21 (12/21/12), known as the Ascension Gateway, during which the planet was flooded with high-frequency light to initiate an accelerated Ascension process.

Ascension is an evolutionary process of ascending to a higher level of consciousness and energetic frequency. The Ascension Gateway was a portal for cosmic light rays containing evolutionary intelligence, or light codes, to propel a mass awakening that is currently gathering momentum and will continue until 2032. This process was initiated in 1987 with the Harmonic Convergence, but the Cosmic Moment saw its intensification. Since the Cosmic Moment, continual light transmissions have supported our awakening. In the process of Ascension, light beings from other dimensions and more advanced worlds are helping us to ascend to a higher level of consciousness. As we integrate the higher energies, many more people are awakening spiritually and psychically.

The Cosmic Moment in December 2012 was a general call to humanity to evolve and a clarion call to lightworkers to wake up and get with the collective program of ushering in fifth-dimensional consciousness for this plane of existence. This is what lightworkers are here for right now. At a personal level, the changes in my life since the Cosmic Moment have been profound and reinforced my intention to move away from the dark energy work. I wasn't sure how this would happen, but I reset my sights on my real work of raising vibration and anchoring higher consciousness in my sphere of influence.

As it turned out, the Cosmic Moment in December 2012 was the beginning of the next seven-year cycle on my journey, during which the hidden pathways to three significant vibratory notes were revealed.

TOWARD THE FIFTH DIMENSION

One way of understanding the Ascension process is that humanity is progressing from third-dimensional to fifth-dimensional consciousness. We can understand dimensions as energy zones that vibrate within a particular frequency range that correlates with states of consciousness, awareness, and perception.

For example, in the Third Dimension, fear is the vibrational keynote. In this vibrational matrix, energies such as anger, greed, and envy flourish. In the Fifth Dimension, love is the vibrational keynote, and qualities of consciousness such as generosity, kindness, and compassion prevail. At a fifth-dimensional frequency, spiritual values inform our relationships and guide our choices.

The Third Dimension is tethered to the material world, where survival and security are of paramount concern. At this level of consciousness, ego-based awareness gives rise to materialistic values and self-interested behavior. We adhere to external power structures and behaviors such as control, competition, and domination. Patriarchy itself, as an expression of masculine dominance, is a third-dimensional power structure. In this paradigm, separation consciousness regulates relationships between individuals, cultures, and nations, and between humans and nature.

The Fifth Dimension co-exists with the material world and incorporates the spiritual world. In this dimension, we view ourselves as spiritual beings. This shift gives rise to spiritual values and collaborative behavior. We are guided by internal sources of power and reach for the more feminine principles of connection, cooperation, and creativity. In this paradigm, unity consciousness regulates relationships between people, cultures, and countries, and with Gaia, our Earth Mother.

The progression from the Third to the Fifth Dimension is, in essence, a shift from ego-based awareness to soul-based awareness, from separation consciousness to unity consciousness. With this shift in consciousness, our paradigms are changing too. We are moving away from patriarchy, in which masculine energies dominate, toward a greater balance between masculine and feminine energies. Our beliefs in a mechanistic universe, governed by Newtonian science, Cartesian principles, and linear causality, are slowly being replaced by the new science, which sees the Universe as a conscious entity where everything is interconnected. Exploration of the quantum universe is changing our understanding of the very nature of reality and our role in co-creating this reality. As we move into the fifth-dimensional paradigm, we are beginning to understand Unity or Oneness consciousness in more visceral ways and feel more directly that we really are all connected. There is a growing shift toward experiencing ourselves and others as aspects of Source energy that is changing interpersonal attitudes and behaviors.

How we operate as fifth-dimensional beings is changing too. Our perception is expanding beyond the five senses to include the non-physical world and a much broader range of sensory awareness. Intuition, for example, is becoming a valid means of knowing. We are becoming multi-sensory, transrational beings, using more than the rational mind to perceive and interpret reality. In becoming more intuitive, we are connecting with multi-temporal experience—jumping timelines will become a normal way of being rather than something unusual or weird.

As we transition into the Fifth Dimension, we will engage more consciously with the role of thoughts, beliefs, and attitudes in creating our experience. It will become common knowledge that consciousness radiates out into the Universe and attracts like energy. Every thought we have is an energetic projection. This mental energy is a frequency that we emit first into our personal auric field and then out into the quantum field, and there it is replicated. How we project thought and frequency into the world is then reflected back to us. Repetition of thoughts, words, and actions magnifies the energy, increasing the power to create and manifest in alignment with the projections. Whether conscious or not, repetition of a particular frequency creates a vibrational groove or pathway that allows energy to return to us. Imprinting the quantum field with a strong frequency through repetitive thought is the equivalent of leaving psychic footprints and asking something to come back along this vibrational pathway to manifest in physical form. It is much like sending out an energetic request. As fifth-dimensional beings, we will become much more conscious and conscientious about how we wield this power of request and manifestation for the highest good.

Currently, we are in a bridging phase between the Third and Fifth Dimensions, between ego-based and soul-based awareness. An evolutionary process of this magnitude takes time. It is a gradual ascension into a higher frequency and consciousness, much like a collective upgrade that is rolled out in phases. Although gradual, it is not a smooth transition; it is more like a push and pull, lurching in fits and starts toward an undefined new identity as a species. Not everyone wants things to change, and like tectonic plates shifting before they come to rest, there is much turbulence and chaos as the world slowly turns. This is not a comfortable process by any measure.

In this collective discomfort, each of us has a choice—either we can become totally overwhelmed and fearful, or we can be part of *creating* the Fifth Dimension. Choosing the path of co-creating our fifth-dimensional reality is nothing short of an evolutionary choice to become awakened humans. As the gateways opened, my personal choice was to start teaching others about this new paradigm and the New Earth that we were being invited to co-create.

Chapter 7 | Light

Since the beginning of 2012, I had been teaching energy management courses as a tutor for the School of Intuition and Healing. Now my spirit guides were spurring me on to develop my own courses and break away from the school. Again, the message was clear. I had to spread my wings and fly solo. Not for nothing had I gone through the muddy waters of initiation and its teachings, and it was time to pass on this knowledge.

Building on my healing work, I started teaching people how to work with their light bodies and raise their frequency. This was groundwork for the evolutionary changes that were already gathering momentum. The more we prepare the energetic ground, as it were, the faster the evolutionary process will take root. From the beginning of 2013, my teaching expanded significantly, and I was able to invite many more seekers to "drink from the river of light" as Mark Nepo so poetically stated.[15]

As the courses grew in popularity, my spirit guides reminded me not to lose sight of the bigger picture of my soul mission to contribute toward anchoring higher frequencies and rolling out the red carpet for the awakened human. After what I had just been through during the Dark Energy Intensive, I felt I still had a long way to go! I was still returning from the abyss and integrating the teachings from the darkness.

A SOUL HELPER APPEARS

At the beginning of this new cycle, Sullivan arrived in my healing room. Little did I know it then, but this soft-spoken man was to play a pivotal role in the shift that was about to happen in my work.

Sullivan was a devout seeker and influential social entrepreneur in Cape Town. Despite his success, he was at a crossroads in his life and wanted to explore his soul path further. The first time I entered his energy field, we went on a spontaneous journey together. I received a vivid vision in which the two of us were sitting in a cave, surrounded by gold coins lying on the ground. In this scenario, he was my teacher, and I

---

[15] Mark Nepo, *Drinking from the River of Light: The Life of Expression* (USA: Sounds True, 2019).

was a novice at his feet, learning the art of spiritual alchemy. He was counting the gold coins, carefully stacking them in neat piles, before placing them in a large treasure chest. The chest was labeled *Souls*, and together we were sorting out the tarnished coins and gathering the gold ones. In the vision, Sullivan said:

> Be careful of ego. I am a guardian of souls, and you, the healer. We can fall prey to the glamour of power. Equally, you can be misled by your call to service. You can't help everyone. See those dull coins lying there amongst the gold coins? Leave them. These are the souls that deliberately stay in the dark. Pick your coins carefully. Go for the gold and guide those souls to the light.

With this, Sullivan shut the chest lid and beamed at me. Lesson delivered.

At the end of the session, I shared the vision I had received with my new client. We looked at each other for a long time before he spoke. "Everything you do is karma," he said gently. "Even helping people. Especially helping people. Choose wisely."

Then he stood up and left.

Soul helpers show up in many guises. For the rest of the year, Sullivan came for energy healing every month. Although I helped him along his path, his role in bolstering my intention to change course was undoubtedly an important part of our work together. Without my asking, he referred a steady stream of clients to me from his extensive network. First, there was a trickle and then a flood of new clients that I could barely keep up with. Everyone was in awe of Sullivan, and I began to get a glimpse of the power and generosity of this quiet, unassuming man of few words who, despite his warning to me about the karmic implications of helping people, was being an active helper in his own way.

CALIFORNIA TEACHINGS

Shortly after meeting Sullivan, I was called to do a training with Denise Whitefeather Linn in California. Part Cherokee herself, Denise is a well-known author and spiritual teacher in the United States. Over the years,

I had read some of her books and even attended one of her workshops in London in the early nineties. She was a significant teacher on my path.

When I say called, it was more like being summonsed. It was one of those epiphanous moments when there is absolutely no doubt that Spirit is at work. Checking my email one day, Denise's newsletter caught my eye. I had been getting her newsletters for years, but something made me pause and read this one more carefully: her residential training program for Soul Coaching® certification was open for bookings. I felt a mounting excitement, and then a rush of wind went right through me, leaving me tingling all over. It was a windless day, with not a breath of wind coming through the open window. This had happened to me only once before when Liam was born, and his name was given to me by my grandmother's spirit in a similar rush of wind. These are moments not to be ignored!

The cost of the residential training and a return flight to California was way more than I could afford. Nevertheless, knowing the ways of Spirit, I booked for the course and paid the deposit on my credit card. Within three days, I had raised the money and booked my flight to Los Angeles. I didn't know it then, but the trip to California would signal the definitive end of doing dark energy work.

Before the Dark Energy Intensive, I had been through a thoroughgoing process of connecting with my Native American past and soul roots as a shamanic healer. Unfortunately, that lifetime was steeped in pain, and I had been saddled with a disempowering vow never to be a shaman again. Although I had done the work to clear this painful lifetime and release the vow, there was one more piece to complete—I had to close the door to my shamanic past and source my power as a healer from elsewhere. Quite unexpectedly, Denise Whitefeather Linn's training, and the soul tribe that gathered at her home at Summerhill Ranch, was the portal to connect me with a more powerful aspect of my soul lineage eight centuries earlier in medieval France. It was here that I found my gold. The dragon was at work again!

When I arrived at Summerhill Ranch, our group of twenty from all over the world gathered in a circle. Denise welcomed us and said that each of us had been called to this training—again, the silent wind brushed my arms. Next, she blessed us with a Native American prayer in her family's native tongue. My heart swelled at the sound of the Cherokee language. There I was on the other side of the world on unfamiliar ground in California, feeling like I had finally come home.

The souls that had gathered at Summerhill Ranch were healers, shamans, or lightworkers of one kind or another. The training was intense and invigorating. Just as intense were the quickly forged bonds with the rest of the group. We were twenty strangers from multiple cultures, yet there was a sense of closeness and belonging that I had seldom experienced. There were deep connections and wonderful conversations late into the night.

At the end of the first week, we had a small feast to celebrate the work we had completed so far. Denise's philosophy was that life should be a celebration, a conscious choice to live joyfully. Flamboyant yet entirely authentic, Denise embodied joy; in this, she was a spiritual teacher of the highest order.

Our celebratory feast started off ordinarily enough, laughing and chatting about our experiences at Summerhill. Even though we had only met a week before, the shared warmth and joy were palpable, like a gathering of long-lost friends. Everyone was part of the joy that flowed like wine; only there wasn't any wine. And then, as if we were swept up together on a wave of joy, we found ourselves in another time.

In one incandescent moment, the veils parted, and we were sitting at a long wooden table in a cellar. The laughter and joy were flowing just as strongly, only in that time, we were meeting in secret. This clandestine rendezvous was a meeting of Cathars in medieval France at a time when persecution by the Roman Catholic church was at its height.[16] Although a dangerous time, the joy of seeing each other after years of separation overrode the fear we must have felt. The joy

---

[16] The Cathars were a Gnostic religious group in southern France, which flourished in the twelfth century. The term Cathar comes from the Greek *katharos* which means 'pure', alluding to their simple form of Christianity, free of the hierarchies and ornate rituals of Catholicism. Deemed as heretics by the increasingly powerful Catholic Church in Rome, the Cathars were systematically persecuted and ultimately eliminated during the Albigensian Crusade (1209-1229) in the early thirteenth century.

between us was so intense that every cell in my body was shimmering as we raised stone mugs and offered thanks for our protection. Just then, someone entered a door at the far end of the room, and the table fell quiet. A trusted messenger, he stretched out his arms in greeting. From across the room, his eyes searched for mine. And there, through the brief parting of the veils, I caught a glimpse of my future husband, a tall man I would meet exactly a year later.

As the vision receded, the magical energy of the feast slowly faded. Emerging from this trance-like experience, we looked at each other with shining eyes, a quiet hush around the long table at Summerhill Ranch. Denise was smiling knowingly as if to say: "You see, the mystery is all around us." She was a past master at creating magic.

Afterward, we all agreed something mystical had happened. Without exception, each of us had experienced the parting of the veils and the escalation of joy in the room. The magical feast—as we started calling it—had been an immersion in the vibration of joy, powerful medicine that each one of us imbibed with delight. In the coming days, I realized that this was the teaching I had come to receive—not the training or new qualification. I was here to retrieve the vibration of joy—the first of three vibratory notes to be revealed in the next seven-year cycle that would take my healing work to the next level. I also realized that the magical feast had opened a portal to my soul roots as a Cathar *parfait* from which I would learn to source my healing work.[17] This was a much deeper soul rooting than my Native American lifetime and one that would keep me anchored into who I really am and attuned to the light work I am here to do.

In addition to this transformative vibrational shift, my journey as a healer also took a significant turn. This was helped along, in no small way, by Wyndham, one of the students at Summerhill Ranch.

---

[17] The Cathars described themselves as Bon Hommes, meaning Good Christians. The Cathar priests (men and women) were called Parfaits (literally perfects), meaning Perfect Christians. In the Cathar faith, there were no churches or formal structures, and the Parfaits served as travelling priests and priestesses, going from village to village to share their gospel-based teachings.

ANOTHER SOUL HELPER ON THE PATH

Wyndham was a mystic who was to become a significant wayshower for the next few years of my life. When we met at Summerhill Ranch, one of the first things he said to me was that I had to change direction and extricate myself from the work I was doing. Fixing me with his steady gaze, he said, "Stop working with those who seek a release from the dark, and work with those who are actively seeking the light."

Wyndham's words hit me like a lightning bolt. Since my experience with Xanthia, I had been more discerning about the clients I took on, but still, dark energy clients found their way to my door. Although I had set an intention to change tack, I had been unable to stem the flow of dark energies completely. Believing myself to be in service to Divine Will, I dutifully did the work. Wyndham taught me that I could choose not only the type of work I wanted to do but also my clients. He said that *being of service* and accepting everything that came my way was an outdated program. I had the right, and the power, to choose. This was an extremely important lesson in spiritual boundaries.

Wyndham taught me a few tricks to create stronger spiritual boundaries and change the tide. First and foremost, I had to set an intention to work only with those actively seeking the light rather than with those seeking a release from the dark. Until then, I hadn't seen my work in these terms and realized this is an important distinction. The second step was reinforcing my new intention, so Wyndham taught me a simple visualization to call in the light seekers.

On our last day at Summerhill Ranch, Wyndham offered the whole group a vision of our soul work. Even though we would be operating from all corners of the globe, we had a group mission to raise humanity's collective vibration and consciousness. Bonded through the vibration of joy, we would continue to journey together in some way. Still in trance, Wyndham gave each one of us a power animal that would guide us on our individual paths. Mine was the Albatross. I was surprised that it wasn't the dragon. Perhaps I had thrown the dragon off my trail!

Chapter 7 | Light

Wyndham explained that the Albatross has a huge wingspan and an extraordinary ability to fly long distances without pause. This was an auspicious totem indeed, though not at all what I expected. For someone who constantly needed grounding, flying around the world didn't exactly resonate with me. It was not until the end of the decade, nearly seven years later, that the Albatross appeared again and took flight in my life. But I'm getting ahead of my story.

MAGICAL FLIGHT

When I returned to South Africa at the end of May, my heart was full. Flying eastward from Los Angeles with the setting sun, the pilot kept low over desert country for nearly an hour, gifting us with breathtaking views of the Grand Canyon and Navajo country below. I felt at once deeply connected to my Native American roots and ready to let go of that long-ago lifetime. It was not my story anymore. Only when it got dark did we ascend to 30,000 feet, and I was left pondering the magic that had happened in California. Surrendering to the long journey ahead, I silently offered thanks for the teachings from Denise Whitefeather Linn, from Wyndham, and from the inspirational group that had assembled at Summerhill Ranch.

Coming into land in Istanbul the next morning, we were held in an interminable holding pattern. We circled around the city for nearly an hour. Looking down over the scenic Bosphorus channel and the Black Sea, I realized with astonishment that I could see the exact spot where I had experienced something traumatic as a young woman that I had completely forgotten.

Toward the end of my Paranormal Gap Year, my travels took me to Turkey, where I stayed with a Turkish friend's family in Istanbul. From this home base, I explored the city and its scenic surrounds. One of my forays was a boat trip up the Bosphorus Strait to the Black Sea. At the end of the waterway, I disembarked at a little village and hiked up the hill to enjoy the spectacular views from the cliffs overlooking the Black Sea. With my attention focused on the seascape, I didn't notice a man in a soldier's uniform approaching until it was too late. He grabbed my shoulder from behind and roughly swung me around. Tapping his gun holster threateningly, he shoved me against the low stone wall at the edge of the cliff. His intentions were clear. I called on my angels to protect me as he tore at my shirt. Just then, another soldier appeared further up the hill and shouted what sounded like an order in Turkish. My attacker swore and shoved me to the ground but left me unharmed. I picked myself up and ran headlong down the hill toward the village. Seeing a little church, I bolted inside. I huddled in the quiet darkness, shaking like a leaf, until finally, I regained my composure just in time to catch the last boat back to Istanbul.

Recalling this event more than twenty years later, I instinctively poured protective light around my younger self. From the vantage point of the plane, I could see clearly where the second soldier must have stood yelling at his miscreant colleague. I imagined him there and thanked him for his timely intervention. I shuddered to think what might have happened had he not chosen to act in my defense. From above, I felt like an angel in the skies looking out for my younger self. And then it dawned on me—what if I was the angel that my younger self had called for at the time? What if the protection I was sending back in time had reached me then in the form of the soldier at the top of the hill who had come to my aid? I had worked with enough past lives to understand how elastic time can be. I just hadn't thought about a future self being able to give assistance to a past self in this way.

This was a revelation to me. The implication was that it is possible for your future older self to change the outcome of an event experienced by your younger self and have a profound impact on the trajectory of your life. In other words, intentional energy can go backward and forwards in time. I wondered how I might apply this principle in the present. If we can affect an outcome in the past, then perhaps we can also go forward in time to create change in our current experience. Could I use this elasticity of time to strengthen my intention to change the direction of my work? It was worth a try!

On the next leg of the journey home, I visualized my future self: the dark energy work was a thing of the past; I was working with clients who were actively seeking the light; the vibration of joy I had experienced in California was reverberating through my life. Above all, my future self was deeply peaceful. This turned out to be a prophetic vision.

ENTER THE LIGHT SEEKERS

Back in South Africa, I was ready to start my work with the light seekers. Without delay, I told all my referral networks that I would not be doing any dark energy cases, no matter how urgent. I communicated with my guides and healing team that from now on, I would only work with clients who were actively seeking the light. To reinforce this message, I did the visualization Wyndham had taught me and energized my intention every single day. My messaging to the Universe was loud and clear.

My part of the bargain was to stand firm, despite the wobbles about the financial implications of my new spiritual boundaries. I could hardly afford a drop in income, especially now that I had a sizeable loan to repay, but I needn't have worried. Over the next few months, I watched in wonder as my clientele changed, like a large ship turning around in the ocean. After an initial dip, my healing practice grew in leaps and bounds. Sullivan played his part without ever being asked, sending more light seekers my way. Somehow, he had got the memo. Within six months, I was busier than ever before and had more energy—for my family and clients—because I wasn't awake half the night, keeping wandering spirits at bay.

Soon after I got back from California, a striking African woman called Celeste, with long braided hair and bangle-covered arms, turned up in my healing room. A local *sangoma*, Celeste had heard about me from one of her clients and booked an appointment out of curiosity more than anything else. When Celeste arrived in my healing room, I was immediately struck by the light in her aura. My guides said she was an *angelic presence*. There wasn't much I could offer Celeste that day, but her visit undoubtedly helped me. Although I have no proof, I am convinced that Celeste opened a portal for my new work, blessing the path for more light seekers to find me.

From then on, I never looked back. I joked that Spirit—aka my healing team—organized my diary. If someone canceled, there was always a corresponding need, either for an emergency appointment or overdue *me-time*. I learned to trust this mysterious ebb and flow. As Wyndham had predicted, as soon as I sent out a clear message, the light seekers found me. Many of these new clients were lightworkers of some sort, and by helping them, the ripple effects, like silent butterfly wings, indirectly touched multitudes of others. It was richly rewarding knowing that many of these clients would go on to help countless others through their own work. Supporting this rippling wave of consciousness was my true calling, and I dived in joyfully.

In the coming years, I worked with hundreds of light seekers. With their thirst for the light, the results of our healing work together were usually profound. Sometimes the results were immediately visible, and sometimes they took years to show. It was always heart-warming when I got to see the results of slow fermentation, as in the case of a spiritual seeker called Alice.

ALICE'S STORY

Alice worked in the fashion industry but felt called to a higher purpose. She thought it had something to do with plants but wasn't sure. Like many spiritual seekers, the call to purpose had taken her into the world of hallucinogenic plant medicine—Ayahuasca and San Pedro were the current vogue in South Africa. By the time Alice came to see me, she was deeply immersed in medicinal ceremonies, her plants of choice being Ayahuasca and an African plant called Iboga. Ayahuasca, she informed me, opened the pineal gland, and activated higher awareness, while Iboga opened the heart. I listened carefully, wondering why she needed me if plant medicine was her chosen path to the light?

When I started the energy work, it soon became clear. Alice's crown chakra was completely blown, leaving a kind of hollow void, and her third eye chakra, which is related to the pineal gland, was whirling like a vortex, drawing in way too much energy. The rest of her chakras were spinning haphazardly, in different directions, and much too fast. On top of this chakric mayhem, Alice's aura was thin and porous, and her energy scattered. It was hard to find her center.

Energetically, it was a dangerous state of affairs. It was not dissimilar to the effects of recreational drugs; the only difference, as far as I could tell, was in the intent.

I set about repairing Alice's blown crown chakra and stabilizing her system. It would take a few sessions before I could ground her. I cautioned her about the destabilizing effects of hallucinogenic plants and suggested that there were less risky, albeit possibly slower, pathways to higher consciousness.

Despite my cautions, Alice was reluctant to give up her explorative journey with hallucinogenic plants. While I respected her wishes, I suggested that some knowledge about managing her energy in this space would not hurt. In our last few sessions together, I taught her some basic tricks for safe journeying—grounding, sealing her aura, and closing her chakras after a ceremony. Despite my concerns, I had a strong sense that Alice needed to follow her path with plant medicine.

Four years later, Alice turned up out of the blue for an energetic check-up. She had been on quite a journey since I had last seen her. She described how her work with Iboga had opened her heart and revealed her true path. She left the fashion industry and was working with plant-based nutrition as a pathway to conscious living. This was a topic close to my heart. After all the years of detoxing, I knew first-hand the direct relationship between food and vibration.

It was heart-warming to hear about the changes Alice had made in her life, and there was no denying that she looked radiant. I was curious to see what was happening in her energy field. This time, Alice's energy system was completely unrecognizable compared to its former state years before. There was no trace of the previous instability. Not only were her chakras in good shape, but she was vibrating at a high frequency. Apart from the angelic Celeste, this was the highest vibration I had ever worked with in a client. While making some minor adjustments, I received a vision of Alice championing a global social movement, initiating a sea change in consciousness among young seekers. Without a doubt, she was on her soul path.

This was the confirmation that Alice needed to pursue her dream. At the end of the session, I hugged her and wished her well, knowing that I wouldn't see her again.

Alice's story ended well. However, I saw many spiritual seekers whose experiences with plant medicine ceremonies had not brought the desired results. While Ayahuasca, and other sacred plant medicines, may well open a portal to higher awareness, the energetic fallout can be severe. Most of the spiritual seekers that sought my help were oblivious to the destabilizing effects of hallucinogenic plants on their energy systems. Few connected the dots with symptoms ranging from anxiety and migraines to nightmares.

It is true that shamans in many indigenous cultures used—and still use—medicinal plants to access non-ordinary reality. There is nothing wrong with this pathway. The salient point is that shamans have years of training in managing their energy and protecting themselves while journeying to other worlds. They are also skilled enough to protect those who journey with them. Without this knowledge, plant medicine ceremonies in the hands of the uninitiated are a somewhat risky tool for attaining higher consciousness. In the end, there are no shortcuts to spiritual connection. You have to do the inner work and lay strong spiritual foundations.

It is also not uncommon for light seekers yearning for spiritual connection to use recreational drugs to access non-ordinary reality. This is a risky pathway with many potential traps, not the least of which is taking the seeker to the astral planes rather than the higher spiritual realms. This creates an illusionary experience of spirituality and carries with it many dangers. Another common and serious pitfall of this pathway is soul loss.

One of my clients, a young man called Kyle, experienced severe soul loss after a bad trip with a party drug. We worked together for about six months through a combination of video calls, remote healing, and guided journey work to reverse the damage.

Chapter 7 | Light

KYLE'S STORY

Kyle was an adventurous young South African working in Zambia as a guide at one of the top-dollar game lodges. When Kyle first contacted me, he was in considerable distress. Having just turned thirty, he was in a crisis of sorts feeling stuck and directionless. Despite a strong sense of calling, Kyle had no vision for his life. He loved his work in the bushveld but felt somehow off track. For the past few months, he had been experiencing persistent headaches and tension down one side of his body with no physical explanation.

In our initial conversation, Kyle shared that as a teenager, he had experimented with LSD and had a bad trip. While he hadn't touched recreational drugs since then, he said that the bad trip had had a lasting impact on his psyche as if some vital part of himself were missing, leaving him in a *psychic slumber*.

When I went into Kyle's energy field, there was a dark shadow on the left side of his aura, creating a split in his auric field. This shadowy patch was particularly dense around Kyle's head—his mental body. When I tried to tune in further, I couldn't see anything. It was as if my clairvoyant sight was being blocked. My spirit guides told me that the LSD trip had taken Kyle to the astral plane, and they wanted me to experience it as Kyle had—as a place of total darkness and cold fear. They guided me with words and sensations to the lowest point of Kyle's experience. It was a strange feeling, a bit like being a blind person with no familiar reference points, but it was here in this void-like space that I was able to glean the root cause of Kyle's malaise.

Listening closely to my guides, I was told that during the LSD trip, Kyle had been bombarded with negative thought-forms. Some of these thought-forms were still perceivable in his etheric mental body, appearing as parasitic attachments. Over time, the negative thought-forms had created thought patterns that were still distorting Kyle's thinking, particularly his view of himself. When the effects of the drug had worn off, it had taken great effort for Kyle to come back from the astral plane, and in the process, a fragment of his soul split off, which left him experiencing low energy ever since.

Persistent low energy is often a sign of soul loss. When we incarnate, we bring with us a certain percentage of our soul energy to fulfill our life purpose, while the rest of our soul energy resides in the higher planes. If we further deplete our soul quotient, we may not have the soul strength to fulfill our life purpose. My guides told me that Kyle brought 80% of his soul strength into this incarnation—that's very high—with the aim of becoming a lightworker and making amends for the misuse of power in previous lifetimes. Using power with ethical integrity was his life lesson. The LSD trip was a kind of sabotage act because he didn't feel equipped to handle so much power. At thirty, Kyle was ready to integrate the lesson and reclaim his power.

Kyle's severe soul loss, as well as the negative thought patterns, had left him powerless to even envision his life purpose. Our work together would address both aspects. The first step was to clear the thought-forms and transmute the lower vibrational energy in his aura. With more light in his field, the scene was set for soul retrieval work. With the help of my guides, I was able to locate a split-off soul fragment in the astral dimension and bring it back into Kyle's current energy body.

Over several sessions, we integrated Kyle's lost part and worked with the split-off consciousness of his younger self. Kyle's inner work between sessions was to forgive his younger self for taking LSD and landing him in trouble. He had, in effect, banished this shameful part of himself. While Kyle worked with forgiveness, my task was to clear the vibrations of shame and guilt and integrate his soul energy. The final step was to anchor Kyle's soul energy into his haric dimension. The hara is considered the energetic core where the physical and spiritual bodies meet. It holds the vibrational keynote of the soul's existence in physical form and provides the foundation for the chakric and auric layers of the energy system. With a stronger energetic core, Kyle's soul energy would radiate throughout his energy field.

After six months of deeply transformative healing work, Kyle was ready to move forward with his life. His energy was strong and vibrant. Having connected with his soul purpose, he was ready to explore how he could use his spiritual power in service of the light.

There are many reasons for soul loss, which may relate to the current lifetime, as in Kyle's case, or to a previous lifetime. Whatever the cause, soul retrieval always involves working with consciousness, requiring the client's active participation. There is a reason that a part of the soul splits off in the first place, and this needs to be resolved in the psyche. It is a process rather than a once-off fix.

In Kyle's case, the positive outcome would not have been possible without his commitment to his healing journey. It took enormous courage to face his shadow and reclaim his power. As light seekers, sometimes it's required that we enter the dragon's cave, no matter how dark, to find the gold. Despite their best efforts, I saw many spiritual seekers who were struggling to connect with their light due to severe soul loss. Maya was one such case. Her soul loss had occurred in a traumatic past life and was severe enough to erode her considerable efforts to find her path in this lifetime.

MAYA'S STORY

Maya was a dedicated spiritual seeker. Her search had taken her to spiritual gurus in India, Tibet, Nepal, and many other far-flung places. Despite decades of devotion to her spiritual practice, she was utterly despondent, feeling that she didn't belong anywhere. In the surface-world, Maya was a landscape gardener. Her beautiful creations spoke volumes about her inner beauty. She was a highly conscious soul, and I wondered what was preventing her progress.

When I entered Maya's energy field, it was evident that her soul energy was fragmented. The cause of her soul loss was a traumatic past life experience of being burned alive on her husband's funeral pyre in India. At that time, widow-burning, called *Sati*, was still widely practiced in parts of India and Nepal. According to ancient Hindu customs, Sati symbolized the ultimate act of devotion and purity when a living wife honored the marriage by following her deceased husband to the afterlife. Initially a voluntary act, Sati became a forced practice until it was outlawed in 1829. Forced Sati was at its peak from the fifteen to eighteenth centuries. During this period, Maya was sent to her death on her deceased husband's pyre while her extended family stood by and watched her burn.

This past life experience was so traumatic that it left an imprint in Maya's auric field. It was also evident that part of Maya's soul energy was still entangled in the residual energy of the traumatic event. After clearing Maya's soul trauma, it was possible to retrieve the part of her soul that was stuck in the past and integrate it into her current energy body. The soul retrieval work went unusually quickly, and I sent Maya off with some homework to further integrate her soul energy.

At her check-up session the following week, I noticed that Maya's lower chakras were stagnant as if the incoming soul energy had only integrated with the upper energy body, while her lower energy body remained cut off. Tuning in to see what the blockage might be, my spirit guides told me that the *vibrational note* of the lower chakras was tied to Maya's old name. At this point, I didn't know Maya had another name, but she confirmed later that she was named Anne at birth and had changed her name when she was traveling in India. The name Maya carries a strong vibration, while her birth name Anne held the vibration of her old soul trauma. Changing her name in India was an inspired act of releasing her past. However, my guides said that her two identities were now to be integrated as Anne needed to belong to the whole.

The energetic frequency to enable this integration process was to be sourced from an even more distant past life. When I asked my guides how to integrate Maya's soul energy, I was shown a mountainous country, which I was told was Tibet and taken to a monastery perched on top of a hill. Inside, a group of young boys in orange robes was sitting cross-legged on the floor. There was a golden light around one of the boys. This was Maya, who was male in this previous incarnation. The young boy lived in the monastery all his life and became a highly revered Buddhist monk and spiritual teacher. I was guided to connect Maya-Anne with the soul energy of the boy-monk and the adult monk. There was a process of vibrationally aligning Maya-Anne with this previous soul aspect and integrating the younger and adult aspects of herself. With this, our work together was done.

This was a complex soul retrieval, but ultimately our work together restored Maya's soul strength to a point where she could connect with her true self and find her way. When I saw Maya a few years later, she looked deeply peaceful. She told me that she was finally living her purpose as a custodian of the land and working with the light grids.

Working with clients who were actively seeking the light was a joy. Many, like Alice, were already vibrating at a high level when they arrived in my healing room. Others like Kyle and Maya felt an intense longing for the light but were hampered by severe soul loss. There were others who were losing their power in all manner of dysfunctional relationships. A common trap for empathic light seekers is the empath-narcissist lock.

Empaths are sensitive souls. Energetically, they tend to have thin skins with porous auras. They absorb negative energy at the drop of a hat and are prone to energy theft. This makes empaths susceptible to fatigue, anxiety, and even illness. More so than any other soul type, it is important for empaths to learn how to protect and restore their energy. When it comes to relationships, empaths are likely to give more than they receive. This is like honey to all manner of bees, the narcissist being the more predatory among them. An inexperienced empath will fall headlong into the narcissist's trap. This is a variation of the victim trap, but one that is especially hard to escape, for the narcissist is a master at manipulation.

One of these empathic light-seeker souls was a talented young actress named Lesedi.

LESEDI'S STORY

Lesedi was a beautiful African woman with a light, vibrant soul energy. Originally from Lesotho, she grew up in Johannesburg and was now based in London, where she was working for a theatre company. Lesedi had performed all over Europe and was currently on tour in South Africa. When she came to see me, she was suffering from extreme fatigue and anxiety. She put this down to the demanding tour schedule but felt worse than usual. She described feeling generally off track in her life, having abandoned her spiritual path amid the demands of her London life.

While Lesedi was talking, I could feel the presence of someone else's energy in her field. I asked about her family and intimate relationships. Lesedi was involved with a married man who had been promising to leave his wife since the start of their relationship a few years back. She described their relationship as intense, adding sheepishly that her lover—let's call him Gerald—was verbally abusive at times. She knew their relationship wasn't healthy, but try as she might, she couldn't break it off. Every time she tried to leave him, he reeled her in again.

No Gold Without The Dragon

When I went into Lesedi's energy field, I found a few rather disturbing things. Her aura was very porous as if she had no energetic boundaries at all. More disturbing was that several energetic cords were wrapped around her torso, plugging into three of her chakras: the sacral, the solar plexus, and the throat—the troublemaker trilogy. These energy cords linked Lesedi to a tall, dark-haired, trim-bearded man, who I could see clairvoyantly in her aura. This man appeared to be holding her in an energetic lock. When I tuned in further, the cords were acting like giant suction pads, draining Lesedi's life force energy. This would account for her tiredness. The energy running through the cords was that of control and manipulation. This was a classic energetic picture of an empath-narcissist lock, and it didn't look good.

I described the man as best I could, and Lesedi nodded, affirming it was Gerald. I asked her permission to cut the cords in order to free her from his energetic hold over her. This would enable her to make a more conscious choice about whether to continue what was proving to be a destructive relationship. In the process of untangling and cutting energy ties, it became apparent that Gerald was not being honest with Lesedi. The giveaway was an energetic cord at her heart chakra; Lesedi's heart energy was flowing toward Gerald, but there was no love flowing back from him. I doubted that he had any intention of leaving his wife.

After cutting the cords and freeing Lesedi from the energetic net, I cleared the three affected chakras and boosted her energy flow. I hoped that with her energy restored and a bit of breathing space in South Africa, Lesedi would find the courage to make a healthier choice. At the end of the session, I sent her off with an exercise to reclaim her energy and reinforce the work we had done together.

When Lesedi got back to London, she emailed to tell me that she had broken it off with Gerald. He had tried his usual tactics to get her back, but she was not persuaded this time. Although she was sad at the way things had turned out, Lesedi was relieved and excited to be free to walk her spiritual path.

Lesedi's story was a classic Bluebeard tale. Lured by a charismatic man, she had fallen into the victim trap. She was blind to Gerald's narcissistic behavior. Coming to see me was a plea from her soul to remove the scales from her eyes. It is not an easy task for the healer to be the one to deliver the blow, but the truth must be told. It doesn't serve a client to shield them from reality. The truth of Lesedi and Gerald's relationship dynamic was found in the multitude of cords that held her captive in an energetic net. The energy body doesn't lie.

WALK-INS

During this period, I encountered another type of light seeker, commonly referred to as a walk-in. A walk-in is a soul who has taken over a living person's body, usually after the person has been in a prolonged coma or had a near-death experience. This is not the same as a possession, which is a hostile takeover. This unusual phenomenon is an exchange that has been agreed upon between the two souls concerned. The reasons are complex and varied, but the walk-ins I encountered wanted to assist with the Ascension process and had arranged to incarnate into an adult body to speed up the growth process. These are light seekers of the most extraordinary kind!

I've seen very few genuine cases of walk-ins. One of these was a young man who'd been in a car accident a few years before he came to see me. He had no memories of his previous life, and his family and friends felt he had undergone a complete personality change. My spirit guides told me that he was a walk-in and that the soul that had taken over his body had a big mission to fulfill. This young man didn't know he was a walk-in, so I had to tread carefully in explaining what my guides had said. My task was to help him to accept the walk-in's soul and life path.

Another genuine case was that of an older woman called Astrid. When I first saw her, I was immediately struck by the dissonance between her appearance and her soul energy. Unlike the young man, Astrid knew she was a walk-in. The soul exchange had occurred after she'd been in a coma as a teenager. Ever since then, she'd had an uneasy knowing that she was "someone else," as she put it. By the time she came to see me, she was ready to accept what she knew in her heart to be true. My task was to help her to connect with the walk-in's soul purpose as a lightworker.

Working with the light seekers was an exciting learning curve, pushing me to experiment with the light spectrum and sound healing. My guides showed me a range of new techniques, including working with various light rays and using sound to reinforce the light effect. One of the light rays I was shown incorporated the full spectrum of color, like a rainbow, and vibrated at a high frequency. I called it the *joy light*. It was particularly effective in opening the heart, and I used it on all those who could receive it, adding a high-frequency sound to amplify the light effect. For most light seekers, opening the heart center was the biggest challenge and the biggest game-changer.

Five years after setting out as a healer, I was doing the work I really wanted to do. This was a confirmation of the power of intention and focused thought to create experience. If you are clear and consistent in your messaging to the Universe, it is entirely possible to manifest your heart's desire. I started to work with these concepts in every aspect of my life and watched how things changed around me. Not only had my healing work taken flight, but I was altogether much happier. My boys were doing well too. At the end of that year, we went on our first, and only, overseas holiday together—a trip to New Zealand to visit family. Life was good. Now it was time for a man at my side.

CALLING IN MY SOULMATE

After cutting soul ties with Brad, I felt free, both as a single woman in the surface-world and at a soul level, to find a soulmate. Applying the principles of focused intention and manifestation, I asked the Universe for a man who would be able to accompany me, as a kindred spirit, on my continuing journey as a healer.

At this point in my story, I want to be very clear that calling in a man is *not* casting a spell to get a particular person to fall in love with you. Spell-weaving is base magic. That kind of manipulation goes against everything I stand for. As a healer, spiritual permission and free will are my guiding principles. The business of calling in a soulmate is utterly respectful of free will. Think of it as sending an etheric *message in*

Chapter 7 | Light

a bottle to a bunch of potential soulmates. Picking it up and answering the message is entirely the other person's choice.

With this caveat in mind, it is important to be very precise and specific in your message. The Universe can't respond to your intentions if you are not clear about what you want. I'd had plenty of time to think about this and made a detailed list of qualities and attributes that I wanted in a partner. What were his values? How did I want to feel when I was with him? What did our life together look like? I energized my wish list and posted my intention on the ethernet. Now all I had to do was let go of the outcome, trusting that when my soulmate was ready, the Universe would make sure that our paths crossed. It would then be up to us, both of us, to recognize each other and exercise free will in our response.

Three months later, I was given a heads-up by my spirit guide Chenoa. On a warm autumn evening, I was enjoying sundowners with friends on the clifftop above Llandudno. The sinking sun was spreading fiery rays across the Atlantic Ocean. It was spectacular, as only an African sunset can be.

"He's coming," Chenoa whispered, interrupting my surface-world conversation.

"Who's he?" I asked, turning my attention inward.

"The one you've been waiting for."

Looking toward the apricot horizon, I knew instinctively that this man was coming from a place far away, from *overseas*, as we say in South Africa.

"How will I recognize him?" I asked, slowing my thoughts down, dropping into the zone of receiving information—perhaps a ring, a bangle?

"By the vibration," came the reply. "Remember California .... "

And then Chenoa was gone, leaving me buzzing with energy and brimful of questions. When was this man going to appear? Would I be able to recognize him? What if I missed the moment? I thought back to that extraordinary time in California, almost a year ago now, and the vibration of joy I had been gifted. So, this was the vibration that would announce my soulmate's arrival.

Two days later, I went to my weekly Bliss Dance class. The dance teacher introduced the theme of the evening—aptly, *Finding your Joy*, and we dived into the dance, whirling, twirling, on our own and with others as the mood took us. At the end of the evening, I literally bumped into a tall man who was new to the class. He held out his hands to me, and we moved together in a slow dance. Suddenly there was a burst of energy, a powerful current that passed between us. I looked up at him, and our eyes locked. He seemed to see right into me. I felt as if I were sinking into the well of his being. In that moment, I knew everything about him; it was like a rush of information that came to me in words, pictures, and feelings. There were no thoughts, just a sense of dropping into the mystery. And then the music stopped, the dance class ended, and we were catapulted back into ordinary reality.

"I'm Sander," he said, introducing himself, a detectable foreign accent in those two words.

"I'm Heather." I smiled and left without another word. It was up to him now. I knew he would find me.

On our first coffee date, one hour quickly turned into four as we exchanged life stories. At our age, there was a lot to share! Sander was Dutch and had come to South Africa for a six-month sabbatical, which was coming to an end. In a few weeks, he was flying back to the Netherlands. This cast some doubt in my mind as to whether he was the man Chenoa had spoken about after all.

After the next dance class, we went out for supper, picking up the thread of our first conversation. There was so much overlap in our journeys. Although we'd spent our lives on different sides of the planet, we discovered that major life changes had happened at the same time—

Chapter 7 | Light

not just the same years, but the same months. We had even crossed paths in France when I was traveling around Europe in my twenties. Synchronicity is a seductive thing.

On the way home, we took the scenic route along the Atlantic Seaboard toward Llandudno. The full moon was rising over the sea. Suddenly Sander veered into a viewing bay, stopping in the exact spot where my spirit guide Chenoa had predicted his arrival. *Why is he stopping here?* I thought. I hadn't told him about my clifftop experience.

"Come," he said, jumping out of the car. "Look at the moon. Isn't she beautiful? And look beyond the horizon; that's where I come from. I've come a very long way to find you."

In the weeks before Sander returned to Holland, we spent as much time as possible together, carefully avoiding the question of future. Just before he left South Africa, we hiked up one of the mountain gorges to my favorite river-listening spot. We leaned against each other, soaking up the pleasure of being together while the river-song washed over us. Each lost in our own thoughts; my heart was burning, a silent struggle raging within. As if in answer, the river gurgled its refrain: *Keep your heart open, keep your heart open.*

Despite my misgivings, I took a deep breath and opened my heart chakra. As I did so, I had the strangest sensation that Sander was dropping into my heart. Then I felt myself falling into a void—a bit like Alice tumbling into Wonderland, before landing in a dimly lit room with a long wooden table, a celebratory feast, and a tall man at the door, his arms stretched out like wings. *It was him!* In a wave of joy, recognition crashed onto the shores of my awareness, and I knew, without any doubt, that Sander was the man I had seen when the veils parted in California, the man my guide had announced on the Llandudno cliff, the man who would find me across time and space. And I knew, too, that my heart was the portal to our shared past *and future*. While this realization washed over me, Sander had a similar experience of non-ordinary reality. As he listened to the river, he found himself falling into my heart, dropping down into a well of joy that he later described as "coming home."

This mystical experience at the river was the moment our souls forged a pact to be together again in this lifetime. But there was a long, uncertain road ahead of us before this could happen. A week later, Sander flew back to Holland. He had big choices to make. Could he give up his life there and leave his grown-up children and extended family for an uncertain future with a woman he had only just met? We left it open. A blink of an eye in the soul-world can take more time in the surface-world.

When we said goodbye at the airport, I didn't know if I would ever see Sander again. It is one thing to be privy to the soul's knowing. It's another being comfortable with not knowing in the surface-world. I belly-flipped between trusting and tenterhooks for the next six months. I told Sander what I wanted—*always best to be clear with the Universe*, then let go, promising I would not interfere with his free will.

This was an important test for us both. Would Sander give up his known world and choose an unknown path with me? Would I be able to keep my heart open to allow him to come back to me? I understood that my heart was the doorway, but it was tempting to slam the door shut in the uncertainty of not knowing whether he would choose me. There was also the not-to-be ignored question of official bureaucracy. Most foreigners can't just waltz into South Africa for longer than six months without a work or residence permit.

By agreement, we had little contact during this period. I knew Sander would contact me when he had made his choice. As I was the one who had sent out the call in the first place, it was important that he choose me. The ball was in his court. My part was to keep my heart open. At times, this was extremely trying. "Hold the faith," my friend Liz said, reminding me of the pact our souls had made at the river.

Six months later, Sander called me out of the blue. "I'm coming to Cape Town," he said. "Do you want to see me?"

That is how I found myself back at Cape Town International airport. Apprehensive doesn't quite capture how I felt about seeing this man in real life again. I thought about our experiences so far, the unfathomable connections, the deep familiarity, his quirkiness that matched mine, and most of all, the feeling of knowing who he was. But would I feel the same way after all these months? And then there he was in front of me. In his embrace, he was so familiar, and all my doubts fell away. For Sander, he said that being together was like coming home. Again, our intuitive soul choice was made in the first few moments, but the surface-world is never so simple.

We spent our first day together in Kalk Bay, enjoying the stirring of spring in Cape Town. Sander spoke about his feeling of coming home, although this was a foreign country for him in every respect, and I was a virtual stranger.

"I know this is my path," he explained. "I could have stayed in my comfortable life, but I got a clear message that it was destination Cape Town. I was guided the same way you describe being guided, only I kept hearing the word *path*. So here I am!"

Sander had a three-month tourist visa and a return flight to Holland at the end of the year. This was the linear time we had been granted to figure out our future. In the allotted three months, Sander's certainty about his path was to be constantly tested. He had a lot to process as he slowly let go of his old life and found his feet in South Africa. Dogging us like a shadow was the niggling bureaucratic question of what happened after Sander's three-month visa expired. He applied for a business permit, usually processed as a three-year work visa, but we didn't hold out much hope. Home Affairs is notoriously inefficient, and extended permits were like hen's teeth. On good days, I trusted that the Universe would support Sander's application if we were meant to be together. There were plenty of bad days too. Miraculously, just before his visa expired, his business permit to work in South Africa came through. Even more astonishing was that he was issued a five-year permit, which was almost unheard of for work permits. The Universe had delivered a miracle through Home Affairs, of all unlikely places!

Now Sander had a real choice. On New Year's Eve, we went out for a romantic dinner, and he put his printed return ticket to Amsterdam on the table. "I'm staying in South Africa," he said. "It's time to create our life together." And with that, he tore his return ticket in half. The choice was made.

AN OBSTACLE ON THE PATH

A few months later, an obstacle appeared on the rosy path. After weeks of mystery bleeding, I was diagnosed with complex atypical endometrial hyperplasia. In plain speak, this meant that my womb lining was too thick, and cancerous cells were present. It is a pre-cancerous condition that is a common precursor to uterine cancer. I had reached an impasse.

In the archetypal Heroine's Journey, the heroine receives a call to change her life in some fundamental way. This is usually in the form of a crisis or life event that makes the heroine question the way she has been living her life and the direction of her path. If she chooses to respond to this call, she leaves her comfort zone and crosses the threshold from her known life into the unknown—and so she begins the transformative cycle of the Heroine's Journey.

Facing the obstacle that has presented itself, the heroine has the opportunity to progress along the road of trials where she will undoubtedly meet dragons and awaken to an aspect of her life that is arid, dried up, or in some way depleted. With this realization, she may need to push on, cajoling the dragons to assist her, and descend into the darkness—the abyss—for a time. While there, chances are she will meet the Goddess and begin the process of reconnecting with her divine feminine nature. Here the heroine dreams the healing dream, which allows her to transform some aspect of her life. On her return from the depths, she gathers the gifts of the Goddess for her onward journey.

Men can go on this journey too. However, the steps in the traditional Hero's Journey are a bit different. The hero's impulse would be to slay the dragons and avoid the abyss at all costs. This is not the heroine's way. She goes to great lengths to befriend the dragons, and when she reaches the abyss, she dives right in, knowing instinctively that this is where she will source what she needs to find her way out of whatever mess she is in.

Chapter 7 | Light

When we receive that call, we all go through a variation of this archetypal cycle more than once in our lives. This time my call came in the form of a cancer warning. My real-life version of the Heroine's Journey threw me into crisis and a new cycle of transformation. When I got the diagnosis, the ob-gyn specialist—let's call her Dr. Jones—suggested surgery. I politely declined, but Dr. Jones insisted that a hysterectomy was the only sensible option. Without it, she explained, the odds were that the cancerous cells would spread to the ovaries.

"Ovarian cancer is a silent killer," she said matter-of-factly.

When I asked about other options, such as a combination of non-invasive treatments, Dr. Jones changed her professional tone and read me the riot act about being irresponsible. Her tirade was peppered with vulgar expletives; I kid you not. Energy healing? That would be playing with fire, she said. *The dragon would be happy.*

"It is patients like you who die," Dr. Jones informed me, perhaps not realizing that her words were like a death threat. With that, she took out her calendar to schedule the extraction of my uterus. My intuition was screaming that anyone who spoke to her patients in this manner was not to be trusted with the surgical knife. Once more, I declined her well-meaning offer and fled from her consulting room as quickly as possible.

I'm not sure what shocked me more—the diagnosis or being handed a death sentence by a cussing doctor. The dragon of fear was uncoiling in my troublesome womb-space. Did I have the courage to face cancer without allopathic medicine? Although I didn't yet have a Plan B up my sleeve, Dr. Jones had struck terror in my heart, and I knew without a doubt that I was not going to submit to her Plan A. This was a pivotal moment. Unwittingly, Dr. Jones had pushed me across the threshold of the known into the unknown.

Crossing this threshold was when I got to test my faith in mind-body medicine. Faced with a potentially life-threatening diagnosis, it is easy to panic and be pressured into conforming with the mainstream medical model, which, frankly, has not had a very high success rate in treating cancer. And if you think it's perfectly fine for women to have hysterectomies at the drop of a hat, then I would suggest that you have been misinformed by said medical model. Dr. Jones's unprofessional tirade had certainly given me reason to pause for thought and consider alternatives. So, I decided to give myself six months before submitting to the knife. During this grace period, I would dive into deep self-healing of my womb-space—a woman's inner well.

Still reeling from the diagnosis, Sander and I went for a long hike through the forest to talk through holistic options. Nothing like a crisis to test a new relationship! I was still in the grip of fear, desperately trying to gather my inner resources, while the awakened dragon breathed down my neck.

Possible cancer, I reminded myself. *A few cancerous cells are peanuts, right?*

This was a different kind of fear from the cold fear I'd experienced during the Dark Energy Intensive. This time, the dragon of fear felt watery, sloshing about in the hidden recesses of my womb, my veins, my blood. Suddenly I was aware of hidden tunnels and wells, vast inner waterways I didn't even know about until this new fear dragon stirred. This was a different beast from the fiery dragon of my earlier years. This was a watery creature, pulling me like an undercurrent into the depths of the unknown.

We stopped to rest at a pond, leaning against a fallen tree trunk. I noticed a pair of dragonflies skimming the water, their rainbow wings shimmering in the light. Just watching them doing their aerial dance lifted my spirits. Soon, more and more dragonflies joined the dance until the very air above the water seemed to shimmer like an iridescent mirage. In that moment, I knew without a doubt that all would be well. I didn't know exactly how I would get through this challenge, but I knew I would move through it without surgery and with relative ease. Whenever I wavered in the six months that followed—and waver I did—I remembered the dragonfly dance and crystal-clear knowing that arose in my heart.

Chapter 7 | Light

In Native American symbology, the dragonfly represents the illusion we accept as reality. When the dragonfly appears, it is a call to break down the restrictive illusions and seek out the perceptions or patterns that need to change. Once thought of as a dragon, the dragonfly holds wisdom and the possibility of magical transformation. What a tricky shapeshifter my tenacious dragon was, but it got my attention. How could I not be awed by the magical display over the pond? The big question was, what did I need to change to step through the veil of illusion?

I didn't know the answer to that question yet, but the dragonflies had given me hope. I decided I didn't need a Plan B so much as a healing dream—a vision of a positive outcome and a willingness to embark on a healing journey. Since my life path was being divinely guided, why wouldn't I be guided in overcoming this latest trial? Perhaps it was a spiritual assignment.

With that, I embarked on a top-priority healing journey. As a start, I cut back on clients to reduce stress and create space for my own healing. Next, I signed up for an intensive holistic cancer healing program to learn everything I could about this cellular entity in my body. Although the course was focused on the physical body, it was a good start. The takeaways? Cancer cells don't grow in a healthy environment. Cellular terrain is key; to improve cell health, we need to focus on nutrition, oxygenation, and detoxification—inside and out.

The external environment was simple enough. I did a clean sweep of toxins in the house: cleaning agents, cosmetics; all the potential suspects went. Although I had long been using natural products, when I put my forensic hat on and weeded out the parabens and carcinogenic suspects, they filled a large garbage bag. I was shocked at the sheer number of chemicals we unthinkingly smear on our skins.

The inner environment was more complex. While I was choosing to honor the body's wisdom and capacity to heal, I would still need some medical assistance. After a few false starts, I found a doctor in Stellenbosch who practiced integrative medicine, specializing in women's health. Dr. Lynette was the wise woman kind of doctor. Her take was that estrogen dominance was the underlying cause of the errant cell growth, and if we could reverse that, we had a good chance of stopping the cancerous spread. She concurred that my condition was serious but was willing to go with the six-month plan.

Off the record, Dr. Lynette said that if she were in my shoes, she wouldn't have her uterus cut out without first exploring other options. This was very reassuring, coming from a doctor. She also suggested that I ask my body to make me aware if there was a significant change. I was warming to this doctor very quickly.

Over the next few months, Dr. Lynette guided me through an alternative treatment protocol, using a combination of bio-identical hormones, nutrition, and monthly detoxes to boost liver and hormone function. What I was putting into my body also had to change. I considered myself a mindful eater, but a cancer prevention, hormone-balancing diet was the next level up. Sander and the boys dived right in with me on a life-changing food journey.

Despite my trust in Dr. Lynette, I still had misgivings. With all the detox I had done over the years, it was hard to believe this was the solution. While it wouldn't do any harm to deep-clean my physical systems, I intuitively felt that my healing lay in the emotional realm. Having taken my physical body in hand, it was time to wade into emotional territory. Reinforcements were needed for this leg of the journey. My support team quickly materialized.

> My body, myself, and my inner healer formed a stronger alliance.
>
> My Chinese spirit guide, Doctor, was always at hand to give instructions.
>
> Dr. Lynette doled out her Wise Woman medicine.
>
> Faye, my faithful colleague, offered vibrational medicine.
>
> Sander was a steady rock.
>
> The dragon of fear reminded me to take this seriously.

Chapter 7 | Light

With little prompting, Faye stepped in to give me weekly energy healing, asking nothing in return. In her wise-crone way, she focused on changing the vibrational terrain of my womb-space and said nothing about my odds.

The intuitive Dr. Lynette suggested her new She-Art program, a guided process of narrative medicine during which I would unearth the lessons, toss out the old story, and write a new story for my life. This was her remedy to subdue the mutinous cells and transform my womb from wound-space to creative cauldron.

For six months, I dove into this multi-faceted healing space, immersing myself in the She-Art process of crafting a new storyline and stoking up the creative fires in service of my healing dream. Every week, I visited Dr. Lynette for my weekly dose of narrative medicine. For these few hours, she settled me in a sunny corner of her consultation room, with colorful paper, aromatic herbal teas—in a dragon teapot, mind you—and healthy snacks and told me to write for my life.

The old storyline was that I had to do it all alone, with little or no support. It transpired that I was heavily addicted to survival mode. The theme of this story was tough-sledding and depletion. This was the classic desert dance, and I was awakening to its aridity. The new storyline was one of nourishment—physically, emotionally, and spiritually. In the new story, I was available to receive support and love. Within a more nourishing container, my wildish nature and creative fire would be rekindled. This was wild woman medicine.

Sourcing my body wisdom and activating my inner healer was a long-winded affair. Before I could make any progress, I had to cajole the dragon and turn fear into faith, believing in miracles rather than prognoses or statistics. This took some doing. Despite my work as a healer, it appeared that the conventional medical model was still firmly entrenched. No one escapes programming. Throughout this healing journey, my biggest battle was dealing with my inner dialogue, which tended to disappear down rabbit holes of fearful thinking. This required vigilant surveillance and redirecting my wayward mind toward positive outcomes.

There was also the small matter of regarding my body as an ally and dismissing the unhelpful notion that it had somehow betrayed me. With gratitude I didn't yet feel, I thanked my body for the early warning before the harbinger cells spread into the ovaries, which, according to Dr. Jones, was the inevitable trajectory. As a peace offering, I flooded my womb-space with love, infusing my cells with light. With no evidence that it was making any difference, I spent hours super-charging the mind-body connection with positive vibes.

During my morning meditations, I turned my attention inward, exploring the murky womb-space. Listening to my body with a new reverence, I strained to hear what it was telling me, open to receiving any little snippet of wisdom. More often than not, I was greeted with silence, but sometimes I was graced with revelations.

One of the first breakthrough insights was that I wasn't healing cancer; I was healing my life. Over the long years of active mothering and being on the client treadmill, I had become depleted—exhausted might be more accurate. The gist was that I was giving out way more energy than I was receiving. My body was running on empty. Had I been listening more carefully, I might have heard my body's loud messaging in the excessive bleeding stage—my life force energy was literally running out in the form of blood. I was drying out!

Now at least I could acknowledge that I was deeply tired, not the kind of tiredness that sleep alleviates; this was bone-tiredness from holding it all together for so long. The antidote was to stop working so hard. I had been in survival mode for too long. It was time to take a breather, do less, have fun, and invite in love. I also had to set some boundaries and take my own nourishment seriously. Nurturing myself meant changing some deeply embedded beliefs that just happened to come from my mother line. My cellular terrain was stuck with some old programming dating back to the 1820 Settler lot.

Undoubtedly a gift from the Goddess, I was prompted to clean up this ancestral wounding and release the disempowering stories passed down through the generations. This stoic line of women had been playing out a full-blown victim drama ever since their original ordeal in Algoa Bay. While I rooted out this dried-up narrative, the taciturn Faye chipped away at the questionable cells. Six months later, she pronounced my womb clear.

Upon Faye's pronouncement, I returned to the medical mainstream and had an ultrasound scan and a biopsy. This was the time of reckoning. After all my focused healing, I was convinced it would be good news, but my heart was in my mouth. An hour later, I walked out of the doctor's room on air. The endometrial lining had returned to normal, and there was no trace of cancerous cells. A few days later, the biopsy results came back clear. My new ob-gyn doctor, though supportive of my holistic approach, warned me that we would have to continue monitoring potential changes. I could live with that.

MIND-BODY MEDICINE: THE NEW NORMAL

Cancer is a wake-up call and a teacher. If you are willing to engage with cancer or any chronic illness from this perspective, the potential for transformation and growth is boundless. I often wondered, had I followed medical advice and had my uterus whipped out, would I have been able to harness the creative energy to write this book, for example?

If I were to distill what I learned into one guiding principle, it would be reversing cancer is possible, but it requires a holistic approach. Holistic healing requires a willingness to delve into every layer of your being and go the distance in rooting out imbalance. We can't expect medical experts, or healers for that matter, to deliver the cure. In a conventional approach and the hyper-focus on cancer itself, the emotional, mental, and spiritual aspects tend to get ignored. It is also true that energy goes where we put our attention. By focusing exclusively on the cancer cells, we may unintentionally be spurring their growth.

Either way, there is no magic wand or quick fix. We must take responsibility for our own healing, digging a little deeper to understand why the body produced disease in the first place and making the inner shifts to kickstart its self-regulatory mechanisms. The mainstream medical model zooms in on the physical manifestation, using the blunt tools of surgery, radiation, or chemo to get rid of the cancerous growth without looking beyond the symptoms. For lasting healing, we need to cast the net a bit wider and deeper before resorting to such crude methods.

It all comes down to clearing up the environment in which the cancer is growing: the cellular terrain of biochemical imbalance, oxygenation, and hydration; the emotional environment of negative emotions and stress; the mental terrain of beliefs and attitudes; and the physical environment in which you live with its assorted toxins. Where there is disease, the cellular terrain is not likely optimal—too much toxicity, too little oxygen, and inadequate hydration. To reverse disease, it's important to change the terrain through a combination of nutrition, detox, lifestyle changes, and emotional processing. Given the right signals and circumstances, the body heals and regenerates itself quite naturally.

An integrated approach requires a willingness to examine the life you are leading and make sweeping changes. Everything that happens in the mind-body occurs in the container of consciousness. The physical body is structured by the energy of vibration and consciousness. This includes the consciousness of the soul across multiple lifetimes. It is possible to reverse disease by changing consciousness and the vibrational terrain in which imbalance arose. In my experience, emotional healing is often the key to unlocking disease. This is because all emotion is carried on a vibrational frequency, which is either harmful or healing. Love, for example, is high-frequency energy that keeps the body in a state of grace.

According to the spiritual Law of Healing, everything is energy, and energy is light. Your energy-consciousness is like a river of light flowing through your body. Ill health arises when the river stops flowing. Heavy emotions such as grief, fear, anger, resentment, jealousy, and hurt are like silt in the river. There is nothing wrong with these emotions; the problem arises when we don't process emotions and heal our wounds. If these dense energies, like base metals, are not alchemized, they block the flow of life force energy and ultimately cause disease. High-frequency healing energy, or love for that matter, clears the debris, so the river of light can flow again.

The powerful role of emotion, or vibration, in restoring health is science, not fanciful thinking. In Candace Pert's groundbreaking book *Molecules of Emotion*, she explains in detail how emotions affect our body chemistry and cellular terrain. In a nutshell, emotions are chemical messengers. Every feeling we have sends a signal to the body. The heart, mind, and body are in a perpetual conversation. When we have recurring emotions, these feelings are communicated to the cells, influencing how they reproduce.

This ongoing mind-body conversation cuts deep grooves into our physical make-up. To undo disease, we must deal with these pesky chemical messengers. Change how you feel and think, and you quite literally change your biology. It is as simple or as complicated as we make it.

THE RIVER OF LIGHT MUST FLOW

I had tested spiritual law and scientific theory with positive results, but now I was being called to guide others through these same treacherous waters. Sometimes we are given challenging assignments to gather knowledge and build resilience so that we can then show others the way. Sure enough, it was not long before a stream of clients with various forms and stages of cancer and other chronic illnesses—HIV/Aids, multiple sclerosis (MS), fibromyalgia, glandular fever, and chronic fatigue syndrome (CFS)—began to show up in my healing room. By now, I knew how this reflective process worked. It was not in the least surprising that the clients who sought my help during this period were reflecting an aspect of my own healing journey. This was simply the spiritual Law of Attraction in action. My focus on cancer was magnetizing similar energies into my orbit. Fortunately, everything I was learning about chronic illness also benefited my clients.

One of the most valuable things I learned during this period was to create circles of support to ensure that my clients had access to holistic healthcare. With the growth of integrative medicine, many mainstream professionals were open to working with energy healers and forming multi-disciplinary teams to support their clients. My approach with any new client was first to assess the severity of their condition, find out what kind of treatment and support they were already getting, and then provide—or refer them to—appropriate complementary support.

Most of the cancer patients were receiving conventional medical treatment, including radiation and chemotherapy. My role was to support them through the grueling medical mill and work with the *vibrational terrain* hosting the cancerous growth. As I listened to my clients' stories, I was struck by two recurring themes—chronic stress and emotional wounding. They seemed to go hand in hand. If my client was willing to stay the course, we worked with the underlying imbalances, whether emotional, mental, or spiritual. Nine times out of ten, the key was emotional healing.

Not everyone was ready to do this deeper work. Some clients saw energy healing as a once-off intervention to help them deal with the stress of the medical treatments, in particular chemotherapy, which hammers the body. There wasn't much I could do beyond providing temporary relief. If someone isn't ready for deep healing, you cannot push the river to flow. Change only happens as fast as the slowest parts of the inner being can go. This calls for the utmost respect. Another aspect of the spiritual Law of Healing is that, even with permission, you cannot impose healing on someone if, at some level, they don't want it. For example, if the illness is serving a karmic lesson, taking it away prematurely may incur more karma for the healer.

That said, the results were overwhelmingly positive for those who dived willingly into a healing journey. No matter how ill, this group of clients came regularly to bathe in the river of light. Invariably, they saw big changes in their lives and looked back with immense gratitude for the gifts that cancer brought them.

One of these clients was Ruth, who came to see me shortly after being diagnosed with breast cancer.

RUTH'S STORY

When Ruth arrived in my healing room, she was still in the shock phase of having received this grim news. Beneath her shy demeanor, there was a steely resolve to do everything in her power to overcome this challenge in her outwardly smooth-running life.

In the first session, I asked Ruth about her personal life to get a picture of the whole woman and what might be contributing to the cancerous growth. Ruth was a professional photographer. She shared a home with her life partner Josie and their three-year-old adopted daughter, Thuli. She described her family life as happy, though she felt that she was more dependent on Josie, emotionally and financially, than she wanted. This pattern of dependency was evident in all her relationships, where she looked for external approval and validation because she felt inadequate and unworthy. As a child, she had lost her mother to cancer, and this core wounding had surfaced with her recent diagnosis. She was feeling very insecure, just as she had as a young child. It was clear that Ruth's healing journey would include inner child healing.

From the outset, we laid out a multi-pronged healing plan, which included medical treatments with the oncologist, regular detoxes under the guidance of a naturopath, and energy healing with me. Then, with a rough map in place, we embarked on a healing journey that lasted nearly two years.

For the first year, Ruth was on a medical rollercoaster. She had opted for surgery, followed by several rounds of chemotherapy. My role was to support her physical body to process the chemo drugs and to boost her immune system, which took a knock after each round of chemotherapy. At the same time, throughout the first year, Ruth was doing stringent detoxes, which were tough physically and left her emotionally vulnerable. The healing room was a space for her to decompress and release the rollercoaster of feelings.

In the first few months, Ruth wasn't in a state to dive into emotional healing, so we worked with her fear. Over time, her energy body relaxed, and the vibration of fear gradually subsided. This naturally led to a process of surfacing the wounding that she had experienced as a young girl. In one of the sessions, I guided Ruth on an inner journey to communicate with her body. It was a powerful process during which Ruth dropped into the well of grief and anger about her mother's untimely death. For the first time, she connected with deeply held feelings of abandonment and her vulnerability growing up without her mother's guidance. This session was a big release for Ruth but also brought her vulnerability to the surface. This was a turning point. Allowing her vulnerability and finding strength within it was the key to Ruth's long-term healing.

Toward the end of the first year, after several rounds of chemo, Ruth's medical team declared her cancer free. She was now officially in remission. This was a huge relief but also brought up new fears about cancer coming back. Many people would have stopped energy healing at this point, but Ruth chose to continue, and our work together went to an even deeper level. Free of the destabilizing effects of the medical rollercoaster, we could dive further into the emotional-spiritual terrain. As the heroine, Ruth was in the transformation phase, and if she were willing to stay a little longer, the gifts of the Goddess would be hers for the asking.

In the second year of our work together, we explored Ruth's pattern of dependency and the beliefs that were keeping it in place. The core belief was that she was not able to survive on her own. Challenging this belief led to a transformative process of redefining herself and developing more inter-dependent relationships in her relationship with Josie and in her professional life. Ruth learned how to acknowledge and take care of her needs, nurture herself, and receive nurturing from others. Asking for her needs to be met without fear of being too dependent was a radical shift. It brought up her deepest fears of abandonment. By connecting with the wounded child and changing her perceptions, Ruth could release this old fear and explore healthier inter-dependent relationships.

Ruth's transformation was a thrill to witness. The Goddess showered her with gifts. She had faced her fears, released her anger and grief, and allowed the emergence of her powerful feminine aspect, who knew how to source her inner world. As our work together came to an end, I had no doubt that whatever the challenges ahead, Ruth would shine in the world and be a strong mother to her young daughter.

Healing is undoubtedly more powerful if the client is willing to respond to the healing crisis and do the inner work of transformation. Ruth had answered cancer's call and embarked on a life-changing journey. In the two years of our work together, I was constantly in awe of her courage to stick with every facet of her healing program. Though the journey was tough, Ruth went through her initiation and found her treasure.

Sadly, there were others who didn't have enough time for a healing journey. One of these clients was Layla, a thirty-something single mother battling an aggressive form of skin cancer.

LAYLA'S STORY

When Layla first sought my help, she had stage four skin cancer, which had spread to the lymphatic system and bone marrow. She had been through the full gamut of available treatment, including chemotherapy, and had recently been given just six months to live. Desperate for a cure, Layla was hoping I could help her.

At a physical level, she was struggling with nausea, extreme fatigue, and frequent colds. Emotionally, she said she was "paralyzed with fear" and felt angry that this had happened to her at such a young age. Understandably, she was also heartbroken that her seven-year-old son might lose his mother. Adding to her load, Layla was very stressed about her interior design business, and despite the advanced stage of the disease, she was still working long hours. This would need to change.

At this advanced stage, I wasn't sure I would be able to help Layla reverse the cancer, but I hoped that with some emotional healing, she would find peace with her transition. I also knew that miraculous healing could happen in an instant if the right mix of factors came together. Not wanting to give Layla false hope or another death sentence, I explained to her that we would focus on emotional and spiritual healing. She was already doing everything possible at a physical level through nutrition and conventional medicine and had a team of specialists supporting her. But as far as I could tell, the root cause of the invasive cancer was emotional rather than physical.

When I went into Layla's energy field, her fear was overwhelming. It was the freeze kind of fear, which is more difficult to shift than the flight or fight kind of fear. The vibration of fear was keeping her in a state of rigid resistance. On top of the fear was a layer of resentment toward her son's father and a layer of anger about her illness and life being unfair. There was also a deep undercurrent of feeling powerless, which had been amplified by cancer.

If Layla was going to have a fighting chance at stopping the spread of cancer in her body, we would have to change the vibrational terrain. This would require some inner work to release dense emotions and the beliefs that were keeping the emotions in place. I could do my part, but Layla would also have to do the inner work.

In our first session, I focused on dissolving Layla's extreme fear and channeling high-vibrational light through her system. Before she left, I emphasized the need for her to process her emotions and make a few lifestyle changes. First and foremost, she had to reduce her stress levels and prioritize her healing. This meant delegating her workload and turning her attention to radical self-care. I suggested that whatever the outcome, she spend as much time as possible with her little boy.

Layla came for one more session. She said she felt lighter and better emotionally but was disappointed that I couldn't offer her a cure. I explained that nothing is impossible, but at the same time, there were no guarantees. Her best shot would be to continue to see me for weekly light infusions while doing the inner work and making the lifestyle changes I had suggested. This was my prescription.

Sadly, Layla didn't come back after the second session. Several months later, I heard that she had passed away. I was deeply saddened. Although Layla had left it far too late to seek my help, I believe that she had a chance, if not to reverse cancer, at least to find acceptance and prepare for a peaceful transition. I was left with feelings of regret that I hadn't been able to do more for her and sadness that she hadn't done more for herself.

While it was very painful to stand by and watch Layla make choices that thwarted her chances of survival, it was an important lesson in detaching from the outcome. Not only did I need to respect Layla's free will, but I also reminded myself that we can never know what is in someone else's highest good or what their soul's agenda might be. Some souls have work to do on the other side. Death is not an ending; it is a transition, and the soul's journey continues. I had to rid myself of *ending thinking* and release my judgments. It is quite possible that Layla's soul was choosing to exit. There is no judgment in that, only another perspective of how we view disease and death. Divine timing is also a factor. Ultimately, if it is our time to go, then there is not much that either conventional or energy medicine can do to change the outcome.

There is yet another aspect to consider in understanding the pervasiveness of serious disease—the role of environmental toxins. Dangerously high toxicity levels in the food chain, the soil, and the very air we breathe are affecting human health. Woman's bodies, with their intricate hormonal balance, are particularly at risk. Take the rapid rise in cancers in the last few decades. This is symptomatic of a far deeper malaise in our world. Our collective body can no longer absorb and process the toxic load.

What is the antidote to this sorry situation?

My view is that we must source a new story from deep within, a collective healing dream. Together, we need to nurture this healing dream for ourselves and for the Earth itself. We must believe that healing is possible and create a vision for a healthy planet, where balance and *right relationship* are restored. Much like the mind-body relationship, the relationship between Mother Earth and her inhabitants requires co-operation, harmony, and mutual respect. Can we reset our collective compass and find a more life-affirming way to live on this beautiful planet?

A VIBRATIONAL COMPASS

My brush with cancer initiated a profound change. The long years of survival mode had depleted my joy. Resetting my vibrational compass, I made a choice for nourishment, abundance, and joy. It helped that the man in my life embodied lightness of being and *joie de vivre*.

A few years later, Sander and I got married. I had never really aspired to being married, but it felt right to formalize our soul bond in the surface-world. Besides, in the three years we had been together, the signs along our path had been unequivocal in pointing us in this direction.

No Gold Without The Dragon

The promise to my boys had been fulfilled. Luca had already left home, and Liam had finished school. They had become young men ready to make their own way in the world. On my wedding day, these precious souls led me down a forest path to a grassy clearing in the embrace of Hout Bay's fire mountains. Sander was waiting for me at our elemental altar, encircled by family and friends. In a simple ceremony, we spoke our vows to each other. In essence, we vowed to keep the joy vibration alive. This was the wellspring of our relationship, which began in medieval France, and would feed our life together now. The joy vibration was our mysterious magnetic force, our glue, and it would be our compass for the journey onward. We were picking up the thread of our original story and weaving new verses and chapters.

In her lyrical style, Clarissa Pinkola Estés implores us:

> *I hope you will go out and let stories, that is life, happen to you, and that you will work these stories from your life — not someone else's life — water them with your blood and tears and your laughter till they bloom, till you yourself burst into bloom.*[18]

Blood and tears and laughter, that's about right. Since answering the call, I had raised my boys and was doing the healing work I really wanted to do. In the process, I found my soul roots as a healer and released my sorrowful shamanic past. I had completed the Dark Energy Intensive and befriended the dragon. I had gone through a cancer scare and lived to tell the tale. It was time to write a new chapter of my story.

Accompanying me into this next chapter was a man who had journeyed with me through time. He grounded me in the deepest possible way. From this firmly rooted place, I could expand into the breadth of my soul mission. It was time to spread my wings and claim the power of the Albatross, the majestic sea bird of the southern oceans.

---

18 Clarissa Pinkola Estés, *Women Who Run With the Wolves: Myths and Stories of the Wild Woman Archetype* (USA: Ballantine Books, 1992).

Chapter 7 | Light

DRAGON'S GOLD
Wisdom teachings from Chapter Seven

- According to the spiritual Law of Healing, everything is energy, and energy is light. Your energy-consciousness is like a river of light flowing through your body. Ill health arises when the river stops flowing. Heavy emotions such as hurt, grief, fear, anger, resentment, and jealousy are like silt in the river. If these dense energies build up through suppression and are not continually alchemized through processing and expression, they block the flow of life force energy and ultimately cause disease. High-frequency healing energy, or love for that matter, clears the debris so the river of light can flow again.

- Another aspect of the spiritual Law of Healing is that, even with permission, you cannot impose healing on someone if, at some level, they don't want it. For example, if the illness is serving a karmic lesson, taking it away prematurely does not serve them and may incur more karma for the healer. In such cases, don't push the river before it is ready to flow. Divine timing is also a factor. If it is our time to go, then there is not much that either conventional or energy medicine can do to change the outcome.

- The physical body is structured by the energy and vibration of consciousness. This includes the soul's consciousness forged over many lifetimes. All changes in the body occur within the container of this multi-temporal consciousness, which is in a constant state of flux. The perpetual mind-body conversation cuts deep grooves into your physical make-up. It is possible to reverse disease by changing this conversation and, with it, the vibrational terrain in which imbalance arose. Change how you think and feel, and you quite literally change your biology.

- Cancer, or any chronic illness, is a wake-up call and a teacher. If you are willing to engage with the teacher as an ally, the potential for transformation and growth is boundless. Reversing cancer is possible but requires a holistic approach to change the vibrational terrain. A hyper-focus on cancer itself ignores the terrain in which it has flourished. Holistic, or integrated, healing, on the other hand, delves into the physical, emotional, mental, and spiritual layers of being to understand why the body produced disease in the first place. While it might not be possible to pinpoint the root cause, there is invariably a complex combination of physiological, biochemical, emotional, mental, and spiritual factors in the mix. Addressing all these aspects changes the vibrational terrain in which these factors interact. This supports the body's self-regulatory mechanisms and innate capacity to heal.

8

SHADOW
January 2017 – June 2019

Still round the corner there may wait
A new road or a secret gate
And though I oft have passed them by
A day will come at last when I
Shall take the hidden paths that run
West of the Moon, East of the Sun.

– J.R.R. Tolkien, author of *The Fellowship of the Ring*

West of the moon, east of the sun, is the mythical place where the sun is eternally sinking in the west, and the moon is forever rising in the east. It symbolizes the eternal threshold of darkness. This is a place of crisis from which one may choose to stay in the darkness or move toward the light. Tolkien's reference to this fabled place comes from an old Norwegian fairy tale about a young woman who journeys into the twilight zone. Here she fights for her values, triumphs in her struggle, claims her just rewards, and returns to the light. This Norse myth is a version of all initiatory stories and the traverse through the dark night of the soul. It is the story of every modern woman's struggle within a patriarchal culture to find her voice, reclaim her truth and rise into her divine feminine power.

Before I found my wings, another initiation was waiting around the corner, another foray into the darkness before I could return to the light. This had been the pattern throughout my healer's journey; before I could guide others, I went through another transformational loop of my own. As it turned out, the next growth spurt was an almost total dissolution of my identity and everything that had structured my life for the last fifteen years.

The journey of a healer is a continual search for the highest path—a life-long dance between personal healing and the healing offered to others. As I grew, the way I worked with my clients changed. Every time I integrated new knowledge, new types of clients would arrive in my healing room as if on cue. Or perhaps it worked the other way round. My clients pushed me forward; then, I expanded to meet the challenge. Either way, my clients were part of the dance: healer and recipient—two sides of the same coin—reflecting, challenging, and pushing each other to stretch and grow. This was the magic of the path.

Like any path, mine was strewn with assorted highs and lows. After the high of retrieving the joy vibration in California and finding Sander again, there was a big dip ahead. Before I could stretch into my wingspan, I would go through another dark night of the soul, the third in my lifetime. By now, I knew that the dark night was an initiation into the next level of awareness. The third time around, I had a map of sorts to find my way through. Nevertheless, it was a challenging time in my life.

I should have known by now that light and shadow go hand in hand. It is a misconception to think that light is a constant state or an attainable endpoint. In a dualistic dimension, there will always be opposites calling for balance. From a non-dualistic perspective, the one encompasses the other. Darkness is only the absence of light, and light is the absence of darkness. Mastery is to give equal opportunity to both, enjoying the light and embracing the shadow. Shadow and light. The spiraling dance.

THE COLLECTIVE SHADOW

After the Dark Energy Intensive, the shadow that hung over my healing room was related to the unresolved trauma of my country's painful history. Most South Africans have experienced violence or trauma in some form or another, and this came out of the shadows in a steady stream of distressing cases.

With the ending of apartheid, South Africa embarked on a grand reconciliation program. When Nelson Mandela came to power in 1994, he preached a message of forgiveness. We hung our hats on the concept of the Rainbow nation and the dizzy hope of healing the past. Inspired by Mandela's almost god-like status, we set to work building bridges between the nation's multiracial, multicultural, multilingual, and highly unequal citizens. The Truth and Reconciliation Commission (1995 - 2002) went some way toward healing old wounds, though most believe it didn't go far enough in redressing the wrongs of apartheid that simmered and seethed beneath the rhetorical surface. We were, and still are, a fractured nation. With time, the mirage of the Rainbow nation faded, and the collective shadow loomed large once again. Democracy did not bridge the inequality gap—one of the largest in the world—and the messy era of state capture corruption during Jacob Zuma's presidency (2009 - 2018) only made matters worse. Our fraught past will not just magically disappear.

Apartheid left no one untouched. Regardless of race, color, or creed, everyone is affected by the unresolved trauma at the heart of the nation. Anger, fear, and anxiety were and still are, to some extent, the vibrational keynotes. In my healing practice, I began to see clients who were tapping into the trauma of their family's unique experience of apartheid or colonialism. Across the racial spectrum, they came out of the woodwork in droves to my healing room. I had to ask myself, *why now?* My answer was that until now, I had not been ready to handle the distressing depths of the nation's wounding. The initiation with dark energies was a necessary preparation to hold a safe space for my clients as they faced their personal and ancestral traumas. Undoubtedly, it was also time to look in the mirror to find the reflection of the unresolved trauma that I might be carrying.

Some of my clients had experienced apartheid-related trauma directly; for others, it was embedded in their family stories and ancestral heritage. The traumatic experiences of one generation can be transferred to the next generation in numerous ways, including conditioning, behaviors, beliefs, and even gene expression. This is known as transgenerational or intergenerational trauma. Transgenerational trauma is largely unconscious. We can think of it as the shadow story; the story that isn't told yet gets handed to the next generation much the same as the family stories that are consciously passed on. The body holds all these family stories. Healing from transgenerational trauma takes some digging to unearth the shadow story and reset the body-mind system.

A poignant case of transgenerational trauma involved Themba, a young Black student struggling with chronic anxiety. During the apartheid years, Themba's grandparents lived in exile in Angola, where they were members of the then-banned African National Congress (ANC) and part of the underground anti-apartheid movement. On one fateful day, Themba's grandmother opened a Christmas parcel, which appeared to have been sent from her family in Soweto. It exploded in her hands, and she was killed instantly. Although Themba wasn't born yet, my young client was carrying the energetic imprints of the tragedy that befell his family in the early eighties. At the time, Themba's mother was ten years old. Losing her mother in this gruesome way, and witnessing her father's devastating grief and anger, was extremely traumatic for Themba's mother. The family never spoke about what happened, and these intense emotions were buried. Seeing Themba nearly forty years later, the echoes of this tragic event were still evident in his energy field.

Sending lethal letter bombs was a common tactic of the apartheid security forces, and many exiles who sought shelter in the country's neighboring states—Angola, Botswana, Zimbabwe, Zambia, and Mozambique—were victims of this type of covert operation. In the 1980s at the height of the anti-apartheid struggle, there were many brutal assassinations within the country and beyond its borders. Anti-apartheid activists of all race groups were targeted. The assassination of Ruth First, a White anti-apartheid activist who suffered a similar fate in Mozambique in 1982, was one of the few to make headlines. As a university student involved in the internal anti-apartheid movement, I was privy to many horrific tales about similar events that didn't make the national news.

Themba's story unlocked something deeply buried inside me, a visceral bone-felt pain. Was I simply feeling Themba's unfelt pain? Was it my own sorrow and guilt about the sins of my White compatriots? Or was it the collective heartache I had tapped into when I worked with Themba?

There isn't a simple answer to these questions. I considered my own family history—a story of privilege by comparison, yet as a privileged White South African, I also carried ancestral trauma and guilt. You cannot live in a country of such contrasts without being affected by the horrors of oppression. The oppressor and the oppressed are bound together, two sides of the same tarnished coin, going right back to our early roots in colonialism.

Working in Cape Town with clients whose families had lived here for centuries, I encountered the impacts of our colonial legacy again and again. At this point, a whistle-stop tour through South Africa's early colonial history might give some context to my ancestral healing work.

THE CAPE'S COLONIAL ROOTS

The first colonizers were Dutch traders, who arrived in the Cape with the Dutch East India Company, or more accurately, the *Vereenigde Oostindische Compagnie* (VOC). Back in the 1600s, the Cape of Good Hope, as it was then known, was nothing more than a stopover on the VOC's lucrative spice route to the Dutch East Indies. But the VOC gardens were so beautiful and the sunny Cape's grape-growing conditions so enticing that the Dutch traders soon settled at the foot of Table Mountain.

Like most colonizers in that era, the Dutch settlers enslaved the local Khoisan people, who by all accounts didn't take to this mistreatment, and many disappeared into the hinterland. This left the Dutch settlers short of labor to cultivate their crops, so their attention turned to importing slaves from the Dutch East Indies. So many slaves arrived on the spice-laden ships they soon formed a new population group known as the Cape Malays. Many Malay slaves were skilled artisans: silversmiths, milliners, cobblers, masons, and tailors. Over a period of about 150 years, until slavery was abolished in 1834, slave labor diversified to include these artisanal jobs. To this day, the Cape Malays have a distinct identity, with the Muslim religion and Malay cuisine deeply embedded in Cape Town's colorful cultural tapestry.

The Cape Malay culture is only one of many other cultural threads in this tapestry. For a few centuries before the first Immorality Act banned interracial sexual relations in 1927, the Dutch interbred with Khoisan locals and Malay slaves, resulting in the mixed-race Colored population that is the majority population group in the Western Cape province. Over time, there was further cultural layering as British colonialists displaced the Dutch population while Black Africans, predominantly Xhosa speaking, migrated from the rural Eastern Cape province to Cape Town in search of work.

In this richly woven tapestry, there are multiple intersections between race, religion, and language. For example, there are English or Afrikaans-speaking Muslims who might identify as Colored; Afrikaans or English-speaking Christians who might identify as White or Colored; Xhosa-speaking Christians or Zionists who identify as Black; and English-speaking Hindus who identify as Indian. Among the city's residents, there are many other religious affiliations, such as Jewish, Buddhist, and Greek Orthodox, to name a few. The astonishing thing is that despite such a racially fraught history, when it comes to religion, South Africans are uniquely tolerant.

Also woven into this cultural tapestry are layers of pain. The colonial legacy is stitched into the very fabric of every community. When it came to my clients, clearing aspects of this complex legacy could take some unstitching, as I discovered when Ayesha came to see me.

Chapter 8 | Shadow

AYESHA'S STORY

Ayesha was a Colored, English-speaking Muslim woman, a mother of three with her own small IT business. When Ayesha came to see me, she was struggling with severe anxiety, depression, and weight gain. She described feeling trapped and hopeless. She felt as if she were constantly holding her breath, waiting for the other shoe to drop. While telling me her story, I noticed she repeatedly used the words *trapped* and *hopeless*.

As the breadwinner in her family, Ayesha worked hard to earn a living and constantly worried about financial security. From a poor family, she was determined to give her children better opportunities than she had growing up on the Cape Flats. Not only was poverty a grinding reality in her childhood, but she had suffered many other hardships. Ayesha had a difficult start in life, having been abandoned at age two by her alcoholic mother. After that, she was cared for by a series of relatives until she was formally adopted at age five by an aunt.

Listening to Ayesha's story, I imagined we were in for some deep inner child work: abandonment, rejection, survival fear. This was the emotional landscape of her childhood. When I entered her energy field, I was shown a series of perplexing images. The first was a female figure sitting hunched forward in a tightly packed row of women, all chained at the ankles. They were barely visible in the dimly lit space, and the stench was overpowering. I was aware of a rocking motion and guessed these prisoners must be in a ship's hull. Then I was bombarded with several rapid-fire images of men and women working in vineyards and fields under the hot sun. I saw several different settings with different people, giving the impression of time moving forward.

Tuning into the woman on the boat, I was told that she was Ayesha's ancestor. She was a Malay slave brought from the Dutch East Indies to the Cape of Good Hope in the early 1700s, where she spent the rest of her life working as a slave on a Dutch-owned farm. Her children were born into slavery, as were their children, and so on until slavery was abolished over a hundred years later in 1834. In other words, several generations in Ayesha's ancestral lineage had been enslaved, which was undoubtedly the root cause of her deep feelings of entrapment and hopelessness.

With Ayesha's permission, we embarked on a process of ancestral healing. The slave woman on the boat was the original, or seed, ancestor in her maternal line. I cut energetic ties with this ancestor and cleared the female lineage until the present generation, including Ayesha's children. I then worked through Ayesha's high heart and soul star chakras to clear ancestral trauma and the vibrations of hopelessness and despair. After the first session, Ayesha reported that she felt that she could breathe and relax for the first time in a long time. This was a good result, but I knew that her healing journey had only just begun.

Ayesha had inherited several disempowering and deeply ingrained beliefs transmitted down her ancestral line that were running like background programs in her psyche: *life is a struggle, it is hopeless, I am trapped*. Not only did Ayesha experience herself as a victim of her tough childhood, but she also suffered from a victim mindset of utter powerlessness that had permeated her lineage for hundreds of years.

I worked with Ayesha for about two years. During this time, we worked on clearing these disempowering beliefs and the childhood wounding that was keeping her stuck in a victim mindset. As Ayesha gradually released her past, she was able to explore new ways of being. Over time she made some important inner and outer shifts, transforming her fear-driven, workaholic lifestyle into one where she could relax and enjoy a newfound sense of freedom.

Ayesha's ancestral story was not uncommon. Many of my clients hailed from slave roots. This shameful episode in South Africa's history was embedded in their family narratives of both spoken and shadow stories.

Despite a privileged position in the history of oppression, my White clients were not immune from the impacts of colonialism and the conflicts *between* oppressors. Around this time, I worked with Liezel, a young Afrikaans woman struggling with alcohol dependency. When I went into Liezel's energy field, I saw her great-grandmother in a British concentration camp during the Anglo-Boer War (1899 - 1902). In these harsh circumstances, this tough *boerevrou* (farmer's wife) watched helplessly as her four young children died one after the other. After the war, Liezel's great-grandmother took to the bottle and drank herself into a numbing stupor. Here was the seed point of my young client's troubles.

Working with Ayesha and Liezel got me thinking about my own family history in the Cape Colony. On my Afrikaans-speaking father's side, my Dutch ancestors arrived in the Cape in the late 1600s with the first wave of Dutch colonists. On my English-speaking mother's side, my lineage is Celtic. On her paternal side, my Irish ancestors landed in Cape Town in the 1840s, about 150 years after my Dutch ancestors. According to my great-great-great grandfather's diary, the Irish lot had fun in the fashionable Cape Colony before jumping on the gold-rush bandwagon. My ancestors on my mother's maternal side came from the south of England and arrived in the Eastern Cape in the 1820s, with the contingent known as the 1820 Settlers. I've already mentioned how tough life was for this group of settlers, and my immigrant ancestors were no exception. This is my transgenerational shadow story—survival mode, fear, and abuse.

ANCESTRAL HEALING

From an energetic point of view, we carry the unresolved issues from the bloodlines of both parents. This is our ancestral inheritance or karma, which is stored in our soul star chakra. From a scientific viewpoint, new research in the field of epigenetics has found that ancestral trauma may be passed on through genes. It is part of our genetic make-up, embedded in our DNA.

You might well wonder how it is possible to clear trauma encoded in the DNA. We have been taught that genes are destiny, making us susceptible to certain diseases, for example. But we are not as much sitting-duck victims of our genes as we have been led to believe. Genes can be switched on or off, depending on the environment and our responses to it. In other words, our biology is more a product of family belief systems than genetics research would have us understand.

In his best-selling book *Biology of Belief*, Dr. Bruce Lipton, explores this notion through the study of epigenetics and has written several books on this fascinating subject.[19] Epigenetics proposes that both

---

19 Dr Bruce Lipton, *The Biology of Belief: Unleashing the Power of Consciousness, Matter & Miracles* (Hay House, Inc., 2008).

physiological traits and environmental factors turn genes on and off and define how our cells *read* our genes. In other words, epigenetics establishes a strong link between the mind's beliefs and attitudes and the body's cellular behavior.

Epigenetics is gaining traction in the scientific world and provides an explanation for how trauma may be passed down through bloodlines. The conventional view is that genetic information is fixed, and we can't change our genetic make-up. In other words, for better or for worse, we are stuck with our genes. Epigenetics contests this notion of genetic determinism, proposing a more responsive genetic structure. At the heart of epigenetic theory is the idea that what people experience switches certain genes on and others off. In other words, an ancestor's experience of and reaction to a traumatic event may change the gene expression, which alters the genetic transmission to the next generation. This altered transmission is the equivalent of the shadow story.

Genes are a bit more chameleon-like than originally assumed; they change the way they express themselves without any changes in the DNA sequence itself. Our amazing genes also contain memory, and this genetic memory is what gets passed down through the bloodline. This is how the experiences of our ancestors, especially trauma, may affect us decades, even centuries later.

That's the bad news. The good news is that we have more control over our genetic inheritance than we have been led to believe. Think of it like this. In genetics—the old paradigm, genes cannot be changed; in epigenetics—the new paradigm, genes can be changed by switching them on or off. We just have to find the switch.

That's the scientific gist. From an energetic point of view, if an ancestor had unresolved trauma, this may be passed on to their descendants through family beliefs, patterns, and behaviors. Much like the unfinished business from a past life, ancestral trauma can persist for many generations. It is an *energetic constellation* for the bloodline. Each member of the family will pick up some aspect of the package to carry and either resolve it or pass it on. Ancestral wounds are also amplified by events along the way, cutting deep grooves in the family psyche, which become our own until we recognize that the roots lie in the ancestral realm.

At a soul level, we choose our birth family and invariably inherit the genetic traits of that family bloodline. Sometimes, a soul will choose a birth family with ancestral wounding that matches the soul's wounding. In this scenario, the lessons the soul needs to learn correspond with family wounds, and there may be an overlap of people, issues, and karma in the soul and ancestral lineages. In my experience, this constellational complexity made for some surprising untangling and unraveling in the healing room.

If there is significant ancestral wounding, the information is available in a client's energy field. So, when offering ancestral healing, I would usually see the seed point clairvoyantly through a series of images, much like viewing a past life, only the protagonist in this approach is the ancestor, not the client. Once or twice, I have come across an ancestor who was the client in a past life—an intersection of ancestral and soul lineage—but this is rare. My guides would usually tell me when the original wounding occurred, and I would get a visceral sense as to whether it was coming through the mother or father lines. Most of my clients were familiar with their family history, at least the surface story, and could verify what I found in the energetic memory banks of their ancestral lineage.

There are many ways to do ancestral healing, especially among the shamanic traditions. My approach was to locate the original trauma—the seed point—in the bloodline and work energetically with the original ancestor to clear the wound. Once the original wounding had been cleared, it was a matter of drawing the purified energy down the family line until it reached the client. The final step was to clear the wounding as it appeared in the client's energetic make-up. This is where the client can flip the cellular switches and clear the genetic memory.

When I first encountered this new knowledge frontier, I trusted my guides to show me what to do. My Chinese guide, Doctor, was especially forthcoming about the mysteries of genetic memory and shared some handy techniques. One of these techniques is DNA coding or *recoding*.

That's right! We can change our DNA coding. DNA strands appear energetically as thin crystal-white lines along the spinal cord. With Doctor's guidance, I was able to dissolve tiny knots in these DNA strands attuning them and the internal coding to a higher vibrational frequency that sustainably replaces the lower frequency of the genetic trauma memory. In this way, it is possible to delink from genetic DNA and align with spiritual DNA, effectively freeing us from ancestral karma.

The concept of spiritual DNA was new to me. A simple explanation is that genetic DNA relates to our biological make-up, while spiritual DNA relates to our spiritual potential—or divine blueprint. Genetic DNA is the outward, physical manifestation of generations of conditioning and third-dimensional programming. These genetic codes, sometimes referred to as *enslavement codes* because they keep us enslaved to an old paradigm, can be altered by energetic means, and attuned to the higher frequencies of incoming light codes. The process of changing the genetic environment is one of activating the dormant information within the strands of DNA and attuning them to these more exalted light codes.

I gained further insight into this recoding process when I worked with Monique, who was suffering from a rare genetic disorder for which there was no medical cure. After fifteen years of suffering from a range of debilitating symptoms, Monique had turned to energy healers and shamans for assistance. She had several incredible breakthroughs on her health journey and was curious to understand more about her soul purpose and asked me for a soul reading. When I offer soul readings, I tune into my client's energy field, their soul energy and channel information from two spirit guides who assist with the readings. My reading guides were clear: Monique's life purpose was to learn how to work with *degraded genes* and embody the higher-frequency light codes. Learning *how* to do this would contribute toward higher consciousness entering and altering the mainstream medical model.

Although I assisted many clients with DNA recoding, Monique was a unique case because she had to learn how to work with the genetic codes herself and, according to my guides, would go on to pioneer this new field.

THE SPIRALING DANCE

Healing work is a dance between energy, consciousness, and karma. Whatever the issue, the task of a healer is as much to transmute the energy as to surface the deep-seated issues into consciousness. With greater awareness, my clients could face their own dragons and move forward on their paths with conscious choice. This is the dance of growth-led change, the spiral of evolutionary consciousness in motion. Karma also plays a role; we can't go faster than karmic lessons allow. However, healing energy is a powerful frequency and can help us move through the wheel of karma at an accelerated pace.

In South Africa, this dance took a particular form. As a nation, we have a lot of bad karma, so the vibratory note that directs the dance is trauma. Across the spectrum of race, class, culture, language, religion, and any combination thereof, trauma is pervasive. From an energetic point of view, it is safe to say that trauma is endemic. So, it's not surprising that I encountered a lot of trauma in my healing room. Underneath every surface-world story, trauma lurked in the shadows like a hidden choreographer. The stories varied, but the vibration was the same, oscillating like a tremor in the energy body. Trauma was so pervasive that a standard question for all my new clients was, have you ever experienced major emotional or physical trauma in your life? With few exceptions, most of them had experienced some degree of trauma. Although trauma is a highly subjective experience, the subjective interpretations associated with it are, at least to some extent, defined by cultural norms. By any measure, South Africa's *trauma norm* is quite extreme.

In psychology, there is a distinction between big-T trauma and small-t trauma. Big-T trauma includes war, accidents, natural disasters, the death of a loved one, physical and sexual abuse, and witnessing or being a victim of violent crime. Small-t trauma arises from repeated low-key events: physical injury, emotional abuse, being ignored or bullied, moving homes, and changing schools frequently, emigrating, losing a job, family conflict, infidelity in a relationship, a divorce, blending families, having a parent or sibling who is mentally ill or suffers from addiction, and more. Experiencing persistent low-key trauma builds up over time and may lead to traumatic stress symptoms.

By these definitions, we are all a little traumatized, and in South Africa, it is safe to say that the vast majority have experienced some variation of big-T trauma. When small-t trauma sits on top of big-T trauma, we are dealing with complex trauma. This, too, was common garden variety stuff in my healing room.

Trauma of whatever type leaves a mark in the psyche and distorts the energy field and its ability to function at an optimal level. Vibrationally, trauma keeps the frequency locked into the lower vibrational range of fear, anxiety, and anger, and the chakric body reflects this vibrational state of affairs. In cases of trauma, a common chakra pattern is that the base chakra will be vibrating with survival fear, the solar plexus with ego-fear, the high heart with anxiety, and the heart chakra will be closed and defended. The good news is that with awareness and energetic recalibration, we are capable of healing from trauma in all its variations.

VIOLENCE AND BIG-T TRAUMA

South Africa's violent culture has left an indelible mark on the nation's psyche. Endemic violence finds expression in a multitude of destructive ways. In my neighborhood, violent crime was surging, with almost nightly home invasions in the immediate area. In South Africa, a home invasion is almost without exception, an armed robbery. It is not uncommon to be held at gunpoint, tied up, or otherwise physically assaulted. You are considered lucky to escape with your life.

The situation is far worse in the Cape Flats' poorer neighborhoods. According to global rankings, Cape Town is one of the most violent cities in the world, with one of the highest murder rates, largely due to gang-related conflict. Ordinary families suffer at the hands of unmitigated gang violence, and all too frequently and tragically, children are caught in the crossfire of gun battles on the streets. So too, the women of South Africa are bleeding. Gender-based violence and rape are endemic, with statistics too horrific to comprehend. What hope is there for the divine feminine in the face of such grotesque expressions of masculine power?

Yet, as a traumatized nation, South Africans have been conditioned to shrug off violent expressions. We have been collectively desensitized to it. Events that in other countries would dominate headlines for weeks barely get a mention in the local press. We are meant to bounce back and carry on. We wear our resilience like a badge of honor, but our hearts have hardened. Invariably, trauma is suppressed, unacknowledged, undealt with, just waiting to erupt.

Working in this vibrational field was demanding, and there were stories that made my blood curdle. What some of my clients had endured was beyond imagining. Energetically, it was harrowing, but not in the same way as the Dark Energy Intensive. In this terrain, there was no fear on my part, only heartache and sorrow. Nevertheless, it demanded everything I had as a healer to hold a strong, safe container for this new wave of clients. The gift they gave me was to open my heart of compassion.

One of these clients was Farouk. He had grown up in what he called a "gangster household" on the Cape Flats and had been both a witness to and a victim of violence throughout his childhood. This had left an indelible mark on his mind, body, and soul.

FAROUK'S STORY

When Farouk arrived in my healing room, he hung his head in shame and pronounced himself a mess. Despite landing a job he enjoyed, he said his life was falling apart, and he felt adrift. Even when things were going well, he felt restless and anxious. After a messy divorce a few years ago, Farouk was struggling to get his life back on track. His ex-wife had recently blocked him from seeing his son, a source of great pain. He was distraught.

When we unpacked his distress, Farouk told me that he had never known his own father, who left him and his mother when he was a baby. He had grown up in a gangster household with his extended family of aunts, uncles, and cousins on his father's side of the family. Although the family had given him and his mother shelter, it was a violent environment for a child to grow up in. He was regularly beaten by one of his uncles, bullied by his older cousins, and witnessed several killings in the line of gangster duty. Farouk left home as soon as he reached adulthood and cut ties with his family and community.

Digging deeper into his family history, Farouk told me that his grandparents had been forcibly removed from District Six in the late sixties, and his grandfather, who had lost his livelihood as a result, joined a gang to survive. This was the root cause of the gangster lifestyle and eviscerated masculinity. Listening to Farouk's story, I reflected that his healing journey would require a combination of ancestral healing, inner child healing, and a process of reclaiming his authentic masculine power.

When I went into Farouk's energy field, his energy body was literally shaking. He had grown up on a diet of violence, and the vibrational keynotes were anxiety, fear, and trauma. Before I could begin a process of ancestral or inner child healing, this vibrational field would need recalibrating. This took a few sessions, but finally, as Farouk's vibration settled, we could address the trauma in his father's lineage and the deep wounding of the traumatized child. Over time, we also looked at the issues playing out with his ex-wife. I encouraged Farouk to work with his own feelings and issues before attempting to confront his ex-wife, who was insisting on a court battle.

About six months into our work together, Farouk received a call from his ex-wife asking for a meeting to discuss their son. I helped him get clear about his intentions for the meeting and an acceptable outcome. It was a breakthrough moment on his healing journey. Not only did he have the first conciliatory conversation with his ex-wife since their separation, but she agreed that their son could spend the day with Farouk every Sunday. Farouk was overjoyed! This was the start of a renewed relationship with his son as well as with his inner child, who longed for a meaningful family connection. Stepping into the role of a father was the starting point of reclaiming his masculine power. It took time, but slowly Farouk regained a stronger sense of self and belonging in his new community.

Farouk's spiritual task was to stand in his power and choose his own path rather than blindly following the one laid out by his family culture. His courageous journey allowed him to heal the distorted masculinity passed down through his male lineage and develop a healthier masculinity for himself and his son. We need more men like Farouk to heal the wounded heart of South African men.

If this seems like a sweeping statement, I saw far too many clients who were on the receiving end of dysfunctional male behavior. Rape is practically endemic in South Africa and poor women, who live in marginal informal settlements, are especially vulnerable to this predatory behavior. For a while, I worked at a healing clinic, a multi-disciplinary pro bono service for women who couldn't afford private care. The aim was to provide emergency intervention and then arrange appropriate support, whether counseling or medical, for vulnerable women who would otherwise not access these services.

At the healing clinic, I saw many women suffering from post-traumatic stress disorder in the wake of sexual assault and various forms of abuse. This was painful work and a sobering reflection of South Africa's ruptured social fabric. One of these pro bono clients was Lindiwe, who arrived at the clinic in a distraught state. The previous week she had been accosted by two men and raped in front of her young daughter. This is her harrowing story.

LINDIWE'S STORY

Lindiwe was from the Eastern Cape. Like many rural South Africans, Lindiwe had come to the city in search of work. She shared a shack in an informal settlement on the Cape Flats with a female cousin and their three children. She eked out a living selling second-hand clothing on the streets. Lindiwe's daughter was eight years old and attended school in the neighboring township. Life was tough, but she got by despite crowded living conditions and a precarious livelihood. "My daughter will have a better future," Lindiwe told me.

Most informal settlements on the Cape Flats are poorly serviced, with no indoor toilets or running water. Sanitation is a public facility, not much more than a tap and a portaloo shared by scores of families. Using these rudimentary facilities, especially at night, can be a risky undertaking. One evening, just after dark, Lindiwe had accompanied her daughter to the toilet at the end of their street. While waiting outside, she was accosted by two young men, barely in their twenties. They jeered at her, asking her why she was hanging around like a prostitute. Just then, her daughter opened the toilet door and stepped outside. The young men flashed a smile and made for the young girl. "It's you or her," they said, holding the girl by the arm. Of course, Lindiwe offered herself and told her daughter to run. Rooted to the spot, her daughter watched while the men, barely more than boys, took turns raping her mother, but eventually, she ran to fetch help.

Lindiwe was racked with sobs while recounting her story. Despite her horrific ordeal, her concern was for her daughter. Since the incident, the little girl hadn't spoken one word, and she refused to go out, not even to school. She was completely traumatized by what she had witnessed. Watching her daughter suffer like this and feeling helpless was a double trauma for Lindiwe. She was also fearful that the perpetrators would come back.

My work was cut out for me. Lindiwe's energy body was visibly shaking. Her base chakra was fractured, and she was completely ungrounded. With only one session at our disposal, I had to focus on stabilizing her. After clearing the perpetrators' energy out of Lindiwe's aura, I repaired her base chakra and grounded her again. I was then able to release the shock and recalibrate her energy. It was not possible to clear such severe trauma in one session, but by grounding her and clearing the worst of the shock, I hoped Lindiwe would be better able to process her ordeal and find the strength to help her daughter.

Sadly, it was beyond my power to change Lindiwe's circumstances. She and her daughter were extremely vulnerable in an environment where violence was the norm. The best I could do was to arrange various interventions for both mother and daughter so that they could receive the support they needed to heal.

Like many poor South Africans, Lindiwe lived in a high-anxiety energy field. As a single mother with a girl child, living with a female cousin, she was particularly vulnerable, having none of the protection that a husband or father or brother might offer. Lindiwe was used to navigating danger. Her instincts were on high alert at the best of times. Her world was a precarious one, where dog eats dog, and predatory young men acted with impunity. As a result, Lindiwe was anxious and hypervigilant. A big-T trauma like the one she had just been through could tip her over the edge, eroding her hard-won resilience. She was going to need a lot of support to heal. I prayed that Lindiwe and her daughter wouldn't fall through the cracks of the over-burdened community service system.

Even privileged South Africans were not immune to violence and the resultant trauma. I worked with many clients who had been subjected to muggings, car-jackings, home invasions, and various other expressions of the nation's violent psyche. One of these clients was a young woman called Chloe, who came to see me after an armed robbery at her home.

CHLOE'S STORY

Chloe was a talented young artist in her twenties who suffered from chronic anxiety and depression. I had been seeing her regularly for a few years. The energy work helped her to maintain balance, and Chloe had made good progress in managing her anxiety and fluctuating moods. Although it had been challenging for her, she had successfully completed a demanding Fine Arts degree, and her future was looking good.

One of the underlying reasons for Chloe's mental health issues was an early trauma when she was just three years old. She had witnessed her father beating her mother black and blue. After that incident, he walked out, abandoning his wife and young daughter. Chloe never saw her father again. This early trauma had left deep scars, including a profound lack of safety. This was Chloe's big-T trauma.

Now Chloe had gone through another big-T trauma. This time the violence was directed at her. Late one evening, three young men armed with knives broke into the apartment she shared with a flatmate. Two of the men tied up Chloe and her flatmate while the third ransacked the apartment. Chloe was shaking when she described how one of their assailants was yelling obscenities at them as the other tied their hands behind their backs. She thought they were high on Tik (crystal methamphetamine), a common scenario in Cape Town. The third man was grabbing laptops and cell phones and demanding cash. When his rucksack was full, the robbers ran off into the night, leaving Chloe and her flatmate in a shocked heap on the living room floor. They managed to untie themselves and call for help on the landline. Fortunately, the young women weren't harmed physically, but the trauma they had both been through was going to take a long time to heal.

Knowing Chloe's low tolerance for any type of stress, I was concerned about the impact of this new trauma. When I went into Chloe's energy field, her energy body was shuddering violently. Before I could begin to release the trauma vibration, I cut energy ties with the man who had tied her up. I also had to clear the energetic imprint of the ropes around her wrists that were still evident in her etheric body. After a lot of clearing, I focused on releasing the vibration of trauma. This I did through Chloe's high heart, which was shrouded in a dense black cloud. Clearing this dense energy and releasing the trauma vibration was slow going, but eventually, the shuddering subsided, and I could channel a higher vibration to recalibrate Chloe's energy field.

Chloe felt much better after that session, but we had to return to the early big-T trauma, which had been reactivated by the recent trauma. Over several sessions, we worked with this deeper layer of trauma. The triggering of the old trauma had resulted in an energy tie to her father that had reformed at the back of her heart chakra. Here the energies of betrayal and distrust were keeping her heart stuck in the past. The silver lining was that the trauma of the home invasion had brought to the surface aspects of the earlier big-T trauma that she hadn't wanted to remember. Chloe could now process this and find a new equilibrium.

After working with so many light seekers, I was wondering why violence and trauma were suddenly so in my face. What had changed in the surface-world? What had changed in my inner world? I found the answer in my worries about the escalating crime and violence in my neighborhood and in Cape Town as a whole. This volatile environment was an inconvenient yet undeniable reality, and I had my head in the sand like the proverbial ostrich. Now my anxiety had surfaced, but I didn't know how best to respond to this situation. Work through my anxiety and carry on with business as usual? Suppress the underlying fear and ignore the disturbing reality? Work energetically to protect my own backyard? In the end, I probably did all three and many variations of this haphazard coping strategy.

None of us were immune from this high-anxiety field. Among the more spiritually minded clientele, I noticed a new phrase creeping into the lexicon: *It is as it is.* What this meant is that things were not so bad, really, and we should just accept whatever was going down and get on with it. This innocent little phrase punctuated the most heart-rending narratives. It was recited like a mantra as if by saying it often enough, the inconvenient reality would just go away. While I understood the Buddhist notion of acceptance and that suffering lies in non-acceptance, this oft-repeated mantra was unsettling me. I suspected it was a form of collective denial, a kind of linguistic cover-up, a clever little spiritual bypass. I had reason for my suspicions because my clients' anxiety-laden energy bodies told a different, more authentic story.

As always, I wondered what my clients were reflecting and teaching me. I kept a running tab of imponderable questions on a little notepad in my healing room. This is what a busy day or a quiet week might yield:

QUESTIONS TO SELF

What is my spiritual bypass?

How do I keep an open, compassionate heart in the face of such horrors?

How do I *not* get sucked into despondency, anger, or White guilt?

How do I keep my vibration stable in an anxiety-charged field?

Is inner peace possible when the field is so fraught?

Sometimes answers come in unexpected ways. If you are alert to the Universe's quirky communication system, answers will always arise to meet your questions, however unfathomable they may seem.

CALL OF THE WILD

That winter, Sander and I went to Botswana on a belated honeymoon. The bushveld was calling. Botswana is like the Garden of Eden. The whole country is teeming with game. North of the Tsetse fly barrier, there are almost no fences. Animals roam free and migrate in vast herds as nature intended. In the winter months, the usually dry Okavango Delta turns into a vast wetland system attracting an abundance of wildlife and birds. In this environment, we quickly dropped into the peace I was craving. After all the trauma work, I desperately needed a reset.

One of the highlights of our visit was an evening bush walk with a Botswanan guide, a skillful tracker and knowledge keeper. He showed us a Giant Eagle Owl—formally known as the Verreaux's Eagle Owl—in her nest with her juveniles. This is a large owl, one of the world's largest, remarkable for its distinctive pink eyelids. From a respectful distance, we watched this pretty mama owl pushing her fledglings out, one by one, headlong into their clumsy flights. Our guide explained that the mother bird had to push the baby owls out; otherwise, they would never leave the nest. I couldn't help feeling that it was an ominous precursor to what was imminent in my own mother-nest.

After two weeks in this pristine wilderness, we flew to Maun in a tiny Cessna. I've always been a nervous flyer, but in the agile Cessna, I succumbed to the thrill of the choppy airwaves. Perhaps I was becoming more at home in the element of air. The dragon, rather silent in the bushveld, would be pleased. When we landed in Maun, we discovered that our flight to Cape Town had left the day before! Our flight had been rescheduled at short notice, and we hadn't received the SMS notification in the bush. We had a good laugh and settled in for the long wait for another flight. Finally, we were rerouted through Johannesburg and headed back to South Africa.

When I walked into the terminal building at Johannesburg's O.R. Tambo International Airport, I was hit by a wave of anxiety that nearly lifted me off my feet and stopped to catch my breath. Working with energy, I was used to discerning what was mine and what was not. This wave of anxiety was certainly not mine. What was going on?

Chapter 8 | Shadow

It dawned on me that anxiety is South Africa's energetic signature. Being in the vibrational soup for so long, I didn't notice the anxiety when I was in that energy matrix. I was like the proverbial frog in the pot of boiling water. Not only was I working with a lot of anxiety and trauma, but I was immersed in the same energetic field. It should have been obvious, but I hadn't really considered the extent of my own immersion until this moment. Although I cleared my energy religiously, I was as much part of the field as anyone else. Like the scientist who observes an experiment, I was inside the vibrational mix, not outside of it. As quantum physics has taught us, there is no such thing as a neutral observer.

This *aha* moment at O.R. Tambo Airport started a running conversation with Sander about living in the city. What did we want to create in our new life together? I wanted to live in a wildish place, where the vibration is soothing, and life is sourced from simple pleasures. Sander had always longed to live in the countryside. We flirted with the idea of leaving the city, but it didn't seem feasible. My whole life was in Cape Town—children, friends, networks, the beloved mountain. There were practical considerations too—work, for example. With an online business and his family in Holland, Sander was more footloose and flexible, traveling more lightly through life than me. Still, I wondered how we could move from impossibility to possibility.

NEW BEGINNINGS

I didn't have to wonder for too long. All sorts of things lined up in the surface-world, and less than a year later, Sander and I moved to Riebeek Kasteel, a small countryside village about an hour from Cape Town. The village nestles in a valley at the foot of Kasteelberg, meaning Castle Mountain, so named because the early Dutch settlers modeled their camp on the mountaintop after the Castle fort in Cape Town. Kasteelberg and Table Mountain are linked by a ley line, and on a clear day, these two landmarks are visible to each other.

Our new home wasn't far from Cape Town, but it might as well have been. It was a different world. The Riebeek Valley is not wild by any stretch of the imagination, being mostly farming country, but it offered the best of both worlds—a country lifestyle within easy reach of Cape Town. Riebeek Kasteel ticked enough boxes to justify leaving the city, which had been my home for the last twenty years.

I wasn't quite ready to move, but is one ever ready for a big change? In the surface-world, the timing was seemingly perfect. Luca was completing his master's degree and preparing to head off to Europe for his gap year. Liam was in his second year at university and chomping at the bit to move into a student house with his friends. With or without me, the constellation was shifting. It made sense to go with the changes and create new beginnings with the man in my life. The time had come to say goodbye to the cozy nest I had created with and for my sons.

Once the wheels were set in motion, change happened rapidly. Within a period of three months, I sold my house, Liam moved into student digs, Luca left for Europe on a one-way ticket, and Sander and I moved to the Riebeek Valley. There was nothing incremental about this transition. It wasn't so much an empty nest as the total dissolution of the nest, and all that was tied to it. Truth be told, I didn't know what had hit me.

EMPTY MOTHER-NEST

My version of an empty nest was rather extreme, as the nest itself didn't exist anymore. It was gone in one *coup de grace*, and with it, my sacred healing room and my identity as a mother—the daily acts of mothering, impromptu chats with my boys, our reassuring rituals, the countless small things that textured our relationships. This was all swept away with the sale of our home. I felt strangely disoriented without these defining roles and rhythms. I had lost my center.

Two weeks after leaving Cape Town, I said goodbye to Luca at the airport, wishing him well on his gap year, knowing in my bones that he would be gone for far longer. Driving back to a place that wasn't yet home, I howled—deep belly-racking sounds I didn't recognize as my own. And then the shock of it was done and what followed was a period of mourning for the triple loss of my home and my two young men.

In the months that followed, I learned that empty-nest syndrome, with or without the nest, was a visceral thing. It was like no other grief I had ever experienced. It was as if my old self was being dismantled as my identity was washed away, and the foundations of my world were being shaken up and rearranged. My boys grounded me; without them around, I felt like a boat slipped from its moorings. For months, I barely knew who I was. During this time, I clung to my healing work for some semblance of sameness, but the form of my work was changing too. No aspect of my former life was left untouched. Even my fledgling marriage underwent a thorough-going transformation. How could it not, when I was in the throes of such an identity meltdown?

I've spoken to many women who've been through the empty-nest phase, and although the narratives vary, it's a universal story of loss and adjustment. It's the unexpectedness of the feelings that knocks one off one's moorings. Nothing prepares you for this moment, perhaps because no one tells you in advance what's coming. Empty-nest syndrome is one of those well-kept secrets about a women's life—like menopause; it's not spoken about very much and quietly endured in the privacy of your home. Often the two coincide, which creates a special kind of craziness. Menopausal or not, mothers are meant to just get on with it, cheerily pushing our children out into the world and celebrating their leaving. This we must do, and fly they must, but there is no rite of passage, no holding place, nothing to bookmark what mothers go through when the home goes eerily quiet.

This time of life is bitter-sweet. It is at once richly rewarding to see your children finding their feet in the world and a supreme act of letting go. Stripped of the active mothering role of tending, nurturing, cajoling, championing, and guiding, women feel as empty as the nest itself. No mother-type is immune from the hollowness that ensues; stay-at-home moms, working moms, and those with a burning purpose are all afflicted by this phenomenon. I thought I could avoid empty-nest syndrome by leaving the nest too, going on my own adventure, and starting a new chapter of my story. But it wasn't quite as I expected.

DARK NIGHT OF THE SOUL, ROUND THREE

Arriving in the Riebeek Valley, I went through a profound process of letting go. This time the breaking down of the old life felt like a dissolution of my old self too. Who was I without the mother role?

My spirit guides told me this dis-integration was necessary to find the "ground of my being" stripped of any ego-identity and attachments. If this sounds like a tall order, it was—this was dark night territory. Sure enough, with every passing day, I could feel myself slipping. The things that defined me were no longer there: my children were no longer orbiting around me, my friends and support systems were out of daily reach, and my old ways of grounding myself simply didn't work anymore. I hadn't yet synced with Riebeek's fluctuating frequency and had nothing to hold onto, just blind faith that I would find my way through. Small comfort was the fact that I had been through a dark night of the soul before. The third time around, I had a rough map, a lantern, and an instinctive feel for it. Thus prepared, it should have been quick passage, but it wasn't.

Some people can skip from one thing to the next, hardly pausing to breathe. I envied them. Ever the tortoise, I took a little longer to transition and find my bearings in a new life. Withdrawing into my shell, I needed to take a long deep breath between stories. This takes time. Something odd happens to time during a dark night of the soul; it collapses, and the time-space of *normal life* comes adrift. Somewhat bewildered by this marital detour, Sander knew not to cajole me out of the dream-tight tortoiseshell or try to fix me. No one else can do the dark night traverse for you. Thankfully, he got this.

Several events in the surface-world plunged me further into the darkness. A few months after we moved to the Riebeek Valley, my dear friend and teacher Frieda passed away after a long struggle with cancer. Her death hit me hard. Knowing that she was at peace in the world of spirit was some comfort, but it didn't take away the numbing grief. Not long after that, Liam was involved in a car crash. Although he was relatively unscathed, the car was a write-off, and it knocked his confidence. It was a big setback on his fledgling flight from home

Chapter 8 | Shadow

and brought to the surface my worst fears about my kids driving on our dangerous roads.

Finding new ground didn't come easily. Every night before I went to sleep, a stream of negative thoughts and fears bubbled to the surface. Without any prompting or direction from me, it arose and kept going, an unbidden, relentless stream of consciousness. Turning the lights off was like opening a floodgate that I was powerless to close. All I could do was observe the flow until I eventually fell into an exhausted sleep. Could this torrent of thought really be arising from within me? The weird thing was that the days were quiet, numbingly so. But at night, when darkness descended, the thoughts gushed to the surface in a kind of mental flood.

What was I to make of the nightly floodwaters? I implored my guides to shed some light. They informed me that it was the next-level purification. They were helping me to let go of old ways of thinking and doing. I had worked on my emotional wounding. Now I had to pay attention to the mind, the hidden recesses, the sub-conscious shadows—all the ingredients that went into the mix of creative manifestation. As within, so without. This is how one of my spirit guides put it:

> It is time to understand the power of thought in creating your experience. Everything in the outer world is an out-picturing of the inner world. Your inner world includes the vast unconscious mind, which is like an iceberg beneath the surface waters. To be a powerful creator, you first need to know your ingredients, sift them like a baker sifts flour, then select what is going into the creative mixture. Choose your thoughts wisely, every single one of them. Treat them as precious jewels. Only then will you truly master the creative process.

When I asked for more light on the subject, there was silence. My erudite guide had gone quiet. There was nothing but to go with the mental purification and wait for the ice-melt floodwaters to subside.

During the day, I kept myself busy. One of the things that tethered me to some sort of ground was working with my hands in the earth. I planted herbs and vegetables in some old crates. After just a few months, my crates were thick with leafy greens and aromatic herbs. Even in the depths of the dark night traverse, there were moments of joy in these simple pleasures.

At the same time, I embarked on a process of energetically clearing our new house and the land around it. Shortly after moving in, we discovered that our property was slap bang in the heart of Oukloof, communal land that belonged to the Colored community, which was forcibly removed in 1965.[20] Back when Oukloof was a thriving Colored community, there was a church on the property next door, and the land around it was communal land. Our house was right in the middle of this patch of seized land. The forced removals in the sixties had seen the Ouklowers displaced, the buildings bulldozed to the ground, and the land seized by the Afrikaans elite. The rightful landowners were moved to a dustbowl on the other side of the railway line.

After nearly six decades, echoes of this trauma were still reverberating in the land around my new home. Tapping into this reservoir of collective pain added to the intensity of my own process, especially at night.

My spirit guides informed me that I was to clear this dense historical imprint. So, bit by bit, I chipped away at the energetic residue in the land. At one point, I tapped into an unfamiliar vein of energy and enlisted a colleague's help. Together we traced an even older imprint, going back as far as colonial times when the Dutch settlers displaced the indigenous KhoiKhoi people and settled in the fertile Riebeek Valley. We were like trackers, combing the Earth for any false notes and flushing out the sticky energies. It took months of sustained clearing, and I couldn't help feeling that it was ancestral karma payback time. My Dutch ancestors, who had come to the Riebeek Valley in the early 1700s, were surely not innocent. But I did this soul work gladly. Clearing the land by day took my mind off the dark night. It helped me find my grounding.

---

[20] With the passing of the Group Areas Act in 1950, the apartheid state went on a rampage of moving Black and Colored families out of the urban centers and dumping whole communities onto fringe wastelands, with no housing, services, or infrastructure. No town was spared this inhumane tearing asunder. Forced removals reached their height in the 1960s, leaving a deep scar on the national psyche. The repercussions in affected communities are evident to this day.

The land was also quietly teaching me. In the process of clearing pockets of pain, I discovered a curious phenomenon that explained the fluctuating frequency in the valley. There were two large vortexes, one situated on the western edge of the village and one outside the village further to the east. The western vortex was particularly powerful. It was doing the job of mopping up low-frequency energy, sucking it into the Earth, and then bringing down higher frequency energy in sporadic bouts. In the build-up between clearings, the frequency in the village could plummet. This energetic pendulum was both puzzling and destabilizing until I found my grounding.

I also discovered a much smaller vortex under our house, right beneath our bedroom, which explained the amplification of thought at night. With the help of a dowser, I was able to clear the vortex and move it to a vacant plot of land. Finally, there was some relief from the mental bulimia.

At the lowest point of this dark night traverse, I had a vivid dream that gave me hope. I was floating in a lake, face down in the water, slowly sinking under, when I felt a tap on my shoulder. Then I heard a calm voice say, "Don't lose heart. All will be well." This dream was a turning point. I have no doubt it was Frieda, busily doing her work on the other side of the veil. She renewed my faith. Frieda's message of hope became my mantra: all will be well—a mental note to self as I slowly found my way out of the abyss.

Despite Frieda's encouragement, the third dark night traverse was an extremely uncomfortable time of my life. I knew discomfort was a necessary element in the alchemy of change, and the degree of discomfort was a measure of how much the old structures had to give way; yet I could feel the resistance to change. Once again, here was the call to surrender to soul-led change and dream a new life into being. It was, in every respect, a waking dreamtime.

SOUL ALCHEMY: BREAKING THE SPELL

No dark night of the soul is easy, but when you understand the nature of it and surrender to the darkness, trusting that you will eventually surface into the light, it is a more manageable crossing. This is not a passive surrender, a docile giving up. It is an alert surrender to the darkness, with all your senses humming. You may not be able to see too well, but this is the time to hone your senses and develop night sight like any wildish being until this new awareness becomes effortless. While your instincts grow accustomed to the dark, you might stumble around a bit, but soon enough, you'll find the pathways. With a little tenacity, you'll make your way through to the other side as surely as day follows night. It may be daunting, terrifying even, but the dark night is a transformational space like no other. It will strip you of everything that no longer serves you, and if you stay long enough in the abyss, it will offer up nuggets of gold.

The most precious gift of a dark night is that it breaks the spell of all the illusionary traps of your old life. It is a rare pause from the automatic life on the surface. It is a soul call to go beyond the surface waters and dive into the rich humus of your being. It is a time of profound growth and soul-led transformation. The wise way is to embrace it as an initiation that will break the spell of your old life and wake you up to something more authentic and life-giving.

The danger is that we may be tempted to resist this kind of deep-dive intimacy. We are conditioned to turn away from the self when we should be turning inward. When we cast our gaze inward, get to know the substance beneath the form, and strip down to our base metal, we can get real and create our life from an authentic source. This is soul alchemy.

Resisting intimacy, we do everything to avoid dark night crossings. More often than not, conditioning overrides the voice of the soul. We'd rather take anti-depressants and bypass the whole unpleasant thing. Not understanding that the dark night itself is medicine, we easily fall prey to false assistance and temptation. We may miss the call to sovereign self-hood and the rare opportunity for soul alchemy. Lured off the path by all manner of distraction, it is all too easy to miss the very thing that we say we most want—a soulful life.

We might break the spell if we are willing to stop all the numbing, resistance, and distraction. A dark night of the soul forces us to slow down, peer inside to discover what's underneath the polished surface, and shatter the illusion. If nothing else will, a dark night initiation will crack your heart right open and lead you to your gold.

That said, going through a dark night takes courage and a wolfish appetite for truth. It demands soul hunger. The trick is to remember the river of light, even when it is obscured, and know that by going within to source your soul light, you shine a light for others.

REVISITING THE HEROINE'S JOURNEY

A dark night of the soul is best understood in the overarching sweep of the Heroine's Journey. From this perspective, it helps to see yourself as the heroine of your story.

When the heroine receives the call, she too must leave the known world and step into the unknown. But while the hero pursues his goals with a flurry of action, the feminine way is a less cut-and-dried affair. Not as precise in her goals, hers is a more open-ended journey. Instead of slaying the dragon when it appears on the path, the heroine is more curious about its nature and what might be hidden in the dark cave where it dwells. She pays homage to the dragon to find out what she can learn. In this respect, her journey is more a pilgrimage than an adventure. If, on her pilgrimage, she can befriend the dragon and enlist its support, all the better.

When the heroine reaches the abyss, she knows instinctively that this is the heart of her journey, and she shouldn't rush too quickly through it. The heroine's abyss is a place of surrender rather than action, a place of deep dreaming, where she begins to see herself and her world with new eyes. It is here that she meets the Goddess and reconnects with her wild feminine nature. From this vantage point, the darkness is a place for reclaiming her true nature and where she gets to change her story if she feels like it. It is nothing less than the crucible of transformation—the heroine's true quest all along.

Returning to the known world, the transformation itself is the gift the Goddess bestows on the heroine. Whatever transpired along the way, she cannot go back to her old life or old way of being. Clear seeing, she can no longer sleepwalk through her days. More alert now, her time in the dark has rekindled her interest in feminine ways of knowing. This new thread of inquiry about her feminine nature, the wildish instinctual aspects of her unconditioned self, helps her to navigate the onward journey. As she heals the wounded feminine and attunes to the divine feminine within—her Goddess energy—she is showered with the gifts of the Goddess. And as she blossoms and grows, she passes these gifts on to others.

Back to my real-life journey, there was another rather elusive gift to retrieve from the depths of time before I could return from the abyss.

RETRIEVING THE VIBRATION OF PEACE

Toward the end of the dark night period, Sander and I went on a road trip through the Languedoc region in France to explore our shared Cathar roots. In the early Middle Ages, the Languedoc region was not part of France, but an independent fiefdom governed by the wealthy Counts of Toulouse. I had wanted to visit Cathar country for as long as I could remember. Excitement bubbled up from the dark night depths.

The Cathars were Christian, but their beliefs deviated from the Roman Catholic church. This infuriated the Pope in Rome, who deemed them heretics. One of the Cathars' *heresies* was that they refused to worship Catholic idols or images of Christ. They believed that Jesus was an ordinary mortal rather than the son of God, who embodied Christ-consciousness and brought the message of love. And here's the rub: Christ's teachings were meant to be directly accessible to everyone, without the Church and its priests acting as intermediaries. Their beliefs put the Cathars on a collision course with the Catholic Church, whose power lay in the message that our sinful souls needed saving and only the Church could intercede. Quite ahead of their times, the Cathars also believed in gender equality, reincarnation, and veganism. They advocated a frugal, almost purist, lifestyle. According to legend, the Holy Grail was entrusted to the purist Cathars by the Knights Templar. It was said to have been spirited away during the Siege of Montségur, becoming part of the Cathar's mystery and inspiring Grail quests ever since.

Arriving in Cathar country, we agreed to do a sensory road trip, selecting a few key sites on the Route de Cathar and, for the rest, following the energy where it took us. We were going on a quest, not a package tour. Sander laughed at my floaty ways, but he was game for the experience. From the moment we landed in Toulouse, I felt at home in France, in my skin somehow. I was delighted that I could still understand French quite well, though my conversational attempts were rather dismal.

Heading south toward the snow-capped Pyrenees in the distance was exhilarating. I love road trips! The Languedoc is mountainous country with spectacular hilltop fortress castles and medieval-style villages tucked into the folds. One of our first stops was the quaint village of Foix, in the Cathar heartland, where we stayed in the home of an Occitan historian. Fascinated, I listened to our host's tales of her family history going right back to Cathar times before France conquered Occitania and French became the dominant language. Over the last eight centuries, the Occitan language has all but died out, but our erudite hostess spoke it fluently and taught the old language at the local primary school.

Every road trip has its own rhythm. Life is languidly slow in the far southwestern corner of the country, and we quickly fell into step with the locals. In the mornings, we visited Cathar sites, later digesting the rich history over long, lazy lunches of delicious French fare on the spring-warm terraces. Though captivating, the first few days of our personal quest were uneventful in terms of resonant energy. I was hoping for a glimpse of our own past-life history in Cathar country, but there was no forcing it.

Following the trail of energy, we headed southeast to Montségur. The old chateau of Montségur is perched on a rocky outcrop—known as the pog—at the top of a steep hill above the village of the same name. Historically, Montségur was the last stronghold of the Cathars. It fell to the Catholic Crusaders in 1244 after a long siege. The siege of

Montségur came right at the end of the Albigensian Crusade—a holy war waged against the Cathars of Occitania in a sustained effort to eradicate their heretical beliefs. In this most unholy of holy wars, the powerful Roman Catholic Church joined forces with the French king and marched against the Cathars in the independent south. This gruesome crusade spanning more than thirty years essentially wiped out the Cathar people—another genocide.

Montségur was the end of the road for the surviving Cathars. Toward the end of the ten-month siege, when the hilltop fortress could no longer hold out, Montségur surrendered, and a truce was reached. The Cathars in the besieged castle were given a choice by their captors— renounce their faith or perish on the pyre. When Montségur fell, more than 200 Cathars chose the Inquisition's pyre. There were others who threw themselves off the ramparts on the sheer northern wall rather than succumb to the Inquisition's fire.

From the moment we arrived in Montségur, I was tingling with excitement. The scent on the trail of energy was getting stronger. With some trepidation, we started the hour-long ascent to the old chateau at the top of the pog. A little way up in a grassy field marked by a simple stone cross is the original site of the Inquisition's pyre, where those who would not renounce their faith were burnt en masse. I expected to feel a charge at the memorial, but there wasn't so much as an energetic murmur.

Somewhat puzzled, we continued to the top, enjoying breath-taking views over the surrounding countryside. Just before we entered the fortress ruins, I stopped to catch my breath, looking toward the Pic de Soulerac to the southwest. Despite the heat of the day, I started shivering, emotion welling up inside me. Here was the charge. I sat for a while and, just as with a past life clearing for a client, the story flowed to me in a transmission of vivid images and words:

> I was a young Cathar woman, about twenty-one years old, living in the chateau at the time of the siege. Having grown up in the area, my role during the siege was as a runner; Sander was an out-rider—*I had never heard either of these terms.* Both of us knew

the countryside like the back of our hands. Many Cathars seeking shelter at Montségur were from further north and relied on our assistance. At the time of the siege, I was one of a few local runners who used the perilous secret pathways on the north-eastern slope to carry messages to the village and back. Ropes had to be used to scale the last section of sheer rockface. As an out-rider, Sander rode further afield, conveying messages to clandestine Cathar groupings and gathering information. In the final weeks of the siege, we were entrusted with the sacred task of smuggling our most treasured holy relics out of the fortress and burying them in the forest near the Pic de Soulerac. The buried treasure was later retrieved by surviving Cathars and taken across the Pyrenees into safe-keeping. When Montségur surrendered, I was one of those who leaped off the cliff face rather than submitting to the Inquisition's pyre. *No wonder I didn't like being airborne!*

Absorbing this old story, we continued up the steep path to the chateau, a bit apprehensive about the pain that I might encounter within its walls. As we entered the old gateway, I felt surprisingly light. Miraculously, we were soon alone, the busload of tourists before us having just departed. After wandering around the ruins, we found a spot below the northern ramparts overlooking the picturesque countryside and lay against the grassy bank. Instead of feeling the pain of this past life experience, I sank into the deepest peace I have ever known.

This peace was like a magnetic force, pulling me into a place of deep rest, almost a surrender. This was not at all what I had expected. In spite of persecutory bloodshed, peace was the dominant note at the Cathar's final stronghold. For me personally, I realized that there was no unfinished business from this cut-short lifetime. As a Cathar *parfait*, I had renounced worldly attachments, and when I leaped off this very cliff with others who had chosen the same fate, I was not attached to life or anything else in the world, not even to Sander, who I had loved in that short lifetime. There was no fear in choosing death. It was, in every respect, a deeply spiritual life and a peaceful transition.

Funny, I mused, in that long-ago life, I chose death at twenty-one years old to honor my life purpose of purity above all else, and in this lifetime, at the very same age, I chose life to complete my soul mission.

If there was nothing to clear from this shared Cathar lifetime, why were we here, I wondered? What had drawn us from the other side of the world nearly eight centuries later? The reason, my spirit guides chipped in, was to retrieve the vibration of peace. Not only did I need to remember this frequency, but I was being guided to embody it once again and to understand what creates inner peace, no matter what is happening in the world.

Non-attachment and sovereign integrity were the teachings from my Cathar past. The vibration of peace was the spiritual key to unlocking the next leg of my journey as a lightworker. These were the gifts of the Goddess, my personal Holy Grail, and I received them gratefully.

Bathed in peace, we lay in the spring sunshine for hours, imbibing Montségur's vibrational imprint into every cell of our twenty-first-century bodies. Up above, a pair of black kites circled around us as if to remind me that the time for wings was coming closer. Little did I know, lying in the soporific May warmth, that inner peace was just the medicine for the Covid crisis that was looming for humanity.

On our return to South Africa, my depression of the past nine months slowly lifted. When I think back, there was a precise moment when the dark night came to an end. One evening, I was locking up my healing room. Being winter, it was dark already, the pathway to the house dimly lit by the light from the kitchen window. As I walked down the path, a Barn Owl flew straight toward me, brushing me on the shoulder with its wing. We both got a fright. I gasped out loud, and the startled owl veered off course, flying into the house through the open back door. Inside, Sander caught the owl with a towel, and together we released it back into the night.

Being touched by an owl felt like an initiatory blessing, a signal that the dark night was done. Thankfully, this uncomfortable time was well and truly over. I had come through the traverse and retrieved the vibration of peace. It was a profound reset. Instead of the mental purging at bedtime, I was waking up to inspirational soul whispers, pearls from the dreamtime, like early morning treasure for the picking.

PICKING UP THE RED THREAD

When Sander and I got married, we wrote our own sacred vows. The essence of our intention was to embed the vibrations of joy, peace, and love in our new life together. After our celebration day with friends and family, we had a short and sweet legal ceremony with a Jewish high priestess. This wise old mystic wrapped a red thread around our wrists as we reiterated our intentions.

The red thread has many layers of meaning. In Jewish mysticism—the Kabbalah—the red thread symbolizes the connection with spirit and the ability to receive it into our being. The thread is tied on the left wrist because energetically, the left side of the body is the feminine side, and it is the feminine aspect of our psyche that feels the flow of spirit through our lives. Being in harmony with spirit is like a river flowing to its destination unimpeded.

From an energetic perspective, the wrists and the hands are an extension of the heart, the beating pulse of our soul's embodiment, the chamber of love. And so, the red thread became quite simply a symbol of love, the last in the trilogy of vibrations we had vowed to cultivate.

The priestess reminded us that when the red thread breaks, as it will, we should tie a new one. Symbolically, this thread-tying is a constant renewal, revitalizing and updating the marriage while keeping the red thread of the original intention alive. Marriage itself becomes a creative process, and any creative process, like life itself, should have a red thread running through it. Sometimes the thread breaks, sometimes you lose it, and sometimes you forget about it. But when you remember and take the time to rethread it, it takes you back to your path, a gentle reminder of your soul's intentions.

After our trip to France, we picked up the thread, and the loftier vibrational notes found their pitch again, a bit like a creaky old piano being tuned. The dark night had obscured the red thread of our intentional life. Almost imperceptibly, like a slow incoming tide, light was dispersing the shadow. Now we could anchor the welcome trilogy of love, peace, and joy in our new life together.

DRAGON'S GOLD
Wisdom teachings from Chapter Eight

- It is a misconception to think that light will ever be a constant state or endpoint. In a dualistic dimension, there will always be opposites calling for balance. This is the spiritual Law of Balance and Polarity in action. From a non-dualistic perspective, the one encompasses the other. Darkness is the absence of light, and light is the absence of darkness. Mastery is to give equal opportunity to both, enjoying the light and embracing the shadow.

- Everything in the outer world is an out-picturing of the inner world. Your inner world includes the vast unconscious mind, which is like an iceberg beneath the surface waters. To be a powerful creator, you need to become conscious of the undercurrents of beliefs, values, narratives, and more, that are informing your picture of reality. Choose your thoughts wisely—treat them as precious jewels. Only then will you truly master the creative process.

- We are walking transmitters; everything that we believe, think, and feel sends a signal out to the Universe and attracts like energy. In this way, we are creating our experience in every moment. Out in the quantum field, our frequency is replicated and offers reflections back to us. Imprinting the quantum field with a frequency is the equivalent of asking something to come back in physical form. Repetition of thought, words, and actions magnifies the request, and therein lies the power of creation and manifestation. As we evolve, it is becoming increasingly important to become super conscious about how we wield this power for the collective good.

- In an anesthetized culture, we tend to avoid dark night crossings and override the voice of the soul with assorted tranquilizers and anti-depressants. Not understanding that the dark night itself is soul medicine, we easily fall prey to false assistance, distraction, and temptation. If we bypass the dark night, we might miss a rare opportunity to find our buried treasure and the very thing that many of us say we most want—a soul-led life of purpose.

9

WINGS

January 2019 – October 2020

A woman in harmony with her spirit is like a river flowing; she goes where she will without pretense and arrives at her destination prepared to be herself and only herself.[21]

– Dr. Maya Angelou, American writer and civil rights activist

While my boys were spreading their wings in the world, I was finding mine in my new life. My family was reconfiguring once again. Like birds in a flock, we were flying in a new formation—solo flights, then merging for a while, tracing novel sky patterns. I could live with that. My sons were doing well on their solo flights. My mother hunch had been correct; Luca stayed in Europe after his gap year and found a job in Berlin. After a challenging year, Liam was back on track and shining.

My wings were spreading in unexpected ways.

In the surface-world, I was traveling more than I had ever done, with several trips to Europe to visit Sander's family in the Netherlands and Luca once he settled in Berlin. These trips opened a portal for me to work with clients in Europe, which quickly snowballed, and in the next

---

21 https://www.insightstate.com/quotes/maya-angelou-quotes/

cycle, I would be reaching people all over the world. Just as Wyndham had predicted, the Albatross would have a large wingspan and far reach, but not in the way I expected.

That elusive sea-crossing Albatross still wasn't resonating with me. I had never been comfortable with the element of air. Wind unsettled me and being airborne scared me. Water was my natural element, not flying high above it. Finding my wings and stepping into the power of the Albatross—never mind the dragon, required that I become a medial being in the more etheric realms too.

As it happened, I wrote this final chapter on Sullivan's farm, in a wood cabin perched on top of a windswept mountain with breathtaking views and icy temperatures. Even on bright spring days, the wind whistled incessantly, and a pair of Black eagles rode the thermals. In African wisdom, the eagle is regarded as the king of birds and a symbol of vision, strength, and light. I felt the stirrings of the thermal-riding pair's message. These Black eagles, formally named the Verreaux's eagle after that ubiquitous French naturalist, are among the largest eagles in the world. With their expansive wingspan, Black eagles can stay airborne for long periods and travel great distances. Unlike other birds, they can fly into strong winds and still maintain aerial control. As one would expect, the Black eagle is mostly black, with a large V-shaped patch of white plumage on its back: shadow and light. I loved them instantly.

Until then, I had never had such a close sighting of Verreaux's eagles. Sullivan deepened my awe when he shared his belief that these eagles present themselves when something profound is afoot. I felt honored by the appearance of this auspicious pair. With their capacity for marathon flight and sharp sight, I felt that the Black eagles were inviting me to embrace the more etheric realms and cultivate my vision. It was time to stretch into my full wingspan and align with the power of the Albatross.

STILL LIFE IN THE RIEBEEK VALLEY

Since surfacing from the dark night slump, I couldn't help but notice the abundance of winged creatures in the Riebeek Valley. At night, the occasional visiting owl hooted. Bird song greeted me every morning and kept going all day. These were happy birds. Our garden was home to a wide variety of bird species, and with its natural pond and prolific lavender, it was a haven for dragonflies, butterflies, and bees. I took heart from the natural world.

My vegetable and herb garden had also proliferated, overflowing into assorted pots and sunlit patches. Working with earth, however piecemeal my gardening efforts, kept me in tune with the undulating growth cycles. Living more closely with the natural rhythms and seasons, I was sourcing my life from a different impulse. Without any planning, our new life had become a creative one. In the spaces between client work, I was writing in my outdoor study, which we called *the wing*, and Sander was painting in his art studio. For both of us, it was a return to our early passions. Drinking at the well of creativity nourished our relationship, too, and joy bubbled up to the surface again.

It was a simple yet rich life. With a slower cadence than the city, I had more time to deviate from the routine. Breaking down the old structures had freed me to create new, truer ways of being and expand my peripheral vision. Moving to the Riebeek Valley was a personal reset. For the first time in many years, I had a chance to catch my breath. Much as I missed my boys and mourned the loss of my active mothering role, I was starting to enjoy the spaciousness. While I regrouped, I had time to think about what I really wanted to create in the next phase of my life. I was still in an uncomfortable place of *not knowing*; only now I trusted the stirring of new beginnings. This was the pause between stories; the old story had ended, and the new story hadn't yet been written. A pause like this is a liminal space of magical potential, and I knew that the wise woman's way was to surrender to the discomfort.

During this period of uncertainty, I clung to a few things I knew for sure. Ever the scribbler, I pinned this note-to-self on the Wall of Inspiration in my study:

THINGS I KNOW

Life is simple; if you stay in the generous, spacious present.

More big change is coming; this is preparation time.

I'm moving from my life purpose of healing myself and others to my soul mission.

My soul mission is to contribute toward the Ascension process.

The *how* of this next-level mission is currently beyond my reference point.

I didn't allow myself to think too much about this tall order, which in all honesty, seemed a bit impossible. The best I could do was focus on what was arising and move with the shifts in my personal life and in my work. I was getting back into harmony with my spirit. Drawing inspiration from Maya Angelou's eloquent statement that "a woman in harmony with her spirit is like a river flowing," I hoped my own river would soon begin to flow.

STEPPING INTO THE FLOW

The journey of a healer is a continual dance to keep the river of light flowing through the veins of everyday life. This is the challenge and magic of the path. Finding new ways of working from a small countryside village was like learning new dance steps. In this lifelong dance, my ongoing quest was to find the highest way of working available to me, the modality, or combination of modalities, that drew on my soul's experience and knowledge but wasn't defined by the past. I was being constantly pulled, as if by an invisible thread, toward the future and an upleveled way of working that would fulfill my soul's mission in this lifetime.

When I started out as a healer, I was plagued by the question of what type of healer I was going to be. Did I source my healing work from my shamanic roots or from my training as a metaphysical healer? At the time, my spirit guides hinted that my highest path would be revealed through the vibration. Over more than a decade of practice, these questions gradually fell away. What mattered was being prepared to be fully myself and aligning with my soul's agenda.

This meant showing up, with all parts of myself, and guiding people on their paths the best way I knew how: standing in the fire with them; holding their feet to the fire when necessary; holding up a mirror; seeing them with eyes of love; revealing to them their own riches. Most important in the transformational space of healing is the vibration—my own vibration and the higher frequencies I channeled to others. The type of healer, the label, and the narrative didn't matter much anymore. This fell away along with the structures of my old life. Finally, I was grasping what my spirit guides had been trying to show me all along, and I could step into the flow of my deepest being.

Increasingly, I was bringing all of myself into the healing space: the young Cathar woman who transcended attachment; the French herbalist who lived alone in the forest; the Native American medicine woman who couldn't save her tribe; the city healer who drew from an eclectic mix of traditions to help others; and now the lightworker who was stepping into a bigger soul mission to anchor higher frequencies on Earth.

QUANTUM HEALING

The first major change in my work was moving from contact healing—working with clients in my healing room, to remote healing. This was largely a practical step. Out in the countryside, there was not the density of population to quickly create a new client base. Most of my clients were in Cape Town, and I was too far away to slot into their busy schedules. Remote healing work wasn't new to me, but now it expanded exponentially. Within a year of moving out of the city, 90% of my work was through the ether or online, and my healing room morphed into a virtual healing space.

The content of my sessions was changing too. The remote healing sessions tended to go deeper, addressing soul-level issues rather than the concerns of the ego-mind. It was something of a surprise that the physical distance served to intensify and deepen the energy work rather than dilute it.

We can understand how remote healing works by considering the basic principles of quantum physics—nonlocality and quantum entanglement. In the quantum world, distance is not an obstacle to the instant exchange of information and light. After connecting with someone's unique vibrational identity, it is possible to tap into their energy field no matter where they are in the world and offer healing that is fine-tuned to their individual needs. While spatial distance doesn't dilute the effectiveness of the healing, the nature of the exchange is different.

Whatever the scientific reasons, remote healing allowed me to go on a multi-dimensional journey with my clients. I thought of it as a sacred journey we undertook together, often with the client leading the way in terms of what was most needed to initiate change. During the journey, I received information about the client's current state of being, their life lessons, and their soul's agenda—an overview of issues that needed to be integrated or resolved for them to progress on their path. In this sense, remote healing was a more multi-dimensional intervention than energy healing. It worked at a higher level, integrating the soul's journey through time with the current energy-body experience. One way of understanding this subtle shift is that the spatial distance between myself and the client created more elasticity in time, allowing me to move more fluidly between timelines.

Because of this quantum-like effect, I called this new way of working quantum healing. As always, my spirit guides were closely involved in guiding me through the light pathways and showing me the *how-to* of operating in quantum space. Working in the quantum field brought several changes. In the beginning, there was a process of recalibrating my intuitive senses to the etheric airwaves, much like changing channels. With this, my intuitive senses intensified, especially clairvoyance, clairaudience, and clairsentience, as information was relayed to me through images, words, and sensations in my body. Instead of simply observing the movie clips of clairvoyant images, accompanying someone on a journey was more like being inside the movie. This sweeping aerial view made it easier to access the big picture of someone's soul journey and identify where and why they were stuck.

Venturing into the arena of the soul's journey had to be relevant for the client and speak to their current concerns. With this shift in my work, I aimed to offer a balance between the deeper soul work and the current energy body, ensuring that every client was left with their energy flowing more strongly, their chakras balanced, and their energy circuits connecting. Along with the soul-level work, these energetic adjustments would automatically leave a client feeling lighter and with more life force energy.

Most importantly, I wanted my clients to experience quantum healing in a tangible way. Some clients reported that they had been on their own journey during the session time-space, and their experiences closely mirrored my own. For these clients, quantum healing was a portal to connect more directly with their souls. For others, the experience of quantum healing was more physical. This was the case for Isobel, an elderly woman in New Zealand who had had a bad fall.

ISOBEL'S STORY

Isobel was in her eighties and enjoyed generally good health. A few months before her quantum healing session, she had fallen and cracked a vertebra in her lower back and had been in a great deal of pain ever since. Isobel had been to doctors, physiotherapists, and osteopaths, but despite all these interventions, she was still in pain and dependent on strong painkillers. After months of debilitating pain, she was feeling increasingly low and was worried about the side effects of the medication. Although skeptical about quantum healing, Isobel was open to anything at this point and thought there was no harm in trying.

With permission granted, I asked Isobel to lie on her bed at the scheduled time and set an intention to receive the healing. When I connected with her energy, I was shown a large etheric knot in her lower spine. Tuning in further, the knot was a dense conglomeration of energy related to Isobel's experience of abuse in her childhood. The fall and cracked vertebra had shaken the knot loose, which was her body's way of bringing stored emotional pain to her attention. Some emotional wounding seeps right into the bones. It was time for Isobel to process this old stuff and release it from her body-mind. My contribution was to untangle the knot, gently pull the threads apart, and dissolve the vibrations of anger and shame.

After the quantum healing, Isobel reported that while she was lying on her bed, as I'd asked her to, her body had jolted up into the air—not once but three times, which would have been while I was untangling the etheric knot in her lower spine. Almost immediately after the healing, the persistent pain Isobel had been experiencing for months on end disappeared, and she was finally able to ween herself off the pain medication.

In Isobel's case, the physical pain reflected unresolved emotional pain. Her very tangible experience of quantum healing initiated a process of conscious emotional healing. Even at her stage of life, Isobel could finally address deeply buried childhood wounding and find more peace.

One of the striking things about quantum healing was that I received even more information than during contact healing sessions. This might be because it was easier to cut through the noise of the ego-mind, which is more present in the physical healing room. In the virtual healing space, the client's soul energy is more accessible and often very vocal too. Increasingly, my clients were interested in what their souls had to say rather than the healing work. In response, I started offering soul reading sessions without the healing.

SOUL READING

The soul readings were offered online, in virtual space. While chatting online, I would simply tap into the client's energy field, and with the help of my spirit guides, the information flowed through me. The soul readings required yet another resetting of my psychic antenna. Compared to the quantum healings, the information was more auditory and came to me in fluid *downloads* interspersed with images, symbols, and feelings. A new spirit guide called Emerald came forward to facilitate this auditory channeling. Mostly I heard her musical voice, but sometimes she appeared to me in flashes of emerald-green light. With Emerald's assistance, the readings took off and soon became the mainstay of my work.

The soul readings focused on connecting people with their soul essence and who they really are beneath their programming. Depending on the client's needs, we would explore their soul purpose and the changes required to walk their highest path. This usually involved identifying the obstacles, temptations, and traps, such as an unhealthy behavior or addiction, a disempowering relationship, or a soul-destroying job. From here, we could identify and reflect on the unconscious patterns underlying a particular attachment or habit. With this kind of information, the readings often initiated change; in some cases, it was small lifestyle tweaks, and in others, it was big changes, such as leaving a job, separating from a partner, or getting out of some type of comfort zone.

By bringing what was hidden to the surface, the readings offered a higher perspective: an overview of what was playing out in someone's life; insight into where their current choices might lead; and other possibilities in line with their soul's agenda. Connecting a person with their soul's agenda was a powerful way to reconnect them with choice and possibility. This usually gave people an entirely new perspective about their dilemmas.

As my readings expanded, I used simple processes to help my clients access their inner wisdom about their burning questions, feeling for themselves where the energy was strongest. Guiding my clients to listen to their hearts and souls was often all that was needed to ignite a different decision-making process. In time, I hoped they would source their own guidance and develop an intuitive compass to navigate an authentic path. My wish was to help people walk a soul-led path rather than a path dictated by conditioning and culture.

Listening to intuition, and acting on it, changes life in unimaginable ways. Instead of feeling lost or stuck, inner guidance is always present to help with taking the next step. The Universe moves to support us in the most unexpected ways. Instead of a scary Survivor Challenge, life becomes a more adventurous Guided Journey, and the Universe becomes a magical place of creative possibility. This shift of perception was the real gift of the readings for my clients.

The gift for me was realizing that the power of the Albatross had been activated, not with journeys through physical space as I had imagined, but journeys through quantum and virtual space. This was my own quantum leap. Little did I know at the time that this new way of working online and through the ether would stand me in good stead when the Covid-19 pandemic hit the world the following year.

THE GLOBAL LIGHTWORKERS

It was through the quantum healing and soul reading work that a new type of client started showing up in my now virtual healing room. With all the changes in my personal life, my vibration was emitting a new signal, and the Universe responded in kind.

Like the first wave of light seekers, these new clients were already on a conscious spiritual path and had a deep yearning for their soul mission. Many of them had a clear purpose to participate in the Ascension process. I called this new wave of clients the global lightworkers. Our work together was inspiring and instructive, and I was often stretched to the edge of my knowledge frontiers.

One of these global lightworkers was a Polish woman called Anja, who was ready to activate her soul mission but needed my help to clear some family baggage and illuminate her path.

ANJA'S STORY

Anja was a successful corporate high-flier. When we started working together, she had a raft of energy-sapping issues, including poor gut health and reactions to many foods, unsatisfying intimate relationships, and complicated family relationships, especially with her mother. She felt constantly drained and desperate for a change. Over the course of the next year, our work together took Anja on a transformative healing journey.

Chapter 9 | Wings

Working with European clients over the years, I gained first-hand insight into the enormous inter-generational impacts of the two world wars. Many were carrying deep scars from the shattered lives of their ancestors, who had suffered greatly during this traumatic period of history. Anja was no exception.

Anja's Polish roots were steeped in suffering. She was carrying unresolved trauma from both her father's and mother's sides of her family. Spanning Russia, East Germany, and Poland, her family story was one of loss and incredible hardship. During the First World War and an intensification of the Polish-German border conflict, her maternal grandmother had fled what was then East Prussia to Poland. With two young children, one just a baby, and a suitcase, she had walked hundreds of miles to cross the border to safety. She died shortly afterward when her baby—Anja's mother—was just one year old. During the Second World War, Anja's paternal grandmother lost her oldest son, Anja's uncle, when he simply vanished during the Nazi occupation of Poland and never returned. Anja's childhood was infused with unspoken grief and survival fear that was deeply ingrained in her family's psyche. Her complex relationship with her parents, and surviving grandparents, had affected her sense of self as well as her intimate relationships.

Slowly, we worked through the multiple layers of Anja's family story, clearing both ancestral lines and the vibration of grief that she had internalized. After lifting this ancestral burden, we turned our attention to her complex relationship with her mother. Anja's father was largely absent, so from a young age, she had been the caretaker of her emotionally crippled and frequently ill mother. The burden of caretaking weighed heavily on her, enmeshed as it was with survivor guilt in a generation that hadn't directly experienced the horrors of war. Eventually, Anja was able to let this pernicious guilt go, freeing herself to walk her own path rather than walking in the shadows of her parents and grandparents.

Our work together yielded big changes in Anja's life. She was committed to her inner work, so her outer world shifted quickly. In just a few months, she made profound changes in her life; she completely changed her diet, which alleviated the gut issues, transformed family relationships, and ended an unhappy romantic partnership. Next, she left a high-paying corporate job and spent time in India with a guru. Anja had connected with her own spirit guides and was receiving high-level guidance in her daily meditations. She was moving ahead on her soul path at lightning speed!

After nine months of fast-paced change, Anja's healing journey took a new turn. She had a big mission and was ready to get going. In one of her meditations, Anja's guides told her that she was an "Earthkeeper," but she wasn't sure how to translate this into something tangible. My role was to help her understand her Earthkeeper mission and make the practical changes to implement it. Our work proceeded with a combination of readings and spiritual coaching sessions with channeled guidance from my guides.

In one of our last sessions together, I was guiding Anja on an inner journey to connect directly with her soul energy. In a semi-hypnotized state, Anja told me that she felt very expansive as if she were plugged into another source of energy. I asked her to describe what was happening. This is what she said:

> I am looking at the Earth. It is my mission to protect it. I am in charge of moving the consciousness level forward. It is not just about the consciousness of the people but of the Earth itself. I collaborate with others in serving cosmic dynamics. There are different cosmic influences, and my role is to coordinate these influences.

I asked Anja to tell me more about her soul mission:

> I'm here to help the Ascension process on Earth, to help others ascend but also to raise the consciousness levels of Earth itself. I'm playing a cosmic role in this transition time, working with other Starseed souls.

With that, she stopped and breathed deeply, realizing that she is a Starseed soul. At this point of realization, my guides said we had to anchor Anja's soul energy-consciousness into her current energy body. They guided me to bring her awareness through her soul star chakra and into her high heart and heart chakras and then anchor it into her hara. Fortunately, we had already worked with all these energy points, and Anja could easily follow these instructions.

At the end of the session, Anja said excitedly, "This is my Earthkeeper mission. But *how* am I going to do this?"

"You just take the next step. You'll be shown exactly what to do. And soon, you won't need me to hold your hand," I said jokingly.

As the words left my mouth, I realized this was true. Our work together was coming to an end. Anja was ready to fly on her own.

Working with Anja, and other global lightworkers, left me pondering the evolution of my work. Not only were the global lightworkers highly conscious, but many of them, like Anja, were Starseed souls.

STARSEED SOULS

Starseed souls originate in realms beyond this planet. While Starseeds may have spent other lifetimes on Earth, they are ultimately connected to different parts of the cosmos. They often have a more advanced consciousness, and by incarnating on Earth, they act in service of the collective. Almost invariably, Starseeds have a big mission and a strong sense of calling to accomplish it.

At this point in human history, Starseed souls are incarnating in increasing numbers. Over the years, I worked with many Starseeds, including Starseed children. However, this new wave of Starseed clients had a sense of urgency about their mission. They joined the ranks of the global lightworkers, but as Starseed lightworkers, their concerns were subtly different. My spirit guides offered this explanation:

> A Starseed soul mission is different from an Earth soul's mission. A Starseed soul is more interested in the cosmic dynamics and the role of Earth within the cosmic system. For this reason, Starseed souls have been incarnating en masse over the last few decades to help with the Ascension process—not only to help humanity but, more fundamentally, to assist with stabilizing the Earth and raising Gaia's consciousness for the good of the planetary system and the Cosmos as a whole.

I welcomed these fresh insights from a Starseed perspective, and the potential for collaboration between Starseed and Earth souls as the global shift in consciousness gathered momentum. While I was helping my Starseed clients get going with their earthly missions, they were teaching me new techniques and alerting me to evolutionary changes. I realized there was more for me to learn from a Starseed perspective, and I was watching this space with growing curiosity.

One of these Starseed lightworker souls was a long-standing client called Melissa. Within the last five years, Melissa had trained as a healer, quit her corporate job, and set up her own healing practice. Melissa's healing work had recently taken a new direction, and her energy field required attuning to a new set of energies.

MELISSA'S STORY

Melissa had been dealing with some deep-seated fear. She had grown up in a violent home environment, and her coping mechanism was to escape to nature to find sanctuary. As a result, Melissa had a strong bond with the natural world, and this was still her go-to safe space.

As I began her quantum healing session, two bluish beings appeared. Their form was vaguely humanoid, but their vibrational frequency was alien. They told me they were Melissa's new guides. I was no longer surprised when a client's alien guides showed up and quickly verified their credentials. After checking the pair's authenticity, I allowed them to guide the session.

The blue beings shared some important information:

> Melissa is a Starseed soul, and her deep connection with nature as a child was a way for her to establish a connection with Earth as a newcomer to the planet. She has done well in anchoring herself in unfamiliar terrain and creating safety. Now is the time for her to understand her Starseed origins and align herself with her soul energy. This will become her source of safety. To align with her soul energy, she needs a Starseed attunement. Once attuned to her Starseed soul energy, she will be able to step into her mission of assisting with the Ascension process through human hearts.

When I started the energy work, Melissa was sitting in front of me—in quantum space—positively glowing with excitement. I realized that this was an important attunement for her. The blue guides proceeded to channel a high-vibrational light that I had never seen before; usually, I saw the light frequency I was being guided to use, but this was off my known spectrum. I could sense its vibration rather than see it. As best as I can describe, it appeared as an electrical pulse going up and down Melissa's spine. After holding this energetic pulse for a while, there was a powerful burst of energy that cleared the vibration of fear from her field.

The next step was to do the Starseed attunement process. The blue guides showed me how to work with Melissa's DNA structure and change the coding. If this sounds far-fetched, those were the exact words they used. It wasn't the same process I used when working with genetic recoding, and the blue guides did most of the work. While I held the energetic space, they combed through the DNA strands with high-frequency light and attuned Melissa to her Starseed blueprint.

The final step was integrating Melissa's new energetic frequency with her earthly energy body. This involved activating her twelve, fifth-dimensional chakras. Her energy body was positively zinging! In closing, I was guided to show Melissa a new way of grounding; rather than grounding through her base chakra with roots into the Earth, she needed to ground through her Earth star chakra and connect with the crystal energy in the Earth's crystalline grids. I instructed her in the new technique while the blue guides were *sparkling* her aura. With that, the blue guides said in unison, "Now her real work can begin." Judging by Melissa's excitement throughout the session, I was absolutely sure that this was true.

After the session, Melissa told me that the two blue guides had shown up in her meditations the previous week, but she hadn't yet connected with them. With the attunement and lines of communication open, she could begin working at a higher level in partnership with her blue guides to assist with the Ascension process.

Around this time, I was also encountering Starseed children—sometimes called Star children—who were already attuned to Starseed frequencies. Working with these children, I was seeing changes in the energy architecture, most notably in the heart chakra. In some cases, the heart chakra was enlarged, and the usual pink color was so pale it was almost white. In a few cases, the heart chakra seemed to have merged with the high heart, sometimes known as the eighth chakra, creating an enlarged heart chakra that vibrated with pure white light—rather than the green or pink of the primary heart chakra. Among these New Children were those whose heart energy was so expansive that their lower chakras were barely visible. As humanity transcends into higher consciousness, it is likely that we'll no longer need the lower chakras, but I digress.

THE AWAKENED HEART

There is undeniably something afoot in the magical human heart; it is evolving! As our heart energy is expanding, the chakric structures are changing. I got the first inklings of this phenomenon when working with Starseed children, but it wasn't until I started working with children born after 2016 that I truly grasped what is happening. The heart chakra (fourth chakra) and the high heart chakra (eighth chakra) are merging to form a new energetic center with its own distinct vibrational frequency. Like harmonic chords in an octave, the fourth and the eighth chakras are beginning to sound one vibrational note. I called this the *awakened heart*.

Many of the new arrivals on Earth appeared to have a partially or fully developed awakened heart. With this new heart template, these children are seeding heart-based consciousness. One of these incoming souls was Amora, born in early 2020. At her mother's request, I did a soul reading for Amora when she was just three weeks old.

AMORA'S STORY

When I connected with baby Amora's soul, I felt a ripple of excitement. I immediately got a sense of her strong soul energy and clear purpose to bring in fifth-dimensional consciousness. As a soul, Amora was a wisdom keeper, and over the course of many lifetimes, she had been instrumental in sharing esoteric wisdom and awakening those around her. My guides said she carried the "wisdom of the awakened heart."

Tuning into my clairvoyant screen, I saw a series of images from Amora's previous lifetimes. First, I saw her in the Peruvian Andes, where she was connected to Machu Picchu. Prior to that, she was a high priestess in the ancient civilization of Atlantis and was involved in bringing its sacred knowledge to Peru. I was also shown a life in Egypt, where she took on some heavy karma that took several lifetimes to work through and transcend.

In this lifetime, Amora had undertaken to work with the vibration of fear and transmute it to love. She would do this for herself, her family, and the world. At a global level, her soul mission was to be part of awakening heart-based consciousness and assisting with the dimensional shift currently underway. In her family, she would play a transformative role by clearing wounding in her female lineage. Her personal task was to transmute residual fear into love and keep her awakened heart open.

Working with Amora, I was struck by her enlarged heart chakra, which appeared to have already merged with the high heart. Tuning in more closely, her merged heart was vibrating at a much higher frequency than the primary heart chakra. My guides said Amora had an awakened heart, which is attuned to fifth-dimensional frequencies. This, they said, is the heart template for the awakened human.

When Amora was older, she would learn the ways of the shaman and use this knowledge to impart heart wisdom. She had extraordinary sensitivity but also fiery passion. Balancing these two aspects was her life lesson. She would learn how to embody both aspects so she could be true to who she was and communicate her message.

After working with baby Amora, my spirit guides offered me this explanation of what I had witnessed:

> In this next phase of human evolution, the heart chakra and the high heart are merging. This signals a major shift in consciousness for humanity. What you witnessed with Amora is something you'll see more often. The merged heart is an expanded heart, the container for heart-based consciousness. Adults can develop this expanded heart, but first, their heart chakras must open. Assisting with opening hearts and merging hearts will accelerate the Ascension process. This is something you are to assist with and teach.

According to my guides, this expanded heart center will have the capacity to hold and calibrate fifth-dimensional energy. In other words, at a chakric level, the gateway to the Fifth Dimension is the arising awakened heart.

THE FIFTH DIMENSION

Awakening to the Fifth Dimension and fifth-dimensional consciousness is an evolutionary imperative. Although we still have much to discover and understand about this next-level destination, there is a growing understanding of its fundamental aspects. Most important to understand is that the Fifth Dimension is not a location—it's a field of vibrational frequency, which creates an energetic parameter for an experience of reality. It's an energetic grid that holds consciousness in place, informing perceptions, attitudes, and feeling states. This fifth-dimensional field vibrates at a higher frequency than the third-dimensional field, which has been the dominant field for about 10,000 years. In the Third Dimension, we have been concerned with the material world and surviving physically and materially, governed by the fight-flight response of the ego-mind. This dimensional field is woven of the energies of fear, greed, and control within a container of separation consciousness. The fifth-dimensional grid is a higher-frequency field woven of the energies of love, peace, and connection, within a container of Oneness consciousness. At a fifth-dimensional frequency, abundance is at the core of perception of how the Universe works, and harmony and co-creation are the guiding principles.

As we move toward the Fifth Dimension, we are beginning to understand that there is more than the material world of visible matter, and we're moving into greater spiritual awareness. We are becoming less bound by the survival concerns of the ego and becoming more interested in our soul purpose and why we are here in human form. We are also beginning to grasp the power of thought in creating our reality, minute by minute. For example, when I left my body after the car crash and entered the gap between dimensions, I only had to *think my choice* and the manifestation of my choice to come back into my body was instant. As we move closer to the Fifth Dimension, manifestation is speeding up.

Chapter 9 | Wings

It might not be instant yet, but it is becoming much faster. When we really get how powerful thought is, we will take greater responsibility as co-creators *through* our human experience and become conscious creators as opposed to unconscious victims.

Most importantly, as fifth-dimensional consciousness rises, we are beginning to understand Oneness consciousness in a more visceral way, feeling, rather than simply understanding, that we are all connected. In the Fifth Dimension, we'll experience ourselves and others as Source energy, profoundly altering perceptions, attitudes, and feeling states, generating greater love and respect between people. This shift from separation to Oneness consciousness is a fundamental paradigm shift and is the very basis of the New Earth paradigm.

This is the nature of the awakening that is sweeping across the planet right now. As awakened humans, we are evolving into conscious creators, which is a very new type of experience for humanity. We are currently in the process of writing this new story.

CROSSING THE DIMENSIONAL FRONTIER

Collectively, we are still in a transition phase, poised to cross the dimensional frontier. We've already perceived another level of reality, we are dipping our toes into this new vibrational field, but we haven't fully inhabited it yet. In a very real sense, we are vibrational pioneers exploring the energetic pathways to the new world.

A useful analogy to understand this dimensional crossing is a radio with multiple stations. Every station has a slightly different frequency. When you tune the radio to your chosen station, you only hear the information being broadcast on that station. When you change stations, you tune into and perceive a different reality. We are in the process of tuning into a completely new station: we are already receiving fragments of information, but the signal is still fuzzy.

While the Fifth Dimension is accessible to us now, it's not stable or firmly anchored yet. Even those who are working with fifth-dimensional frequencies are not holding them in a consistent manner. Collectively, we are still swinging wildly between the lower notes of fear and resistance and the higher notes of spiritual awareness and expansion. The energies are turbulent and unstable. It's not an easy crossing.

But as we know, instability in any system precedes change and offers the opportunity for quantum leaps. This is the evolutionary impulse in action. When more people emanate fifth-dimensional consciousness and consistently hold higher frequencies, the vibrational field will become more stable. Gradually, we will learn how to embody fifth-dimensional frequencies, and this will create stability in the collective field. This is an evolutionary process, and the crossing may take years or even decades.

Frontiers are, by nature, tricky places, a necessary but uncomfortable transition between the known and the unknown. A frontier is also a highly charged place of choice and infinite possibility. We can choose to go onward into the unknown or return to the safe zone of the known world. There is so much support from higher dimensions—and more advanced worlds—for humanity to cross the dimensional frontier. Ultimately, however, the rate of our evolution is about the individual and collective choices we make along the way. We have been gifted with free will, and choice is key. The higher dimensions are all about choice and our power to exercise choice, but at far subtler levels than we have learned in the Third Dimension. Choice in the Fifth Dimension is much more about how we think and what we put out into the universal field.

One of the choices we can make to move more swiftly into the Fifth Dimension is to consciously activate the energetic template underpinning fifth-dimensional consciousness.

A MAP FOR CONSCIOUS EVOLUTION

As we move toward the Fifth Dimension, the fifth-dimensional chakra system has become more visible and accessible. Many awakening souls are already working with their fifth-dimensional chakras. As more people activate and work with this energetic template, consciousness will move to a higher level, and as consciousness expands, so too, our energetic structures will continue to evolve. It's two sides of the same coin.

The chakra system is a map for living life in a human body. It is an energetic template, or blueprint, that relates to our soul history, life story, states of consciousness, and general functionality. As such, it is an operating system that goes right to the core of all levels of being—mind, body, and spirit. In other words, the chakra system is integral to who we are in human form, and it is integral to our collective experience of being incarnated on the Earth plane.

Knowing how to access this map is sacred knowledge. In the Third Dimension, we have been operating with seven primary chakras and learning the lessons of these chakras. Now we are ready for the next section of the map—the fifth-dimensional chakra column, which is a twelve-chakra system. By guiding us to embody the higher frequencies, this part of the map will help us to navigate from the Third Dimension into the Fifth Dimension.

When we were in the depths of the Third Dimension, it wasn't possible to raise frequency to a fifth-dimensional level and stay in a physical body. Now we can ascend to the higher frequencies and remain in physical form in order to serve humankind and the planet itself. This is what Ascension means—vibrating at a much higher frequency while being embodied. Human evolution is gathering momentum as the fifth-dimensional energies are more widely embodied. We are literally becoming new humans with a new energetic template. Think of it as our hardware being upgraded to support a more advanced software program.

The twelve-chakra system includes the seven primary chakras, which start to vibrate at a higher frequency, as well as five additional chakras: the Earth star chakra below the feet; the navel chakra (or hara) just above the sacral chakra; and the causal, soul star, and stellar gateway chakras above the crown chakra. It is essentially an evolution of the primary chakras, which are incorporated into an extended higher-frequency system. As the frequency of the primary chakras change, the chakra colors also change to reflect the higher frequencies on the light spectrum.

This fifth-dimensional chakra column, which includes the awakened heart, is the energetic template for fifth-dimensional consciousness that will enable the co-creation of a higher frequency future for humanity. At a collective level, the fifth-dimensional chakras are a gateway for further awakening and Ascension. At an individual level, these chakras are portals to access and embody the higher frequencies. Activating them is a way of unlocking personal potential and moving across the dimensional frontier.

Activating the fifth-dimensional chakras is an incremental process. The awakened heart is one of the first major changes. As this new energy center forms, our capacity to align with higher frequencies expands. An activated awakened heart has the capacity for advanced spiritual perception and heart wisdom. Like the top note of a fragrant perfume, the awakened heart is a high-frequency note in the energy body, guiding us across the dimensional frontier toward the New Earth.

This expanded heart is a guiding light, calling us to wake up! Through it and other light pathways, human evolution is happening. But first, we must consider the role of the primary heart chakra in this awakening process.

HEART WISDOM

Children born since 2016 are leading the way toward the New Earth. They embody the higher frequency capacity that is enabling humanity's next evolutionary leap. Now that the template is available to us, everyone can develop an awakened heart. But first, our primary heart chakras must open. It's the missing piece in the mind-body-spirit trilogy. The heart is the center point of this holy trinity. It is a vastly under-used and not yet understood sensory organ as well as a portal between dimensions.

We know from science that the heart is more powerful than the brain. According to research conducted by the HeartMath Institute, the heart generates the largest electromagnetic field in the body. The heart's electrical field is about sixty times greater in amplitude than the brain, and the heart's magnetic field is around 5,000 times stronger than that of the brain.[22] This heart field envelops every single cell of the body and extends outwards into the field around us, up to several feet away from the body.

The energetic heart creates a kind of toroidal field that arcs out from the heart and back in a continual flow. As such, the heart center is a powerful transmitter and receiver of information. It is even more powerful when there is coherence between mind and heart, thoughts, and feelings. In other words, our thoughts, as electric pulses, and feelings, as magnetic energy, affect our heart's electromagnetic field, which in turn energetically affects our environment and everything in it, whether we are conscious of this or not.

In the future, everyone will be able to tune into each other's heart fields and exchange information. We do this naturally already, but mostly we are not consciously aware of this exchange or what we are capable of co-creating with this awareness. Unlocking the full power of the heart is the next evolutionary step in human consciousness.

At this point in our evolution, many awakening souls are busy with heart-opening work in one way or another. In my work with clients over the last decade, the phrase that I've repeated the most often is: "You're on a journey to open your heart." This was offered not as an instruction but as a higher perspective for engaging with the challenges of opening the heart. In the third-dimensional structures and belief systems, we have been conditioned to close our hearts to protect ourselves. As a result, it is not unusual to have layers of energetic armor covering the heart chakra. As we move toward the Fifth Dimension, the challenge is to dismantle this protective armor and open our hearts again. This is the precursor to activating the fifth-dimensional awakened heart.

We appear to have arrived at a pivot point where the collective journey to open our hearts is not only a key to healing but an evolutionary imperative. Without heart-consciousness, we will remain in the Third Dimension, stuck in the ego-mind and the lower vibrational pull that

---

22 Rollin McCraty, Ph.D. *The Energetic Heart: Bioelectromagnetic Interactions Within and Between People* (HeartMath Research Center, Institute of HeartMath, USA, 2003).

is currently destabilizing the planet. Stepping into the vibrational frequencies of the heart—love, wisdom, truth, and compassion—is our only hope.

Opening the heart can take an instant or a lifetime. Like anything in life, it's a matter of choice. As the great master Jesus Christ taught, the energies of love and forgiveness hold the key. The secret knowledge of the heart is love. It is important to understand that love is more than a feeling; it is a vibrational pathway. It is the unifying substance that flows like water through the Universe. We, too, must learn to flow like water, becoming a vast river of light. When our hearts open, the way into the Fifth Dimension will be illuminated. Every human heart will become a portal, connected to other human hearts through the Universe's light pathways.

For this, we need to cultivate heart wisdom. Heart wisdom is based on spiritual understanding, which has nothing to do with age or experience and everything to do with vibration and spiritual law. With heart wisdom, we can apply spiritual values and spiritual law. This is what is required to anchor higher consciousness on Earth. My spirit guide Emerald said that even the word consciousness needs to be redefined, as it is currently associated with the mind. She suggested that a more accurate term for higher consciousness is heart-based consciousness, which exists in the spaces within and between human hearts. We are leaving the era of the mind and entering the era of the heart. In fact, the mind cannot fathom the evolutionary shifts that are ahead of us.

Opening the heart is a pivotal next step on our evolutionary journey toward heart-based consciousness. Merging the heart chakra and the high heart to form the expanded awakened heart comes next. This merging will occur naturally when both the heart and high heart chakras are open and vibrating at a higher frequency. In my healing work, I have come across many people whose heart chakras are open but whose high heart chakras are not ready to open. It is important never to force an opening of the high heart if someone isn't ready for it. One of the reasons for this is that the high heart is where we tend to hold anxiety, which may be keeping a lid on deeply held trauma. This is why the high heart, which sits above the thymus gland, is one of the main tapping points used by the Emotional Freedom Technique (EFT Tapping) to release stress and anxiety. Extreme anxiety and underlying trauma must be released first before safely opening the high heart.

And so, I believe it is no coincidence that fear was the energy that hit humanity full force in early 2020. This is exactly the vibration that needs to be surfaced and purged from our individual and collective fields to pave the way for humanity's next evolutionary leap.

THE COVID-19 PANDEMIC

When the Coronavirus pandemic swept the world, it traveled on a vibration of fear. Amid rising panic, widespread lockdowns and increasing government control elicited more fear and anger. The intensity of these dense energies amplified instability and chaos in the third-dimensional matrix. The spiritual perspective of this turmoil is that the pandemic offered a window of opportunity to change course as humanity. It was a call to open our hearts to each other and to Gaia and to make more conscious choices about how we live on our planet. In evolutionary terms, the Covid pandemic can be seen as a trigger event that pushed us toward the fifth-dimensional frontier. From this perspective, the pandemic can be seen as an important milestone on the Ascension pathway.

In many ways, the Covid-19 pandemic threw us into a collective dark night of the soul, and as we well know, the dark night is a transformational space where we get to reflect and find our way to the next level of consciousness. In other words, the pandemic was a time of collective initiation with the potential for mass awakening to a higher level of consciousness. If we understand initiation as the breaking down of identity, then the big question is, what is the new identity we are creating? What is humanity's new story going to be? At its most fundamental, the nature of this collective initiation was a push to drop the old dense energies of separation consciousness—fear, anger, hatred, and greed, and move toward unity consciousness—opening our hearts to each other and the Earth and experiencing oneness. We are being initiated into listening to our hearts and souls and waking up to our potential as fifth-dimensional beings. This is the awakened human.

Above all, the awakened human is a sovereign being. This is the new high-frequency identity being forged in the collective furnace. At its most basic, sovereignty refers to mastery of self. As Kate had taught me all those years ago, mastery of self is the heart of the evolutionary path. As souls incarnating into a physical body, self-mastery is, in fact, our primary purpose in attending Earth school. But we also have a duty to the Earth, a debt of gratitude perhaps, to lift the frequency that holds us in sacred connection with all of life—with each other, the planet, and the cosmos. As sovereign beings, we are now being called to weave together our human and divine qualities and create a world based on a higher perception of humanity's potential. A sovereign being goes beyond self-mastery to become a conscious creator. From this perspective, the pandemic was a collective test and growth opportunity. The essential question is will we rise to the evolutionary challenge and co-create a higher frequency pathway for humanity?

At a personal level, the pandemic was a call to step more fully into my soul mission of assisting with the Ascension process. During the first hard lockdown, it was business as usual in some respects, as my work with clients was already online. But as the pandemic deepened, I started linking with other lightworkers in South Africa and around the world to anchor more light on the planet.

By the time we descended into the collective dark night, I had already done my time in the darkness, and it was time for me to hold the light. Throughout the pandemic, I consciously delinked from the matrix of fear and processed my own latent fears when they arose. My soul journey looping back to Montségur to retrieve the vibration of peace held me in good stead in transmuting many layers of fear, my own and in the collective field. The inner peace I found in France was my touchstone, my go-to place whenever I wobbled in the surface-world. From this place, I could be a source of strength for others. And indeed, during the pandemic, I worked with many people struggling with high anxiety levels or who had contracted Covid-19 with varying degrees of severity.

The worst case of Covid-19 that I worked with was that of Amy, a young nurse who fell ill soon after the pandemic took hold in South Africa. Her mother, Jess, was an old friend, and I had known Amy since she was a toddler. When she was hospitalized, Jess asked if I could help. Much to her distress, Amy was so critically ill that we thought she wouldn't make it.

AMY'S STORY

When I tuned into Amy's energy, there was a large dent on the left side of her aura. Within the etheric layer, there were clusters of dandelion-shaped structures, which I took to be the virus. The viral load was high. While Amy was usually a calm person, accustomed to working with other people's medical trauma, I was struck by the vibration of fear permeating her energy field. This was not the Amy I knew. Tuning in further, I was told that she had been under a lot of strain, working long hours in difficult conditions since the start of the pandemic. This had made her vulnerable to the high viral loads she was being exposed to on a daily basis.

At a physical level, Amy was experiencing extreme nausea, headaches, and fatigue. Tuning in further, I was surprised to see that her respiratory tract was completely clear. The virus was concentrated in her abdominal area and intestinal tract and was affecting her digestive system more than anything else. Her chakras had shut down, and the flow of energy through her system was very weak.

Working through Amy's high heart, I released the worst of her anxiety. Once her energy settled, I tackled the virus. Having very little experience with the coronavirus, I was guided by my spirit guide, Doctor, who, with his usual amused look, fired off instructions. First, I was to create a cauldron of heat in Amy's abdominal area to contain the virus, followed by a process of *nuking* the virus with an infrared light ray. I had used infrared with the Epstein Barr virus before, so I was familiar with this virus-defeating frequency. However, Doctor said infrared would not be enough to dissolve the coronavirus. He reminded me that it travels on a vibration of fear and thrives in this environment. The only way to eradicate it was to work with fifth-dimensional energy, specifically the frequency of 432 hertz, which is the vibration of pure love. According to Doctor, this frequency would *outwit* the virus; it would not be able to survive or replicate in this vibrational terrain. After disabling the virus in this manner, I was guided to place Amy in a *healing light bath* to change her frequency at a cellular level and unhook the virus from the affected cells.

Once the vibrational terrain had shifted sufficiently, I turned my attention to Amy's physical body: relaxing her stomach muscles to alleviate nausea, opening the diaphragm, and boosting her immune system.

After the first session, Amy seemed to rally, but after a few days, the intense nausea was back. I worked with her three times in quick succession while she drifted in and out of consciousness. Each time, there was a process of clearing residual fear and recalibrating her vibrational terrain to a higher frequency. I also disconnected all the contact points with the virus, including thought-forms visible in her mental body. At a chakric level, I was guided to focus on Amy's heart and high heart chakras, attuning these centers to fifth-dimensional frequencies. This attunement, Doctor explained, would provide lasting protection from the virus.

At the end of the fourth session, Doctor announced that Amy would recover. All she had to do was rest deeply and surrender. This she did, and a few weeks later, she was discharged from the hospital. Mercifully, Amy pulled through, and after a long convalescence period, she went back to work at the frontline in the hospital's Covid ward.

The clear message throughout my work with Amy was that the coronavirus is a third-dimensional entity, vibrating at the same frequency as fear, and it was possible to dissolve it with the frequency of love. This was a type of energetic alchemy.

There are other ways to work with the coronavirus. One of these is to find all the contact points between the virus and the client's energy body and cut energy cords. It is also helpful to cut cords between the client and the collective consciousness in relation to the pandemic. This is a useful strategy to disarm the virus and give the client's immune system time to rally. However, in my experience, this approach offered little more than a temporary reprieve. Ultimately, it is more effective to transmute the client's vibrational terrain.

Our best protection against the coronavirus, and I suspect any other novel viruses that might come our way, are these higher frequencies, particularly the vibration of love. According to David Hawkins' Map of Consciousness, fear calibrates at a frequency of 100 hertz, while love calibrates at a frequency of 500 hertz.[23] Diana Cooper asserts that the vibration of pure Source love is 432 hertz, while fear calibrates at 60 hertz. Without splitting hairs about the precise measurement, the energy of love clearly vibrates at a far higher frequency than fear.[24] Of course, there is a broad spectrum of vibrational states between these polarities.

The frequency we emit reflects a vibrational range, which correlates with a state of consciousness. This personal frequency setting also determines the vibrational terrain of the physical body, which affects overall health and immunity. Whatever the role of vaccines, reaching for a higher frequency will also have countless benefits for humanity. "If only we could grasp this," Doctor said.

Put simply, a strong heart chakra boosts the immune system and protects against the coronavirus. Once again, all my work was pointing to the heart chakra being the gateway for our next best step as humanity. Love is the most powerful force in the Universe. If enough people choose to open their hearts to love, collectively, we will create the tipping point to move onto a higher timeline as a species.

THE ASCENSION PATHWAY

The pandemic was a call to humanity to wake up and change course. The task of conscious awakening people is to rise above fear and step into the power of heart-based consciousness. When enough people do this and we reach a critical mass of higher consciousness, we will have a unique opportunity to anchor the fifth-dimensional energies on Earth. This is the Ascension pathway. If you are reading this book, this is what you are here to do. The time is right now.

This transitional time is more than a shift in consciousness. We have reached a dimensional splitting point, a fork in the road where one path leads to the Fifth Dimension and the other continues within the Third

---

23 David Hawkins, *Power vs Force: The Hidden Determinants of Human Behavior* (Hay House, Inc., 2014)

24 Diana Cooper's March Newsletter, March 3, 2020 (https://dianacooper.com/diana-coopers-march-newsletter/).

Dimension. Part of humanity is still attached to the Third Dimension. Some people fear change, while others actively resist change and seek to control how we evolve. Another group is consciously moving into the Fifth Dimension. There might be a tipping point where one level of consciousness defines the future, or if these groupings take different routes to the future and move further apart vibrationally, it is possible that the two realities may no longer be visible to each other.

Like any fork in the road, we get to choose our route. Although it is a collective choice point, we each get to play our part. Will we choose the path of heart? Or will we stay hooked into the third-dimensional matrix of fear and perpetuate more of the same?

At an individual level, your path will be determined by the choices you make in your everyday life. If your choice is to walk the fifth-dimensional path, then choose high-frequency thoughts, situations, and people. Process your fears and denser emotions. Delink from the third-dimensional matrix and open your heart of love. Like all dimensional pathways, the *substance* is vibration. The keys to entering the Fifth Dimension are the higher frequencies of love, peace, joy, gratitude, compassion, and co-creation. This is the Ascension pathway—the highest path available to us as a collective. Once a hidden pathway in the Universe, it is now visible to anyone who cares to look.

At the level of consciousness, the gateway to the Ascension path is the ability to delink from third-dimensional power struggles and see the higher perspective of what is currently unfolding on the planet. By asserting spiritual values, we have an opportunity to bring balance to a world that has reeled out of balance, redress the distortions of patriarchy, rebalance masculine and feminine energies, and restore *right relationship* with the Earth itself.

From an energetic perspective, the vibration of fear has served to hold the third-dimensional matrix in place. The antidote is the energy of love and other higher frequencies. Learning to hold a higher vibration within the turbulence, and linking with others doing the same, will take you down the higher path. Everyone can play a role in anchoring light on the Earth plane and co-creating a stable fifth-dimensional grid.

ACTIVATING THE LIGHT GRID

When I moved to the Riebeek Valley in 2018, there were times when I wondered why I was there. Apart from tearing down old structures, my spirit guides told me I had to start working with energetic nodes in the Earth's grid. The starting point was a specific triangle in South Africa, which was needed to stabilize the very unstable energies in the country. This, my spirit guides said, was my preparation for working with sacred sites around the Earth that needed recharging and reconnecting. These physical sacred sites would, in turn, serve as anchor points for the energetic nodes in the light grid. Here was the thread looping back to my initiation as a teenager into the sacred sites of England. How I wished I had paid more attention back then!

Activating the light nodes, my guides informed me, was preparation for the next leg of my soul mission. Lightworkers around the world were activating this grid of light to anchor the fifth-dimensional energies. Back in 2018, I was rather submerged in the dark night, but whenever I had the energy, I turned my attention to this spiritual task.

When the Covid-19 pandemic gripped the world in early 2020, doing this grid work with the light nodes took on a new urgency. Joining forces with other lightworkers, it soon became part of my morning practice. It was like weaving a worldwide web of light, sending fifth-dimensional energy to the light nodes and through the light pathways, and in this way, setting up a template for a fifth-dimensional grid. Lightworkers all over the world have upped their game and, like artists, are busily weaving the new paradigm into being.

This handiwork reminded me of Indra's net in Buddhist mythology. In this ancient story, Indra's knotted net encircles the Earth. Every knot in the net is a jewel, and in every jewel is both the entirety and the reflection of the other jewels signaling like beacons to each other. This Buddhist myth perfectly describes what the Fifth Dimension is all about—the oneness, the reflections, the threads that hold dimensional space together.

Indra's net is a metaphor for the structure of reality, consistent with the holographic nature of the Universe. Think of the jeweled net as a giant hologram, with every jewel in the net a point of the hologram. In a hologram, each point contains the whole and reflects all the other points, thus reflecting the entirety of all the light and information in the Universe. Staying with this analogy, when any jewel in the net is activated, all the other jewels are affected; change in one jewel initiates change in every other jewel. This phenomenon is explained by the quantum theory of nonlocality, which describes the ability of separate entities to instantaneously know about changes to each other's state, even when separated by large distances—potentially even billions of light-years. This suggests that everything in the Universe is interconnected and interdependent in a vast field of Oneness consciousness. Indra's jeweled net perfectly illustrates this unity field.

Working with the light nodes, I imagined I was working with reflective jewels, polishing them so they could sparkle again and radiate the frequencies of love, peace, and unity. Encircling the Earth in a vast etheric net, these sparkling jewels are the portals for humanity to enter the Fifth Dimension. They are like the Earth's illuminated heart centers. Just as the body has an etheric template, the sacred light nodes are the Earth's etheric template for a new consciousness. It is the vibrational safety net for our next evolutionary leap.

CULTIVATING OUR GARDENS

Writing this final chapter on Sullivan's farm, I took a few tea breaks at the main farmhouse when weather permitted. The path down the windswept mountainside led to Sullivan's magnificent garden. This sudden burst of color amid otherwise rocky terrain reminded me of the importance of cultivating our gardens, actual or metaphorical.

When I was a student, I came across this little gem of a book called *Candide*, a satirical novella by Voltaire, published in 1759. This haunting work has stayed with me. At the end of the story, after a series of misadventures, the main character Candide retires to a simple life on a farm where he finds meaning and happiness in cultivating his garden. His garden becomes a metaphor for grounding life in simplicity and beauty. At the time, Voltaire's novella was a scathing attack on metaphysical optimism and the excessive idealism of the Age of Enlightenment. I understood Voltaire's commentary as a directly opposing philosophy to what my soul mission was all about, and yet I found it ultimately balancing—a reminder that we are made of spirit, but we are of the Earth. We are at once human and divine and being grounded in both is the art of living a whole-hearted, soulful life.

My friend Sullivan reminded me of Candide. On his farm, in an extreme mountain climate, Sullivan cultivated his garden with humble pride. Here, where you least expected to find a garden of any sort, was the most spectacular array of flowering plants imaginable. Sipping tea from simple pottery mugs in Sullivan's garden was like drinking at the river of light. The divine feminine has many faces.

Enjoying this simple tea ritual with Sullivan one afternoon, he asked, "Do you remember the gold coins?" *Yes, of course I did.* He was referring to a vision I'd received of the two of us sifting through a treasure chest of gold coins. That seemed like a lifetime ago. "This is the gold, right here in front of us," he said, then fell silent again while the penny dropped.

Sullivan's garden was his soul-place. In full bloom, the garden was a beautiful out-picturing of his heart; the flowers, stone pathways, and crystal-clear ponds his visual story. After all those years of important busy-ness in the city and traveling around the world to find himself, Sullivan's heart had burst into bloom right here on this rocky patch of land. Through the simple act of cultivating his garden, he had found his path of heart.

We all have a metaphorical garden, the place where our hearts flower and bloom. Through the daily watering, mindful tending, and inevitable ups and downs, we find the simple, satisfying pleasures that bring joy. Our treasures may not be as visible to the world as Sullivan's bountiful garden, but we know when we have tapped into the magical vein of creation. This is the path of heart. It is usually right in front of us.

This is the heroine's destination, the place where she uncovers her heart's wisdom and lives in a deep heart state. As the medicine woman foretold, this is the sacred feminine knowledge that will heal the collective female psyche and restore balance to the world. When we as individuals and humanity, both women and men, align with the field of the heart and rise into heart-based consciousness, when we merge our humanness and divine essence, then we will truly awaken.

Back at my mountain-top cabin, I gazed at the mountain range across the valley, purplish-blue in the late afternoon haze. In the distance, the Black eagles glided in graceful circles—ground and air, earth and spirit. It was time for me to get airborne.

A NEW CALL

As writing this book came to an end, I was being nudged to take another leap of faith, leaving behind healing with my hands and joining forces with lightworkers around the world to open the gateways to the Fifth Dimension.

"You are to be a wayshower to the Fifth Dimension," my spirit guides announced. "You will be one of many lightworker souls that have come here at this time of mass awakening to guide others across the threshold to the Fifth Dimension."

I had no idea how I would answer this new call. It was rather an inscrutable mission.

"Never mind," my guides said, dismissing this most human of concerns. "We will show you the way."

As much as I was to be a wayshower, I would have my spirit team showing me the way. Well, that was reassurance, at least!

My path was taking a new turn. I had come a long way since being shipwrecked on a desert island without a map or even a compass to find my way. After much backtracking, looping, stumbling, falling into traps, and scrambling over obstacles, I now have a magical map to navigate my path. I don't have it all worked out—none of us has—but

Chapter 9 | Wings

I trust that I will be shown the next step, and the next one after that, and given everything I need to keep walking this path of heart.

When I set out on my journey as a healer, I would never have guessed that the destination would be a dimension. Thanks to my trusty navigation team, I am no longer afraid of the unknown, the seemingly impossible, or the dragon, for that matter. After many trials and tribulations, the dragon was more likely to offer friendly assistance than force a showdown. Now, at the end of this story, my multifarious dragon had become a valuable ally when it chose to grace me with its presence.

If my story sounds glamourous, it wasn't—mystical yes, enviable no. Mine was not an easy path, but it was a true path, magical and richly rewarding at times and deeply painful at others. The Wounded Healer archetype is not meant to be a walk in the park. It requires deep healing, multiple initiations, and facing the inner dragon at every turn. Make no mistake, dragons are unpredictable and demanding, and making friends with this capricious creature has been a lifelong undertaking. It would have been easier to slay it, like the hero on his journey, but that is not the heroine's way.

The heroine's way is guided by a different impulse. Above all, she seeks transformation. On her return from the unknown world, the gift of the Goddess is the retrieval of her feminine nature. The heroine's rebirthing is ultimately an awakening to the divine feminine within. The awakened heroine befriends the dragon rather than slaying it because she knows that the dragon is the keeper of gold and jeweled treasures. If she dares to venture into the darkness of the dragon's lair and reach its glittering depths, she is rewarded beyond imagining with the dragon's gold.

At the end of the day, paying homage to the dragon is a wise path. The dragon is a guardian of treasures, a storehouse of inner wisdom for anyone who cares to go for this spiritual gold. Dragons have largely been mistreated by myth. In truth, they are wayshowers, not villains as depicted. Rainer Rilke was onto something back in the early 1900s when he wrote in his inspiring *Letters to a Young Poet*:

No Gold Without The Dragon

> *Perhaps all the dragons in our lives*
> *Are princesses who are only waiting to*
> *See us act, just once, with beauty and courage.*
> *Perhaps everything that frightens us*
> *Is in its deepest essence*
> *Something helpless that wants our love.*[25]

Perhaps not helpless, but you get the gist of it—even that fierce, frightening, fire-wielding dragon needs love. Thus charmed, the dragon, with its many faces, obliged me by pointing out the hidden pathways in the Universe. Leading me onward, the way-showing dragon revealed the trilogy of vibrations that had been my North star cluster—joy, peace, love. These were the deepest treasures, the gold that surely any self-respecting alchemist would be overjoyed to forge in their furnace.

The dragon's gold had been there all along, tucked inside my Wounded Healer heart. A bit of alchemy perhaps, a bit of dragon's breath, but there it was—gold under my nose. It's there for all of us, deep within each magnificent, bursting-into-bloom heart.

---

25 Rainer Maria Rilke, *Letters to a Young Poet* (USA: Vintage, 1984).

Chapter 9 | Wings

DRAGON'S GOLD
Wisdom teachings from Chapter Nine

- Over the last few decades, Starseed souls have been incarnating en masse to help with the Ascension process. The focus of a Starseed's soul mission differs from an Earth soul's mission. While Earth souls might focus on raising humanity's consciousness, Starseed souls are more interested in the cosmic dynamics and the role of Earth *within* the cosmic system. They might be called to raise Gaia's consciousness itself. Conscious collaboration between Starseed and Earth souls holds enormous potential for accelerating evolution.

- As we evolve, our energetic structures are changing too. One of the most visible changes is the merging of the heart chakra and the high heart chakra to form a new energetic center with a distinct vibrational frequency. This new heart center, the awakened heart, is the energetic template for the awakened human and a portal to the Fifth Dimension. Many recently incoming souls have a fully developed awakened heart. These New Children are seeding heart-based consciousness in their orbits. An awakened heart has the capacity for advanced spiritual perception and heart wisdom, guiding us through a mass spiritual awakening and across the next dimensional frontier.

- As we transition to the Fifth Dimension, the fifth-dimensional chakra system has become more visible and accessible. This is the energetic template for our next evolutionary leap. Many awakening souls are already working with their fifth-dimensional chakras. As more people activate their fifth-dimensional chakras and embody the fifth-dimensional energies, evolution will gather momentum, and the higher frequencies will become more stable. Think of it as our hardware being upgraded to support a more advanced software program.

- Look no further than your own heart to find your gold. The elusive holy grail lies within.

EPILOGUE

While writing the first draft of this book, the coronavirus pandemic swept across the world. As an initiatory event, the pandemic was a general call to examine the lives we were leading and to interrogate our personal and collective values. Amid the turbulence, it was a window of opportunity to rethink the direction we were going in and reach for higher ground. From a higher perspective, the pandemic served as a major evolutionary choice point.

For me, the pandemic was a catalyst for change and a new direction in my work. Initially, it tested my capacity to build fear immunity and hold the light for others who sought my help. During this period, I started working more intentionally with fifth-dimensional energies and joined thousands of lightworkers around the planet in attuning the light grids to a higher frequency. This collective grid work fed my faith that it is possible to weave a higher-frequency matrix, though we had a long road ahead of us.

And so it was that after writing this book, my attention turned to a new call to become a wayshower to the Fifth Dimension and beyond. Instead of choosing this new role, it pulled me toward the future with an increasing sense of urgency. I felt honored by this spiritual assignment and recognized a sense of duty to respond to the best of my ability, even though the *how-to* of being a wayshower was still unclear.

Once I said *Yes* to the call, events unfolded swiftly and in surprising ways. Listening closely to my spirit guides, I started taking steps, big and small, in the surface-world to ground their guidance in action. The first big step was another move to a more wildish place. Much as the Riebeek Valley had been a place of rest and reset, an opportunity to unearth the ancestral shadow and connect with a deeper current of creativity, I was longing for a wilder place. It was a deep soul yearning that I could no longer ignore. This rising tide of longing took me to Scarborough, a seaside conservation village at the southern end of the Cape Peninsula, at the tip of Africa. Moving to the Deep South, as this part of greater Cape Town is known, was a homecoming.

In this wildish place, I felt deeply rooted, connected to the elements, and supported by the higher frequencies of a more pristine natural environment. Here, I sourced my life from nature: the Atlantic Ocean to the south, the surrounding fynbos-covered mountains, the neighboring Cape Point Nature Reserve, the coastal dunes and wetlands, and the ever-present wind. On this windswept peninsula, the undulating elements—Earth, Air, Fire, and Water—are a visceral part of daily life. There is a palpable sense of sharing habitat with the Earth's many inhabitants. Baboons, caracals, genets, porcupines, tortoises, otters, and a wide variety of bird species are as much part of the community as are the people who have chosen to live here, in close relationship with the natural world.

No matter the season, Scarborough is a windswept place. In winter, sporadic cold fronts roll in from the Atlantic Ocean, reaching land with a stormy blast; in summer, the prevailing south-easter blows more often than not. Never my favorite element, I had to make friends with the wind. The ubiquitous seabirds were a daily reminder of the Albatross totem. As I acclimatized to my new home, there was a rising resonance with the Albatross and its message to fulfill my mission in the more etheric realms.

The second major action to align with the new call to be a wayshower was founding the Emerald Wisdom School. Many years ago, the name *Emerald Wisdom School* was given to me in a soul vision channeled by my mentor, Dreaming Wolf. In the intervening years, the vision for the Emerald Wisdom School took shape through dreams and more channeled information, but the big push came when my guides primed me to become a New Earth wayshower and join the many lightworkers here for this same purpose. The Emerald Wisdom School would be the vehicle for me to direct my energy toward this bigger-picture mission.

My intention with the Emerald Wisdom School is to contribute toward accelerating the evolutionary shift from third-dimensional to fifth-dimensional consciousness and to anchor the New Earth paradigm. As a wayshower, my role is to teach the energetics of the Fifth Dimension, facilitating light body evolution and strengthening the energetic template underpinning the shift to heart-based consciousness. Core to these energetic teachings is activating the fifth-dimensional heart and chakra column to help people embody the higher frequencies and incoming light codes. We are building a bridge to the New Earth *through* our light bodies, bringing higher cosmic frequencies *and information* into embodied form and anchoring this new energetic matrix into the Earth grids. This energetic recalibration is shaping our next evolutionary leap.

While my soul business was blossoming, my personal life was in flux. When I followed the call to move to Scarborough, Sander elected to stay in the Riebeek Valley until we sold our house. During the first two years in Scarborough, I moved five times from one rented beach house to another. I was longing to find a more permanent home and put down roots, but despite using every manifestation trick in the book, nothing was showing up. *Why was it taking so long?*

When we can't manifest our heart's desire, it might be that there is an inner block preventing the desired outcome. Or it might be that the timing isn't right. Sometimes, there are lessons to learn in the uncomfortable waiting zone. I realized that I had been absorbing new lessons about multidimensional grounding. The waiting zone was an opportunity to initiate the next level of soul embodiment and consolidate a deeper sense of being at home in my body no matter where I found myself on the planet.

One day, I woke up to a soft whisper: *Your house is coming.* I waited eagerly for it to show up in the outer world. Within two weeks, a private house sale surfaced on a local chat group. By this time, Sander had moved to Scarborough, and when we walked in the door, we knew it was the house we'd been waiting for. The decision was made before we'd even finished the viewing. It was an instant yes, and the sale was agreed the next day. When things are flowing, there is no mistaking it. Little did I know that another initiatory event was around the corner, this time through the element of fire.

In December 2023, a massive wildfire swept across Cape Town's southern peninsula. With strong winds and tinder-dry fynbos—the vegetation in the Cape Floral Kingdom biome—firefighters struggled to subdue the blaze, which raged for days on end. As the fire veered this way and that, we were keeping a watchful eye on the nearby mountain range but saw no imminent threat to Scarborough.

We moved into our new house on the day of the Summer Solstice. Just as we were bringing in the last of the moving boxes, our village was put on high alert. Although the wind was still blowing away from Scarborough, gale-force blasts were expected later in the day. The element of air is a dangerous consort to fire. Sander headed out with the volunteer firefighters to support the city's Fire and Rescue Service. I started fireproofing our new home: watering the wooden deck, turning off the gas, and preparing for possible evacuation. Just before midnight, the by-now gale force wind changed direction. Like a mythical dragon, the runaway fire raced down the valley at terrifying speed, and within fifteen minutes, the flames were licking at the edges of the village, just fifty meters from our new house. The night sky was bright red, the heat intense, and thick smoke filled the air.

Just after midnight, the call to evacuate went out. I grabbed my bewildered cat and backpack of valuables and raced to my car. We drove through thick, choking smoke and joined the convoy leaving the village. Being evacuated from my new home so soon after moving in was a moment I'll never forget. In a nanosecond, I made peace with losing everything and said goodbye.

The next morning, we returned to a charred wasteland as far as the eye could see. It was a devastating sight. The wildfire had surrounded the village, yet miraculously, no homes had been lost. Our new house was still standing! I breathed a deep sigh of gratitude and set about putting out embers and cleaning up the pervasive ash.

The wildfire was a poignant reminder that life can turn in an instant, and it was a powerful initiation into my new home. The dragon was still at work. This time, it wreaked havoc, giving me pause for thought about the meaning for me and the village. If I were to befriend this version of the dragon, what would be the teaching?

The answer was hiding in plain sight. The wildfire had left a devastating imprint on the landscape and the small wildlife that couldn't make it to safety, yet beneath the smoldering surface, new growth was already preparing to burst forth. Fynbos vegetation needs fire every few years to release seeds and generate new growth. If fynbos goes without fire for too long, the seed reserves get depleted, and growth stagnates. We are much like the fynbos. Sometimes, we need a powerful outside force, a dramatic clearing, and a major reset to activate the next level of soul growth.

Fire is the quintessential purification energy, initiating renewal and rebirth, and the Solstice Fires were no exception. They had served to purify the old energetic fabric and prime us for new growth and awakening. And this time, my guides said, *it is the end of a cycle*. Their message resonated deeply on a personal and collective level.

Having dropped into deeper soul embodiment in my new energetically aligned home, my next level of personal growth was to fully embrace the call to be a New Earth wayshower and align with my highest soul timeline. Stepping into a more visible expression of New Earth leadership meant shedding some tenacious limiting beliefs. First and foremost, my identification with the Wounded Healer archetype, which had shaped my journey as a healer, and any old programming that kept this identity alive would have to go. It was indeed the end of an old cycle and long-running story.

As we enter the second wave of Ascension, we are all being asked to interrogate and dissolve our old programming—and the identities—that keep us tied into the third-dimensional matrix and to step into the next level of awakening and soul embodiment.

The time is ripe to cross the dimensional frontier and co-create an entirely new future for humanity. There is a perceptible longing for a better way of living on the planet. As this shift in perception gains currency, we have an unprecedented opportunity to write a new story for humanity. Anyone can be part of writing humanity's new story; we are all alchemists of the future. Like the alchemists of old, forging base metal into gold, we are called to fashion the new golden age. Our forge is the heart field; our alchemical tools are consciousness, imagination, thought, and feeling. The alchemical process is transformation and evolution, and the gold we are seeking is a stable high-frequency state within a container of heart-based consciousness. Now more than ever, we have an opportunity—perhaps a spiritual assignment—to forge this higher frequency pathway and weave it into a new grid for our Earth home.

As more souls awaken to this potential, the call to dream the New Earth into being is gaining momentum. Like the green shoots slowly transforming the fire-scarred land, the New Earth is appearing and transforming the visible landscape for our continued evolution.

I invite you to join the legions of lightworkers and New Earth leaders and step into your own creative mastery to birth a radical new world on the Earth plane.

When I was writing this book, this note-to-self on my pinboard was my daily inspiration:

> Imagine words like thousands of tiny dragonflies fluttering into the ether, touching lives, reminding readers of their deep-heart wisdom and soul's longing. And then these dragonflies lay their eggs, seeding new waves of dragon magic, and so it goes, ripple after ripple, until a new world is born.

And now, this is my prayer from my heart to yours.

Blessed be.

Heather

BOOK CLUB QUESTIONS

1. Which aspects of the author's journey could you most relate to and why?

2. Did any part of the book elicit a strong emotional response? If so, which part or parts, and what emotions did the book make you feel?

3. How did the author's dragon first appear? Can you relate to this version of the dragon? Was her way of handling the dragon instructive?

4. Did you conjure up your own dragon as a result of your reading? How did it appear? What thoughts, emotions, or memories did it stir in you?

5. What does your dragon have to teach you? Can you think of ways in which you might befriend your dragon rather than slaying it?

6. What new discoveries did you find in the Dragon's Gold sections at the end of each chapter?

7. Were your prior perceptions about yourself or about the nature of reality changed in any meaningful way? What did you learn that was completely new?

8. What did you learn about the world of energy? How can you apply these insights to your own life and your perceptions of reality?

9. How did the case studies add to your understanding of healing and working with energy?

10. What are the major waystations on the Heroine's Journey? How does it differ from the classic Hero's Journey?

11. How can you apply the Heroine's Journey to your own life? What stage of this archetypal journey is most relevant to you? What insights does this transformation schema yield?

12. The author experienced several spiritual initiations. What were they? What was their significance in the overall arc of the author's journey? Can you relate these initiations to your own life experience?

13. Were there any parts of the book that were difficult to get into? Why do you think that was?

14. Do you have a favorite quote or quotes? If so, which ones and why?

15. Are there lingering questions from the book you're still thinking about? If you could ask the author anything, what would it be?

16. Is this a book you would someday re-read? Why, or why not?

17. What surprised you the most about the book?

GRATITUDES

Although it comes right at the end, this is one of the most important pages where I get to express my gratitude to everyone who played a role in the manifestation of this book. Some played an active role in the birthing process, while others were indirectly involved in shaping my journey as a healer. I am truly blessed by their presence in my life and their gifts.

To the radiant book doulas at Sacred Dragon Publishing, my heartfelt thanks for bringing my book into the world. To Andi Rosenau, my erudite editor, your artful wordsmithing and incisive commentary exacted my best effort. Thank you for making a tough task so much fun. I'll miss your flurry of inspirational emails in my inbox. To Francine Marie-Sheppard, and your design team, thank you for creating a beautiful book and for parachuting into the editorial space with pearls of wisdom whenever needed. Your vision, intuition, and creative flair were vital ingredients. Thank you, Sacred Dragon team!

Special thanks go to all my clients who agreed to have their healing stories included in the book. I can't name you, but you know who you are. Thank you for having so much courage and for sharing a part of yourself for the benefit of others. I'm deeply grateful to every one of my clients. It's been a privilege to witness your healing journeys and a deep honor to be of service. Every single person who showed up in my healing room taught me something of value and offered a profound reflection. I bow to these many teachers. Without you, there would be no book.

There are a few significant others who deserve special mention for their magnanimous behind-the-scenes contributions to the creative process.

To my beloved husband, Sander Mahieu, thank you for believing in me and for your whole-hearted support every step of the way. A steady stream of insights and morning coffee deliveries to my writing desk kept me going. Your patience during the long birthing process was way beyond reasonable expectations. You are the love of my life and my rock. To my beautiful sons, thank you for cheering me on from the sidelines and having faith in me no matter what. I love you two with all my heart.

I am immensely grateful to Marilyn Hager for listening to my book idea and pushing me to the starting line. To Michael Stevenson, for providing a writing sanctuary to nudge me to the finish line. To Louise Grantham, for reading the first draft and being so generous with your professional publishing advice. And to Jocelyn Star Feather for helping me to find an aligned publisher.

This book would not have come into being without the special souls who have played a significant role on my journey and shaped my development as a healer.

I'm deeply grateful to these mentors, helpers, and spiritual allies. To my parents, Ben and Dawn, for giving me a childhood steeped in the mythical and the sacred—and so much more. To my brother Tim, for being an ally and friend. To the teachers at the Buddhist Retreat Centre in Ixopo for inspiring a lifelong meditation practice. To Val Moon for teaching me to listen to my body. To Clare Condy for introducing me to every available healing modality during the London years. To Chatelaine Taylor for handing me the spiritual keys and rattling them in my face. To Claudia Rauber for holding me through the fires of transformation. To Lance for the vision questing. To Vanessa Rockey for being a spiritual ally in an unlikely place. To Kate Martiny for your energy wizardry and compassionate wisdom. To Yvette de Villiers for being a spiritual taskmaster of the highest order. To Brent Burgoyne for helping me to complete unfinished soul business. To Cindy Holmes for opening doors. To Sue Allen for teaching me to overcome my fear. To Denise Linn for sharing your magic and unlocking the vibration of joy. To Bill Woodward for your profound visions and loving support over many years. To Kali Widd for your sublime dance classes. To Dr. Lynette Steele for your wild woman medicine when I needed it most. To Margaret Tregidga for your wise words and clearing my energy more times than I can count. To Michelle Hawkins, Natasha Wojnow, Lilah Wolpert, and Janet Homan for your lightworker assistance.

I'm indebted to a luminous band of sisters who have generously shared their gifts at various stages of my journey. To Lee Rossini for all the adventures and being a five-star listener. To Bastienne Klein for showing me the ways of the medial being. To Rebecca Johns for loyal friendship and music. To Natasha Wilson for showering my reconfigured family with love. To Nombulelo Kila for your loving care. To Gilly Siebert and Gillian Mitri for being the best team ever. You were like family through the single-mothering years. To Liz McKenzie and Debbie Ludik for all the ceremonies and so much more. To Kenau Allen for your warm-hearted embrace. And to Petra Becker for walking alongside me once again. Thank you, dear ones, for being there at the right time.

My gratitude list would not be complete without mentioning my light being team in the invisible realms—the consummate supporting act. My eternal gratitude to my spirit guides for their instructive guidance and high-level care. And to the dragon, of course, for leading me deeper into the mystery and to the spiritual gold that has made it all worthwhile.

And thank you to all my readers for your love of our human story and for giving this book its wings.

ABOUT THE AUTHOR

Heather Linn is a quantum healer, psychic reader, spiritual teacher, grid keeper, and writer. Her passion is facilitating journeys of transformation and assisting people in living a soul-led life.

Heather is the founder of the Emerald Wisdom School, a high-frequency portal to the New Earth paradigm, and brings a wealth of experience as a healer to the school's online programs. She also offers one-to-one Soul Readings and works online with clients worldwide.

Heather holds a Master's degree in Development Studies from the School of Oriental and African Studies, University of London, United Kingdom and a Bachelor of Arts Honors degree in English Literature (*cum laude*) from the University of Natal, South Africa. She has also trained extensively in the healing arts in South Africa, the United Kingdom, and the United States.

Heather is the mother of two sons, a role that has been the most profound teacher on her path of heart. She lives with her Dutch husband and Tonkinese cat in Scarborough, a seaside conservation village at the southern tip of Africa. Early morning walks on the beach, cold plunges in the icy Atlantic, and wandering in the fynbos-covered mountains are her daily wellsprings of joy and creative inspiration.

Find out more about Heather and the Emerald Wisdom School at https://www.emeraldwisdomschool.com

INVITATION TO CONNECT

Thank you so much for engaging with my journey as a healer. I hope you enjoyed *No Gold Without the Dragon* and found inspiration and guidance for your own journey of transformation and continued awakening.

Please share your comments about *No Gold Without the Dragon* on your favorite book review sites and social media groups.

I invite you to connect with me personally through the Emerald Wisdom School.

The Emerald Wisdom School website
https://www.emeraldwisdomschool.com

Instagram
https://www.instagram.com/heatherlinn_emeraldwisdom/

YouTube
https://www.youtube.com/c/EmeraldWisdomSchool

www.ingramcontent.com/pod-product-compliance
Lightning Source LLC
Chambersburg PA
CBHW070458120526
44590CB00013B/681